Sadlier

WE·BELIEVE™

We Are
God's People

WITH PROJECT DISCIPLE

Pray
Learn
Celebrate
Share
Choose
Live

Grade Six

S® Sadlier

Nihil Obstat

Monsignor Michael F. Hull, S.T.D.
Censor Librorum

Imprimatur

✠ Most Reverend Dennis J. Sullivan, D.D.
Vicar General of the Archdiocese of New York
January 27, 2010

The *Nihil Obstat* and *Imprimatur* are official declaration that these books are free of doctrinal or moral error. No implications contained therein that those who have granted the *Nihil Obstat* and *Imprimatur* agree with the content, opinion or statements expressed.

Acknowledgments

Excerpts from the English translation of *The Roman Missal*, © 2010, International Committee on English in the Liturgy, Inc. All rights reserved.

Excerpts from the English translation of the *Catechism of the Catholic Church* for the United States of America, copyright © 1994, United States Catholic Conference, Inc.—Libreria Editrice Vaticana. English translation of the *Catechism of the Catholic Church: Modifications from the Editio Typica* copyright © 1997, United States Catholic Conference, Inc.—Libreria Editrice Vaticana. Used with permission.

Scripture excerpts are taken from the *New American Bible with Revised New Testament and Psalms* Copyright © 1991, 1986, 1970, Confraternity of Christian Doctrine, Inc., Washington, D.C. Used with permission. All rights reserved. No part of the *New American Bible* may be reproduced by any means without permission in writing from the copyright owner.

Excerpts from the English translation of *Lectionary for Mass* © 1969, 1981, International Committee on English in the Liturgy, Inc. (ICEL); excerpts from the English translation of *Rite of Holy Week* © 1972, ICEL; excerpts from the English translation of *Rite of Penance* © 1974, ICEL; excerpts from the English translation of *The Liturgy of the Hours* © 1974, ICEL; excerpts from the English translation of *A Book of Prayers* © 1982, ICEL; excerpts from the English translation of *Order of Christian Funerals* © 1985, ICEL; excerpts from the English translation of *Book of Blessings* © 1988, ICEL All rights reserved.

Excerpts from *Catholic Household Blessings and Prayers* © 1988, United States Catholic Conference, Inc. Washington, D.C. Used with permission. All rights reserved.

English translation of the Glory to the Father, Lord's Prayer, Apostles' Creed, Nicene Creed, *Te Deum Laudamus,* and the *Sanctus* by the International Consultation on English Texts (ICET).

"We Believe, We Believe in God," © 1979, North American Liturgy Resources (NALR), 5536 NE Hassalo, Portland, OR 97213. All rights reserved. Used with permission. "God, Creator, God Most High," © 1998, Janet Vogt. Published by OCP Publications, 5536 NE Hassalo, Portland OR 97213. All rights reserved. Used with permission. "I Know You Are God," © 1995, Janet Vogt. Published by OCP Publications, 5536 NE Hassalo, Portland OR 97213. All rights reserved. Used with permission. "Be Not Afraid," © 1975, 1978, Robert J. Dufford, SJ and New Dawn Music, 5536 NE Hassalo, Portland, OR 97213. All rights reserved. "City of God," © 1981, Daniel L. Schutte and New Dawn Music, 5536 NE Hassalo, Portland, OR 97213. All rights reserved. Used with permission. "Psalm 122: Qué Alegría/I Rejoiced," Music and verse text © 1997, Jaime Cortez. Published by OCP Publications, 5536 NE Hassalo, Portland, OR 97213. All rights reserved. Used with permission. English refrain © 1969, 1981, ICEL. Spanish refrain © 1982, Sobicain. All rights reserved. Used with permission. The English translation of Psalm 122 response from *Lectionary for Mass* © 1969, 1981, 1997, International Committee on English in the Liturgy, Inc. All rights reserved. "Prepare the Way," © 1997, Paul Inwood. Published by OCP Publications, 5536 NE Hassalo, Portland, OR 97213. All rights reserved. Used with permission. "Psalm 98: All the Ends of the Earth," Music © 1999, 2000, Barbara Bridge. Published by OCP Publications, 5536 NE Hassalo, Portland, OR 97213. All rights reserved. Used with permission. Refrain © 1969, ICEL. Verse © 1970, CCD. All rights reserved. The English translation of Psalm 98 response from *Lectionary for Mass* © 1969, 1981, 1997, International Committee on English in the Liturgy, Inc. All rights reserved. "Though the Mountains May Fall," © 1975, Daniel L. Schutte and New Dawn Music, 5536 NE Hassalo, Portland, OR 97213. All rights reserved. Used with permission. "Christ, Be Our Light," © 1993, Bernadette Farrell. Published by OCP Publications, 5536 NE Hassalo, Portland, OR 97213. All rights reserved. Used with permission. "My God, My God," © 1988, 1989, 1990, Christopher Walker. Published by OCP Publications, 5536 NE Hassalo, Portland, OR 97213. All rights reserved. Used with permission. "Resucitó/He Is Risen," Music © 1973, Ediciones Musical Pax. Sole U.S. Agent: OCP Publications. English text © 1988, OCP Publications, 5536 NE Hassalo, Portland, OR 97213. All rights reserved. Used with permission. "Pescador de Hombres/Lord, You Have Come," Spanish text and music © 1979, Cesáreo Gabaráin. English translation by Robert C. Trupia, © 1987 by OCP Publications, 5536 NE Hassalo, Portland, OR 97213. All rights reserved. Used with permission. "Jesus Is Risen," Music © 1992, Barbara Bridge. Text © 1992, Barbara Bridge and Owen Alstott. Published by OCP Publications, 5536 NE Hassalo, Portland, OR 97213. All rights reserved. Used with permission. "God Has Chosen Me," © 1990, Bernadette Farrell. Published by OCP Publications, 5536 NE Hassalo, Portland, OR 97213. All rights reserved. Used with permission. "Who Am I?" Music and text © 1999, Christopher Walker and Paule Freeburg, DC. Published by OCP Publications, 5536 NE Hassalo, Portland, OR 97213. All rights reserved. Used with permission. "Envía Tu Espíritu," © 1988, Bob Hurd. Published by OCP Publications, 5536 NE Hassalo, Portland, OR 97213. All rights reserved. Used with permission.

William H. Sadlier, Inc.
9 Pine Street
New York, NY 10005-4700

ISBN: 978-0-8215-6406-6

6 7 8 9 10 WEBC 16 15 14 13

The Subcommittee on the Catechism, United States Conference of Catholic Bishops, has found this catechetical series, copyright 2011, to be in conformity with the *Catechism of the Catholic Church.*

The Sadlier *We Believe* Program was drawn from the wisdom of the community. It was developed by nationally recognized experts in catechesis, curriculum, and child development. These teachers of the faith and practitioners helped us to frame every lesson to be age-appropriate and appealing. In addition, a team including respected catechetical, liturgical, pastoral, and theological experts shared their insights and inspired the development of the program.

Contributors to the inspiration and development are:

Dr. Gerard F. Baumbach
Director, Center for Catechetical Initiatives
Concurrent Professor of Theology
University of Notre Dame
Notre Dame, Indiana

Carole M. Eipers, D.Min.
Vice President, Executive Director
  of Catechetics
William H. Sadlier, Inc.

Catechetical and Liturgical Consultants

Patricia Andrews
Director of Religious Education
Our Lady of Lourdes Church,
Slidell, LA

Reverend Monsignor John F. Barry, P.A.
Pastor, American Martyrs Parish
Manhattan Beach, CA

Mary Jo Tully
Chancellor, Archdiocese of Portland

Reverend Monsignor John M. Unger
Deputy Superintendent for Catechesis
and Evangelization
Archdiocese of St. Louis

Curriculum and Child Development Consultants

Brother Robert R. Bimonte, FSC
Executive Director
NCEA Department of Elementary Schools

Sr. Carol Cimino, SSJ, Ed.D.
National Consultant
William H. Sadlier

Gini Shimabukuro, Ed.D.
Associate Professor
Catholic Educational Leadership Program
School of Education
University of San Francisco

Catholic Social Teaching Consultants

John Carr
Executive Director
Department of Justice, Peace,
and Human Development
United States Conference of Catholic Bishops
Washington, D.C.

Joan Rosenhauer
Associate Director
Department of Justice, Peace,
and Human Development
United States Conference of Catholic Bishops
Washington, D.C.

Inculturation Consultants

Allan Figueroa Deck, S.J., Ph.D., S.T.D.
Executive Director
Secretariat of Cultural Diversity in the Church
United States Conference of Catholic Bishops
Washington, D.C.

Kirk P. Gaddy, Ed.D.
Educational Consultant
Baltimore, MD

Reverend Nguyễn Việt Hưng
Vietnamese Catechetical Committee

Dulce M. Jiménez-Abreu
Director of Bilingual Programs
William H. Sadlier, Inc.

Scriptural Consultant

Reverend Donald Senior, CP, Ph.D., S.T.D.
Member, Pontifical Biblical Commission
President, The Catholic Theological Union
Chicago, IL

Theological Consultants

Most Reverend Edward K. Braxton, Ph.D., S.T.D.
Official Theological Consultant
Bishop of Belleville

Norman F. Josaitis, S.T.D.
Theological Consultant

Reverend Joseph A. Komonchak, Ph.D.
Professor, School of Theology and Religious Studies
The Catholic University of America

Most Reverend Richard J. Malone, Th.D.
Bishop of Portland, ME

Sister Maureen Sullivan, OP, Ph.D.
Associate Professor
St. Anselm College
Manchester, NH

Mariology Consultant

Sister M. Jean Frisk, ISSM, S.T.L.
International Marian Research Institute
Dayton, OH

Media/Technology Consultants

Sister Judith Dieterle, SSL
Past President, National Association of
Catechetical Media Professionals

Sister Jane Keegan, RDC
Technology Consultant

Michael Ferejohn
Director of Electronic Media
William H. Sadlier, Inc.

Robert T. Carson
Electronic Media Design Director
William H. Sadlier, Inc.

Erik Bowie
Electronic Media Production Manager
William H. Sadlier, Inc.

Writing/Development Team

Rosemary K. Calicchio
Vice President, Publications

Blake Bergen
Editorial Director

Melissa D. Gibbons
Director of Research and
Development

Joanne McDonald
Senior Editor, Project Director

Christian Garcia
Contributing Writer

MaryAnn Trevaskiss
Supervising Editor

Maureen Gallo
Senior Editor

Kathy Hendricks
Contributing Writer

William M. Ippolito
Executive Consultant

Allison Johnston
Senior Editor

Margherita Rotondi
Editorial Assistant

Sadlier Consulting Team

Michaela Burke Barry
Director of Consultant Services

Judith A. Devine
National Sales Consultant

Kenneth Doran
National Religion Consultant

Saundra Kennedy, Ed.D.
National Religion Consultant

Victor Valenzuela
National Religion Consultant

Publishing Operations Team

Deborah Jones
Vice President,
Publishing Operations

Vince Gallo
Creative Director

Francesca O'Malley
Associate Art Director

Jim Saylor
Photography Manager

Design/Photo Staff
Andrea Brown, Kevin Butler,
Debrah Kaiser, Susan Ligertwood,
Cesar Llacuna, Bob Schatz

Production Staff
Diane Ali, Monica Bernier,
Barbara Brown, Brent Burket,
Robin D'Amato, Stephen Flanagan,
Joyce Gaskin, Cheryl Golding,
Maria Jimenez, Joe Justus,
Vincent McDonough, Yolanda
Miley, Maureen Morgan, Jovito
Pagkalinawan, Monica Reece,
Julie Riley, Martin Smith

We are grateful to our loyal *We Believe* users whose insights and suggestions have inspired **PROJECT DISCIPLE**—the premier faith formation tool built on the six tasks of catechesis.

Contents

SEASONAL CHAPTERS

UNIT 2

Building the Covenant Nation

WE·BELIEVE

The *We Believe* program will help us to

learn

celebrate

share

and

live our Catholic faith.

Throughout the year we will hear about many saints and holy people.

Saint Agnes	Saint Jerome
Saint Alphonsus Liguori	Saint Lawrence
Saint Angela de Merici	Saint Martin of Tours
Saint Bonaventure	Mary, Mother of God
Saint Catherine of Siena	Saint Mary Magdalene
Saint Catherine Laboure	Saint Maximilian Kolbe
Saint Cecilia	Saint Paul
Saint Elizabeth of Portugal	Venerable Pierre Toussaint
Saint Genevieve of Paris	Saint Stephen
Saint Ignatius of Loyola	Saint Thomas Aquinas
Saint John	

Together, let us grow as a community of faith.

Welcome!

WE GATHER

✝ **Leader:** Welcome, everyone, to Grade 6 *We Believe*. As we begin each chapter, we gather in prayer. We pray to God together. Sometimes, we will read from Scripture; other times we will say the prayers of the Church or sing a song of thanks and praise to God.

Today, let us sing the *We Believe* song!

♫ We Believe, We Believe in God

Refrain:

We believe in God;
We believe, we believe in Jesus;
We believe in the Spirit who gives us life.
We believe, we believe in God.

We believe in the Holy Spirit,
Who renews the face of the earth.
We believe we are part of a living Church,
And forever we will live with God.

(Refrain)

11

We also focus on life.

 means it's time to

think about
talk about
act out
Life
draw about
write about

at school
at home
in our parish
in our world
in our neighborhood

Talk about your life right now. What groups, teams, or clubs do you belong to?

Why do you like being a part of these groups?

What does belonging to these groups tell other people about you?

When we see **We Gather**, we come together as a class

When we see **We Believe** we learn more about our Catholic faith.

Each day we learn more about God.

WE BELIEVE

We learn about:

- the Blessed Trinity—God the Father, God the Son, and God the Holy Spirit

- Jesus, the Son of God, who became one of us

- the Church and its history and teachings

- the Mass and the sacraments

- our call to be a disciple of Jesus.

UNIT 1

Forming the Covenant
"I praise you, so wonderfully you made me;
wonderful are your works!" (Psalm 139:14)

 UNIT 2

Building the Covenant Nation
"Sing to the LORD, for he is gloriously
triumphant." (Exodus 15:21)

 UNIT 3

Redefining the Covenant People
"Rise up in splendor! Your light has come,
the glory of the Lord shines upon you." (Isaiah 60:1)

 UNIT 4

The Covenant Fulfilled in Jesus
"And a voice came from the heavens, saying, 'This is my
beloved Son, with whom I am well pleased.'"(Matthew 3:17)

> A major theme in your *We Believe* textbook this year is learning more about God's love for his people, and his action in their lives throughout history. Your book is divided into four units.

Watch for these special signs:

Whenever we see ✝ we make the Sign of the Cross. We pray and begin our day's lesson.

📖 is an open Bible . When we see it, or a reference like this (John 13:34), we hear the Word of God. We hear about God and his people. We hear about Jesus and the Holy Spirit.

When we see 🏃 we do an activity .
We might:

• talk together

• write a story

• draw a picture

• act out a story or situation

• imagine ourselves doing something

• sing a song together, or make up one

• work together on a special project.

There are all kinds of activities! We might see 🏃 in any part of our day's lesson. Be on the lookout!

Can you guess what 🎵 means? That's right, it means it is time to sing, or listen to music . We sing songs we know, make up our own, and sing along with those in our *We Believe* music program.

When we see Key Words we review the meanings of important faith words we have learned in the day's lesson.

As Catholics...

Here we discover something special about our faith. We reflect on what we have discovered and try to make it a part of our life. Don't forget to read it!

WE RESPOND

We can respond by:

- thinking about ways our faith affects the things we say and do

- sharing our thoughts and feelings

- praying to God.

Then in our home, neighborhood, school, parish, and world, we say and do the things that show love for God and others.

When we see **We Respond** we reflect and act on what we have learned about God and our Catholic faith.

Draw yourself doing something that shows you are a disciple of Jesus Christ.

We are so happy you are with us!

We sharpen our disciple skills with each chapter's Project Disciple pages!

Show What you Know

We "show what we know" about each chapter's content. A disciple is always learning more about his or her faith.

Celebrate!

As disciples, we worship God.

DISCIPLE CHALLENGE

We take our disciple skills one step further.

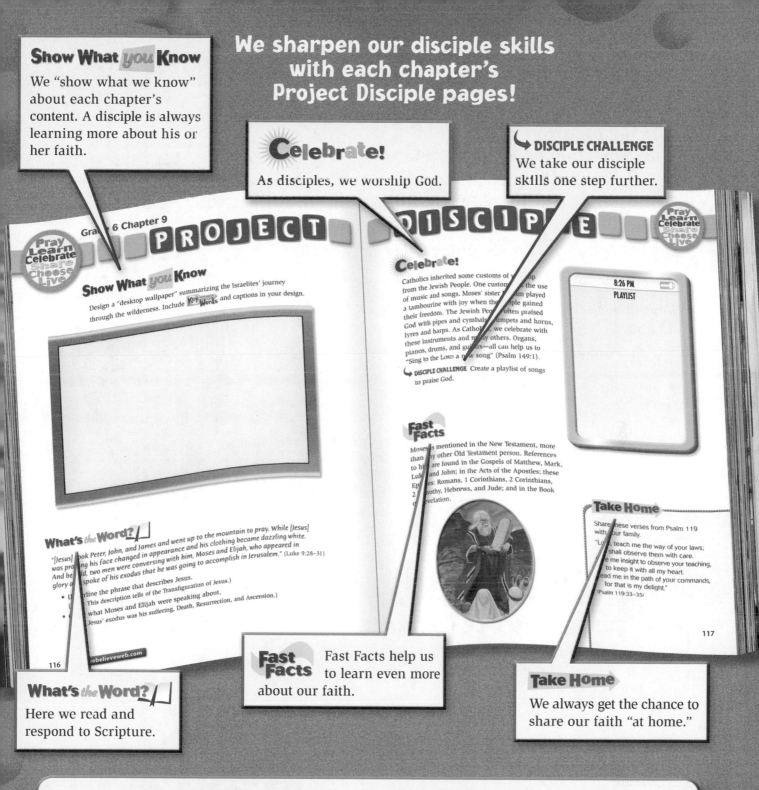

What's the Word?

Here we read and respond to Scripture.

Fast Facts

Fast Facts help us to learn even more about our faith.

Take Home

We always get the chance to share our faith "at home."

There are **LOADS** of **ACTIVITIES** that make us better disciples! Just look at this additional list.

Question Corner—take a quiz

Make It Happen!—living out what we have learned

What Would You Do?—making the right choices

Reality Check—here we can express our ideas and choices

Picture This—a great way for us to see and show our disciple skills

Pray Today—talking and listening to God

Saint Stories—finding great role models

More to Explore—activities to develop our comprehension and Internet skills

Now, Pass It On!—invites us to witness to our faith

And every chapter ends with a Chapter Test!

PROJECT DISCIPLE

You are on a journey this year to become a disciple of Jesus Christ. This year you will:

- **learn** about God's people in the Bible and their lessons for today.

- **pray** to do as God asks, as the patriarchs and prophets did.

- **celebrate** our Catholic heritage of faith and its expression today.

- **choose** to be united to all Catholics, to be holy, to be welcoming and faithful.

- **share** our Catholic faith with others.

- **live out** Jesus' ministry within the Church by working for social justice.

Have a great year!

And remember, you can always visit **www.webelieveweb.com** for all kinds of activities, games, study guides, and resources.

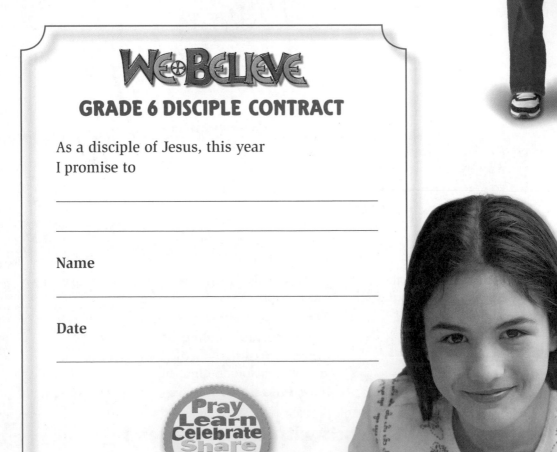

We BELIEVE

GRADE 6 DISCIPLE CONTRACT

As a disciple of Jesus, this year I promise to

_____

_____

Name

_____

Date

_____

Pray
Learn
Celebrate
Share
Choose
Live

Forming the Covenant

Seasonal Chapters

Pray
Learn
Celebrate
Share
Choose
Live

PROJECT DISCIPLE

DEAR FAMILY

In Unit 1 your child will grow as a disciple of Jesus by:

- appreciating Scripture and Tradition as God's Revelation of himself
- praising God as the source of all life and living as the image of God
- recognizing the truths taught in the Genesis stories of creation and of Original Sin
- understanding God's promise to send a Savior and his covenant with Noah
- learning about the patriarchs, our ancestors in faith, and Abraham, the father of God's people.

What's *the* Word?

All of Sacred Scripture is the Word of God. We learn about God through Scripture in ways similar to the ways we learn about characters in books: what the person says, what the person does, how the person acts, what the person thinks, what others say about the person, how others react to the person. For each one of these ways, give an example of what we learn about God from the Bible.

Picture This

In each of the Units there is a timeline of our faith. Look at the timeline on pages 20–21. Go over it as a family and invite members to share what they remember of each of the Scripture events cited. If there is an event that no one recalls, read it in your Bible (or look for it in your child's book) and share it with your family. At the end of Unit 1, return to this timeline and have your child share one event they learned about.

Reality Check

"The relationships within the family bring an affinity of feelings, affections, and interests, arising above all from the members' respect for one another."
(*Catechism of the Catholic Church*, 2206)

Show That You Care

God created us in his image and likeness and so every person reflects God's goodness. As a family, name the ways each member of your family reflects God. Say a prayer of thanks for each member and the God-given gifts they have.

Question Corner

Chapter 5 introduces men and women who were important to God's people in the Old Testament: Abraham, Isaac, Jacob and Joseph, Sarah, Rebekah, Rachel, and Leah. Who are the men and women who have been important to your family through generations? Tell some of their stories to your children. Pray for all of your ancestors together.

Take Home

Be ready for this unit's Take Home:

Chapter 1: Discussing the readings for next Sunday's Mass

Chapter 2: Planning a family "movie night"

Chapter 3: Sharing ways to be a steward

Chapter 4: Recognizing the Good News

Chapter 5: Going where God leads

God's Revelation

WE GATHER

✠ **Leader:** O living God,
Our journey of faith leads us on
the path to you.
Your magnificent deeds are
words of strength and hope for us.
Open our hearts to listen to your
living Word.

Reader 1: "You formed my inmost being;
you knit me in my mother's womb.
I praise you, so wonderfully you made me;
wonderful are your works!"
(Psalm 139:13–14)

All: Your Word is a light to my path, O Lord.

Reader 2: "I raise my eyes toward the mountains.
From where will my help come?
My help comes from the LORD,
the maker of heaven and earth."
(Psalm 121:1–2)

All: Your Word is a light to my path,
O Lord.

Leader: O God of creation, you made
all things good. Help us to see
the work of your hands in the
world and in our lives. May we
always praise you for your
wonderful deeds!

☀ What are some of the ways
that you discover new ideas
or gain new information?

♫ **God, Creator, God Most High**

Refrain:
God, Creator, God Most High,
be our ever present light.
Be among us, here before us, God
within us.

You are light for the world.
You are light for the lost to see.
Out of darkness we come to the
light of your love,
for your word is a lamp unto our feet
to guide us. (Refrain)

You restored night to day.
You commanded the dark to cease.
By your promise of love we shall
not walk in fear.
We shall walk in the light of hope
and peace to guide us. (Refrain)

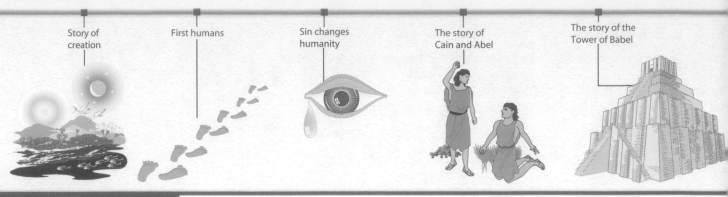

Story of creation

First humans

Sin changes humanity

The story of Cain and Abel

The story of the Tower of Babel

Timeline for Chapters 1–5

WE BELIEVE
We can know God through his creation.

When we think, we are using our natural ability to reason and to come to sound conclusions. The ability to reason is a gift that all human beings have. And through reason humans have drawn many conclusions about God. For centuries, great thinkers have developed reasonable theories for God's existence. The simplest of these theories is based on the idea that a machine, such as a watch or a computer, does not make itself.

It has a maker. The reasonable conclusion is that the universe has a maker. We believe that the maker, or Creator, of the universe is God.

In his writings Saint Paul reminds us that the human mind can find God "in what he has made" (Romans 1:20). By looking at the vast expanses of space through a telescope we get to know something of God's power. By discovering more about the universe we get to know about God's knowledge and wisdom.

POSTCARD

WE ARE GOD'S PEOPLE

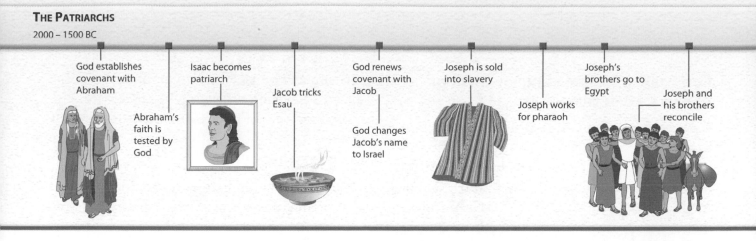

God establishes covenant with Abraham

Abraham's faith is tested by God

Isaac becomes patriarch

Jacob tricks Esau

God renews covenant with Jacob

God changes Jacob's name to Israel

Joseph is sold into slavery

Joseph works for pharaoh

Joseph's brothers go to Egypt

Joseph and his brothers reconcile

We notice the great variety of plant and animal life in the world. We observe human life, the greatest and most astounding creation in the universe. Learning about who we are, how we think and behave, and what we hope for helps us to think about what God must be like.

So by making use of all of our natural gifts, and those of other people, we get to know about our world, about ourselves, and about God.

Yet, natural means of learning about God are all limited. We need God himself to tell us who he is and what he is like.

Which pictures on these pages help you to know what God is like? Why?

God makes himself known through Divine Revelation.

God loves us so much that he told us about himself. He revealed himself to us. *Reveal* means "to make known." **Divine Revelation** is God's making himself known to us. God has made himself known to us through his mighty deeds and by his interactions with his people throughout time.

Although God spoke to individual men and women about himself and his plan for his people, his message was for the whole community. God made it clear that he wanted to have a loving relationship with all people. God made it possible for humans to know him more deeply and to respond to him in a way that was otherwise not possible.

God made himself known gradually over time. God's Revelation began with the creation of the first human beings and their descendants. It continued through the ancient Israelites and the Jewish People.

God's Revelation is full and complete in his only Son, Jesus Christ. By sending his Son, God tells us what we need to know about himself. In the Gospel of John we read, "No one has ever seen God. The only Son, God, who is at the Father's side, has revealed him" (John 1:18).

Jesus Christ is the only Son of God who became man. Jesus shows us God his Father. Together with the Father, Jesus sends God the Holy Spirit who helps us respond to God's great love for us. God the Father, God the Son, and God the Holy Spirit are the Blessed Trinity. The **Blessed Trinity** is the Three Persons in One God.

The Holy Spirit guides the Church to understand God's Revelation and to apply it in our lives. We live in hope of eternal life with God—where we will have a clearer understanding of God's loving plan. It is only in eternal life that we will completely know God. As Saint John said, "Now this is eternal life, that they should know you, the only true God, and the one whom you sent, Jesus Christ" (John 17:3).

Reread pages 22 and 23. Highlight or underline ways God revealed himself.

Key Words

Divine Revelation (p. 330)
Blessed Trinity (p. 330)

God's Revelation is handed down through the Bible and Tradition.

The events and the recollections that people had of God were passed on from generation to generation. People's living experience of God helped to shape what would eventually be written down.

The **Bible**, also called *Sacred Scripture* or simply *Scripture*, is the written record of God's Revelation and his relationship with his people. The Bible has a divine author, God, and many human authors, or biblical writers. These writers used their own words and expressions. As the human writers wrote, they were guided by God the Holy Spirit. The special guidance that the Holy Spirit gave to the human writers of the Bible is called **Divine Inspiration**. It guaranteed that the human writers wrote without any error God's saving truth. For that reason God is the true author of the whole Bible. Thus, the Bible is the *Word of God*.

Tradition is the Revelation of the Good News of Jesus Christ as lived out in the Church, past and present. Tradition includes teachings and practices handed on orally from the time of Jesus and his Apostles. It includes the creeds, or statements, of Christian beliefs. It also includes the teachings and documents of the Church, the Church's worship, and other practices. Tradition is the source of the Church's ongoing understanding of the meaning of Revelation and the ways to apply it to our lives.

The written message of Scripture and the spoken message of Tradition have been handed on by the Apostles to the whole Church. The bishops are the successors of the Apostles. With the pope as their head, they form the *Magisterium*, the living, teaching office of the Church. In Jesus' name and with the help of the Holy Spirit, the Magisterium interprets both Scripture and Tradition. Through the centuries the Church has continued to share and build on the faith of the Apostles. The Church community in every generation believes and lives this faith and passes it on to future generations.

Key Words

Bible (p. 330)
Divine Inspiration (p. 330)
Tradition (p. 331)

In groups discuss the ways the Bible and Tradition are the same or different. Write your notes here.

The Bible is a collection of books.

The biblical writer used literary forms to help us to learn about God in a unique way. A *literary form* is a type of writing used to get a message across.

Talk about how the writers of these books get messages across to their readers.

From a
Poetry Book

From a
Science Book

From an
Adventure Book

_____
(Add your own)

The Bible contains all kind of literary forms: ancient folktales, histories, novels, short stories, advice on living, codes of law, letters, prophecy, visions, poetry, hymns, and many other types of writing.

The word *bible* means "books." The Bible is not just one book but a small library of sacred, or holy, books. The Bible has seventy-three separate books. It is divided into two parts. The *Old Testament* contains forty-six books and the *New Testament* contains twenty-seven books.

In the Old Testament we learn about God's relationship with the people of Israel. The New Testament contains the story of Jesus, his mission, his first followers, and the beginning of the Church.

When we refer to a reading from the Bible we refer to the book, the chapter of the book, and verse of the chapter. The citation Genesis 1:1–2 refers to the Book of Genesis, chapter 1, verses 1 and 2.

What does the citation Revelation 21:1–3 mean?

_____

_____

_____

_____

WE RESPOND

What are some ways that you have come to know God? How can you share what you know about God with others?

Books of the Bible

The Old Testament
Pentateuch ("Five Scrolls")

These books tell about the formation of the covenant and describe basic laws and beliefs of the Israelites.

Genesis	Exodus	Leviticus	Numbers	Deuteronomy

Historical Books

These books deal with the history of Israel.

Joshua	1 Samuel	1 Chronicles	Nehemiah	Esther
Judges	2 Samuel	2 Chronicles	Tobit	1 Maccabees
Ruth	1 Kings	Ezra	Judith	2 Maccabees
	2 Kings			

Wisdom Books

These books explain God's role in everyday life.

Job	Proverbs	Song of Songs	Wisdom	Sirach
Psalms	Ecclesiastes			

Prophetic Books

These books contain writings of the great prophets who spoke God's Word to the people of Israel.

Isaiah	Ezekiel	Amos	Nahum	Haggai
Jeremiah	Daniel	Obadiah	Habakkuk	Zechariah
Lamentations	Hosea	Jonah	Zephaniah	Malachi
Baruch	Joel	Micah		

The New Testament
Gospels

These books contain the message and key events in the life of Jesus Christ. Because of this, the Gospels hold a central place in the New Testament.

Matthew	Mark	Luke	John

Letters

These books contain letters written by Saint Paul and other leaders to individual Christians or to early Christian communities.

Romans	Colossians	Titus	2 Peter
1 Corinthians	1 Thessalonians	Philemon	1 John
2 Corinthians	2 Thessalonians	Hebrews	2 John
Galatians	1 Timothy	James	3 John
Ephesians	2 Timothy	1 Peter	Jude
Philippians			

Other Writings

Acts of the Apostles	Revelation

PROJECT

Show What *you* Know

Complete the crossword puzzle using the Key Words.

Across

3. the Three Persons in One God: God the Father, God the Son, and God the Holy Spirit

Down

1. the Revelation of the Good News of Jesus Christ as lived out in the Church, past and present

2. The special guidance that the Holy Spirit gave to the human writers of the Bible is known as Divine _____.

3. the written record of God's Revelation and his relationship with his people

4. Divine _____ is God's making himself known to us.

Picture This

A *logo* is a uniquely designed symbol to represent a name, a company, etc. Design a logo to represent the Blessed Trinity.

Saint Stories

Saint Jerome was born in the fourth century. He studied in Rome and learned Greek and Latin. He became a monk, and went to live in the desert to fast, pray, and focus on God. Jerome studied the writings of the Old Testament and the Hebrew language. With his skill in Hebrew and Greek, Jerome translated the Bible into Latin. Many people were able to read and study Scripture because of Jerome's translation. Saint Jerome is one of the Church's great biblical scholars. We celebrate his feast day on September 30.

↳ DISCIPLE CHALLENGE

- Underline the phrase that describes why Jerome went to live in the desert
- What helped Jerome translate the Bible into Latin?

_____

_____

Fast Facts

The shortest book in the Bible is the Second Letter of John. It has only 13 verses. The Book of Psalms, with 150 psalms, is the longest book in the Bible.

Make it Happen

Look at the chart on page 27. Take the time to become more familiar with the books of the Bible.

Now, pass it on!

Take Home

Visit *This Week's Liturgy* on www.webelieveweb.com for the Sunday Mass readings and holy day liturgies, as well as activities. Find this week's readings. Read and talk about them. Select an activity to do together.

Write the letter that best defines each term.

1. __D__ Divine Revelation

2. __A__ Bible

3. __E__ Tradition

4. __C__ Divine Inspiration

a. written record of God's Revelation and his relationship with his people

b. a type of writing used to get a message across

c. the special guidance that the Holy Spirit gave to the human writers of the Bible

d. God's making himself known to us

e. the Revelation of the Good News of Jesus Christ as lived out in the Church, past and present

Write True or False next to the following sentences.
Then change the false sentences to make them true.

5. __T__ The Magisterium is the living, teaching office of the Church.

6. __T__ The Blessed Trinity is the Three Persons in One God.

7. __F__ We learn about God's relationship with the people of Israel in the New Testament.

Old Testament

8. __F__ Tradition is the written record of God's Revelation and his relationship with his people.

~~Old~~ New Testament

Write a paragraph to answer this question.

9–10. How has God revealed himself to us?

_____

_____

_____

_____

Creation

WE GATHER

✝ **Leader:** O God of creation, You have given us wonderful gifts! We praise and thank you for all that you have created.

Reader: "All good giving and every perfect gift is from above, coming down from the Father of lights." (James 1:17)

Leader: We thank you for our gift of life.

All: We praise you God.

Leader: We thank you for our sense of smell, hearing, and touch.

All: We praise you God.

Leader: We thank you for our families and friends.

All: We praise you God.

Leader: We thank you for our abilities and talents.

All: We praise you God.

♫ **I Know You Are God**

In the morning's first sunlight, I know you are God.
In the gentle and starry night, I know you are God.
I see in your majesty all that you are to me, in each and ev'rything, I know you are God.
In your loving forgiveness I know you are God.

In your kindness, compassion I know you are God.
My trust rests in you alone, source of all peace and hope;
bless the Lord, O my soul, I know you are God.

✹ Describe your earliest memories or something your family has told you about your early life.

31

The Book of Genesis is about beginnings.

The history of God and his people which is recorded in the Bible covers over thousands of years. Each part, or period, of this story connects in a special way with the **covenant**, an agreement between God and his people.

This chart divides this lengthy history into smaller periods. The chart lists historical periods that are presented in the Bible and indicates some books of the Bible that describe each period.

Historical Period	Books of the Bible
Prehistory	Genesis
The Patriarchs	Genesis
Israel in Egypt	Exodus
The Wilderness Experience	Exodus, Leviticus, Numbers, Deuteronomy
Settling the Land	Joshua, Judges, Ruth
The United Kingdom	1–2 Samuel, 1–2 Kings, 1–2 Chronicles, Psalms
The Divided Kingdom	2 Kings, 2 Chronicles, Amos, Hosea, Micah, Isaiah, Jeremiah, Nahum
The Babylonian Captivity	Lamentations, Ezekiel, Isaiah, Daniel, Esther
Return to the Homeland	Ezra, Nehemiah, Tobit, Judith, Jonah, Ecclesiastes
Israel Among the Nations	1–2 Maccabees, Daniel, Sirach
Jesus' Earthly Ministry	Matthew, Mark, Luke, John
The Early Church	Acts of the Apostles, Letters, Revelation

Genesis means beginning. The **Book of Genesis** is the first book in the Bible, and it is about beginnings. In the first eleven chapters of Genesis, we read about prehistory, the events from creation to the time of Abraham. These chapters contain stories that describe the beginning of God's relationship with humanity. These stories are very old and are not necessarily about factual events. The stories contain vivid descriptions and imagery, repeat details often, and have simple plots with few characters. Thus, it was easy for people to understand the meaning of the stories, remember them, and pass them on down through the ages.

The biblical writer used symbols to tell a realistic story and at the same time to give the deeper meaning of the story. The symbols used in the stories of the Bible express ideas and beliefs about God and his actions throughout history.

The Gates of Paradise, by Lorenzo Ghiberti (1378–1455), depict Old Testament scenes. Baptistery of the Duomo, Florence, Italy

Key Words

covenant (p. 330)
Book of Genesis (p. 330)

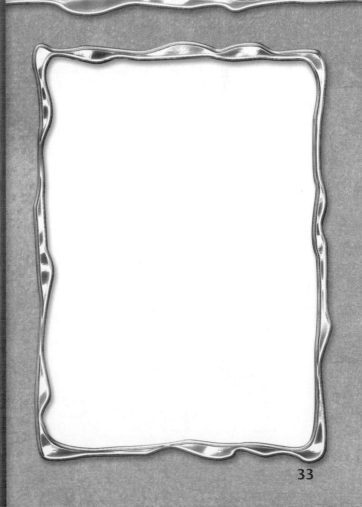 What are some of the stories found in the first eleven chapters of Genesis? Choose one of them. Design a panel for a Genesis door.

33

God created the universe.

Genesis 1:1–31; 2:1–4

The Book of Genesis contains two very symbolic stories of creation. In the first, Genesis 1:1—2:4, the biblical writer tells us in simple but poetic language that God freely created the universe over a six-day period. A *day* in this story does not mean twenty-four hours. In fact, day does not represent any definite period of time. Scholars think the biblical writer showed God creating the universe in six days because that was the normal workweek of the Israelites who lived at the time the story was written.

In this creation story God spoke and everything was created: light, sun, moon, stars, sky, water, earth, sea, fish, plants, animals, and humans. By God's word the universe came into being. And at each stage God saw that what he created was good. Then on the seventh day God rested, just as the Israelites rested after their long workweek.

This creation story is not meant to be a scientific study of creation. It is not an exact recording of God's work within a certain time frame. Instead, it is the story that revealed to God's people the truths about creation: everything in existence is created by God, and everything that God created is good and depends on him.

After you read this story of creation, portray the events in a dramatic presentation. Write the plan for your presentation here.

Day 1

"God said, 'Let there be light,' and there was light." (Genesis 1:3)

Day 4

"God said: 'Let there be lights in the dome of the sky . . .' God made the two great lights, the greater one to govern the day, and the lesser one to govern the night; and he made the stars." (Genesis 1:14, 16)

_____   _____
_____   _____
_____   _____
_____   _____
_____   _____

First Story of Creation

"In the beginning, when God created the heavens and the earth, the earth was a formless wasteland, and darkness covered the abyss, while a mighty wind swept over the waters."

(Genesis 1:1–2)

Day 2

"God said, 'Let there be a dome in the middle of the waters, to separate one body of water from the other.' And so it happened." (Genesis 1:6)

Day 3

"God said, 'Let the water under the sky be gathered into a single basin, so that the dry land may appear . . .' Then God said, 'Let the earth bring forth vegetation: every kind of plant that bears seed and every kind of fruit tree on earth that bears fruit with its seed in it.' " (Genesis 1:9, 11)

Day 5

"God said, 'Let the water teem with an abundance of living creatures, and on the earth let birds fly beneath the dome of the sky.' " (Genesis 1:20)

Day 6

"God said, 'Let the earth bring forth all kinds of living creatures: cattle, creeping things, and wild animals of all kinds' . . . Then God said: 'Let us make man in our image, after our likeness' . . . male and female he created them.

God blessed them, saying: 'Be fertile and multiply; fill the earth and subdue it. Have dominion over the fish of the sea, the birds of the air, and all the living things that move on the earth.' . . . God looked at everything he had made, and he found it very good." (Genesis 1:24, 26, 27, 28, 31)

Day 7

"Thus the heavens and the earth and all their array were completed. Since on the seventh day God was finished with the work he had been doing, he rested on the seventh day from all the work he had undertaken. So God blessed the seventh day and made it holy, because on it he rested from all the work he had done in creation.
Such is the story of the heavens and the earth at their creation." (Genesis 2:1–4)

God is the source of all life.

The first story of creation in Genesis 1:1—2:4 not only tells us about creation, it also tells us about God. To begin with, it shows us that God is the one, true God. There is no other God. This understanding of God is very different from the one held by other ancient peoples. They believed that there were many gods and even thought of objects as gods. They often worshiped the sun or moon, the weather, or ideas like fate or justice.

The first creation story also makes it clear that the God we worship is a personal God, not an object or an idea. God is a living being, and is the source of all life. In fact, God is the supreme being who creates all life and keeps it in existence.

The first story of creation also helps us to know some of God's attributes, or characteristics.

- God is eternal. This means that God always was and always will be. God is changeless and timeless. Change and time are part of creation, and God is *not* part of creation.

The Israelites' view of God was very different from the one held by other ancient peoples. They worshiped false gods that they thought were a part of creation. They believed these gods were born, usually in some fantastic way, and could die.

Throughout history God has continued to reveal himself as the one who is the source of all creation. In the Bible we find many references to God as Creator.

Old Testament	New Testament
"Our help is in the name of the LORD, the maker of heaven and earth." (Psalm 124:8)	"The God who made the world and all that is in it, the Lord of heaven and earth, does not dwell in sanctuaries made by human hands, nor is he served by human hands because he needs anything. Rather it is he who gives to everyone life and breath and everything." (Acts of the Apostles 17:24–25)

- God is all-powerful. This means that God can do anything. God is perfect.

Here again God differs from the false gods that people believed in. These false gods made mistakes and sometimes failed and were often pictured as guilty of terrible evils.

- God is all-knowing. This means that God knows everything—past, present, and future. Yet God's knowledge never keeps people from choosing and acting freely.

Unlike the Israelites, other people believed in false gods that did not know everything, could not do everything, and often tried to keep the people from making their own decisions.

- God is ever-present. This means that God is everywhere at all times.

Again the false gods that other people believed in did not have this quality. They could not be present everywhere and always. They were often described as traveling from place to place, just like human beings.

Words and ideas only explain so much about God. In this life we will never have full and complete knowledge of God. That is why God will remain a mystery to us.

To help you remember the attributes of God, use words and images to complete this diagram.

God is . . .

Which of these attributes best describe your own experience of God? Why?

Human beings are created in God's image and likeness.

In the story of creation we see something strikingly different in the creation of humans.

"God created man in his image;
 in the divine image he created him;
 male and female he created them."
(Genesis 1:27)

The biblical writer is telling us that only human beings are made in the image and likeness of God. We are like God because as human beings each of us has been created as someone, not something.

Each one of us is a unique person who possesses a human dignity. **Human dignity** is the value and worth that comes from being made in God's image and likeness. Both males and females are created in God's image and likeness. God created humans different but equal, all sharing the same human dignity. And God found that good.

Each one of us is created to be like God and to share in his friendship. Of all the creatures we alone are created by God with **free will**—the freedom and ability to choose—and with **conscience**—the ability to know the difference between good and evil, right and wrong. We alone are able to think and love and form relationships. We alone can know and love our Creator.

Being made in the image and likeness of God carries with it serious responsibilities. We are called to respect and care for all that God has given us. And since our free will makes us responsible for our own thoughts and actions, we must make our choices carefully. We are called to choose what is good and right and to act in the image and likeness of our Creator.

human dignity (p. 330)
free will (p. 330)
conscience (p. 330)

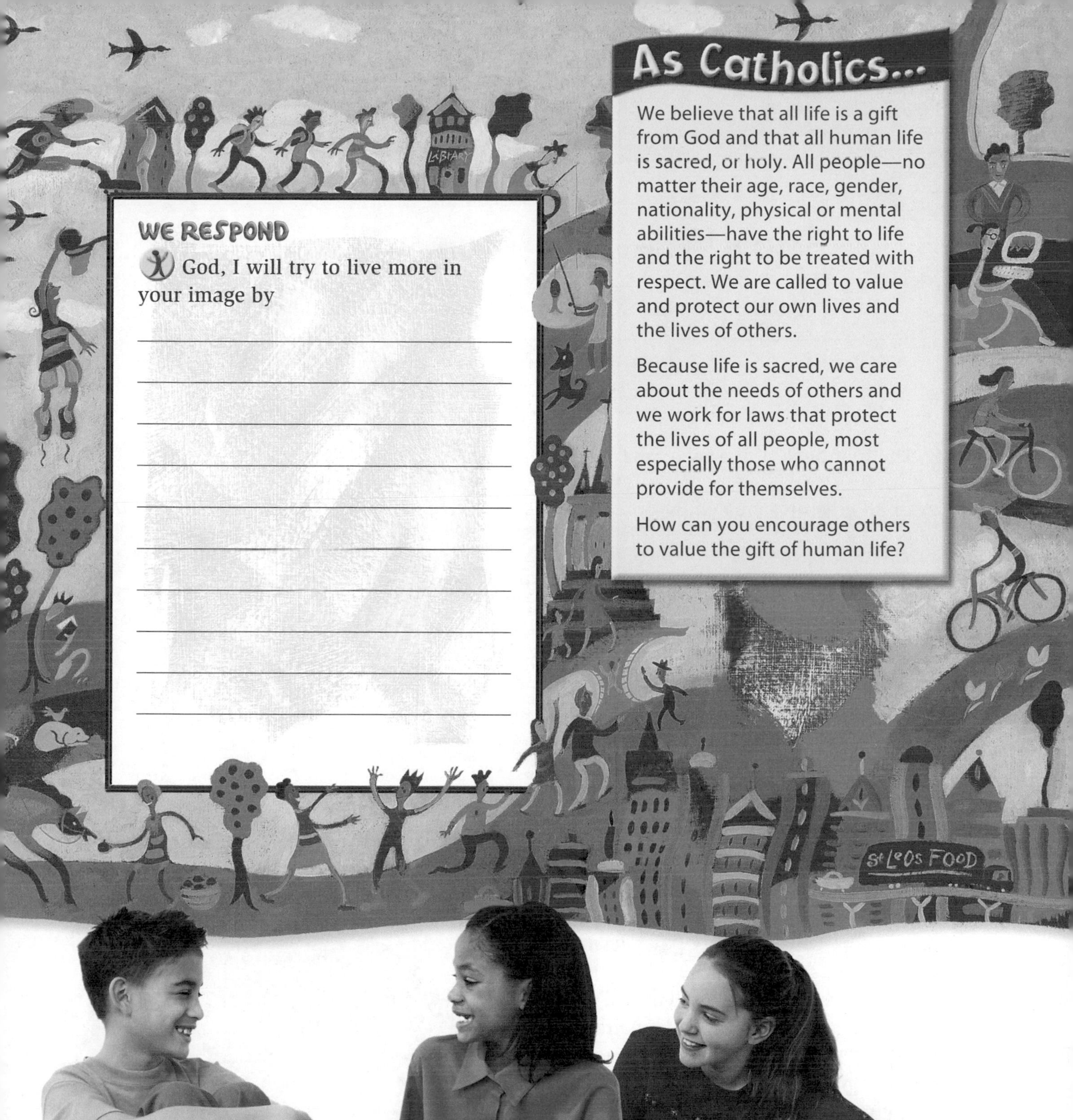

WE RESPOND

✗ God, I will try to live more in your image by

_____

_____

_____

_____

_____

_____

_____

_____

_____

We believe that all life is a gift from God and that all human life is sacred, or holy. All people—no matter their age, race, gender, nationality, physical or mental abilities—have the right to life and the right to be treated with respect. We are called to value and protect our own lives and the lives of others.

Because life is sacred, we care about the needs of others and we work for laws that protect the lives of all people, most especially those who cannot provide for themselves.

How can you encourage others to value the gift of human life?

Pray
Learn
Celebrate
Share
Choose
Live

PROJECT

Show What *you* Know

Unscramble the **Key Words** to complete the sentences below.

| EREF LILW | NUHAM GNYIIDT | KOBO ISESGNE FO |
| ECCNICSENO | | VATNNEOC |

1. The first book of the Bible, the _____, contains two accounts of creation.

2. Of all creatures created by God, we alone were created with _____, the freedom and ability to choose, and with _____, the ability to know the difference between good and evil, right and wrong.

3. The _____ is an agreement between God and his people.

4. Each one of us is a unique person who possesses _____, the value that comes from being made in God's image and likeness.

Celebrate!

On or around the feast day of Saint Francis of Assisi, many parishes hold a special ceremony. Parishioners take their animals, including pets and even work animals, to church. Some churches have a procession. Others simply have the animals gather for a blessing. Saint Francis of Assisi believed that humanity was connected to all of God's creation in a brotherhood. Saint Francis is the patron saint of animals and of ecology, which is the study of the relationship between living things and their environment.

↳ **DISCIPLE CHALLENGE**

• When is Saint Francis of Assisi's feast day?

_____

• Does your parish have a special ceremony or procession for the blessing of animals? If so, describe it.

_____

DISCIPLE

More to Explore

The Vatican Observatory is one of the world's oldest astronomical institutes. It was founded in 1582. The observatory has two research centers, one in Castel Gandolfo, Italy, and one in Tucson, Arizona. The Tucson center telescope is the first optical-infrared telescope to be used to study light at the farthest points of the universe. The center in Italy has a unique collection of meteorites that are used to study the history of the solar system. Studying science is a way to grow closer to God by appreciating the wonders of God's creation.

What are other ways to appreciate the wonders of God's creation?

_____

_____

 **Pray Today**

Write a prayer thanking God for the wonders of the universe.

_____

_____

_____

What's the Word?

What attribute of God is identified in the Scripture passage?

*"Lord, you have been our refuge
  through all generations.
Before the mountains were born,
  the earth and the world brought forth."*
(Psalm 90:1–2)

_____

Take Home

Is there a current movie that shows the main character(s) choosing to do what is right and good, and acting in the image and likeness of God?

_____

_____

Plan a family "movie night" to view and discuss this movie.

CHAPTER TEST

Circle the letter of the correct answer.

1. The _____ is an agreement between God and his people.

    a. Bible   **b.** creation   **c.** covenant

2. Biblical writers used _____ to tell a realistic story and at the same time to give the deeper meaning of the story.

    a. attributes   **b.** symbols   **c.** scholars

3. _____ is the freedom and ability to choose.

    a. Genesis   **b.** Free will   **c.** Conscience

4. _____ is the source of all life.

    a. The Bible   **b.** The Book of Genesis   **c.** God

Short Answers

5. Why is Genesis an appropriate name for the first book of the Bible?

    _____

6. What is a truth that the first creation story reveals to us?

    _____

7. God has many attributes; list three.

    _____

8. What is human dignity?

    _____

Write a paragraph to answer this question.

9–10. Because we were created in the image and likeness of God, what responsibilities do we have?

_____

_____

_____

_____

People Turn from God

3

WE GATHER

✝ **Leader:** Blessed be the God of creation who forms us like clay in the hands of a potter.

All: Blessed be God now and for ever.

Reader 1: "This word came to Jeremiah from the LORD:

Rise up, be off to the potter's house; there I will give you my message.

Reader 2: I went down to the potter's house and there he was, working at the wheel. Whenever the object of clay which he was making turned out badly in his hand, he tried again, making of the clay another object of whatever sort he pleased.

Reader 3: Then the word of the Lord came to me: Can I not do to you, house of Israel, as this potter has done? says the LORD.

Reader 4: Indeed, like clay in the hand of the potter, so are you in my hand, house of Israel." (Jeremiah 18:1–6)

The word of the Lord.

All: Thanks be to God.

☀ What can you do that other creatures cannot do?

WE BELIEVE
God created human beings, body and soul.

The Book of Genesis provides a second story of creation. We can read it in Genesis 2:5–25. In this story the biblical writer tells us that God created humans *before* he created plants and other creatures. Thus, the two creation stories differ. Yet both make the same point: God created humanity as the high point of creation.

The following words about humanity are from another book of Scripture. They make it clear that God gave great dignity and power to all humans.

"Yet you have made them little less than a god,
   crowned them with glory and honor." (Psalm 8:6)

In the second creation story, the biblical writer describes God creating humans by taking a lump of clay from the earth and using it to form the body of the first man. This creation story is very old, yet it agrees with the idea from today's modern scientific study: Our human bodies are made out of the same elements as the rest of the universe.

In this story we read "the LORD God formed man out of the clay of the ground and blew into his nostrils the breath of life, and so man became a living being" (Genesis 2:7). This breath of life from God refers to our **soul**, the invisible spiritual reality that makes each of us human. The soul is immortal; it will never die.

Humans are a union of a visible, physical body and an invisible, spiritual soul. Every human being is unique, yet each of us is made body and soul. One day we will die, and our bodies will turn to dust. But our souls, the breath of God in us, will live forever. At the end of time, our body and soul will be reunited when Christ comes again at the Last Judgment.

We also find in this second story of creation that God said, "It is not good for the man to be alone. I will make a suitable partner for him"

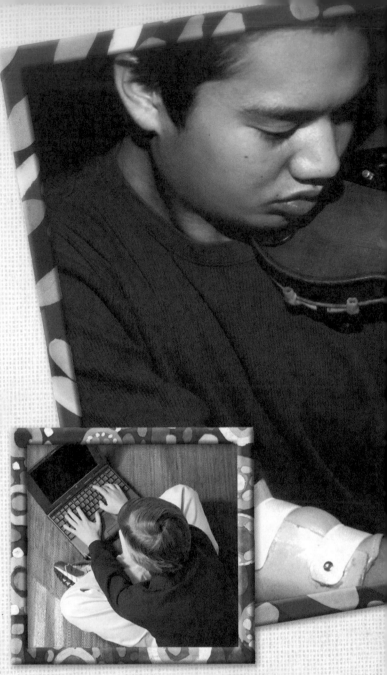

(Genesis 2:18). So God created many wild animals and birds and then finally, while the man slept, God took one of his ribs and created the first woman. When the man woke up and saw this woman, he said,

"This one, at last, is bone of my bones
   and flesh of my flesh" (Genesis 2:23).

God's creation of woman from the rib of man symbolizes that females and males share the same human dignity and are equal. It also reminds us that all humans are united to one another. We all have one true Father—God. We are all created to share in God's own life, and to help one another to know and love God.

Key Word

soul (p. 331)

God makes each of us with gifts and abilities. What gift do you have that can help others know and love God? Draw or write about it here.

God called us to be stewards of creation.

God told the first human beings, "Be fertile and multiply; fill the earth and subdue it. Have dominion over the fish of the sea, the birds of the air, and all the living things that move on the earth" (Genesis 1:28).

God told the first man and woman to bring new life into the world and thus create the human family. He asked them to be responsible for the earth and all the living things in it. Then God allowed humans to be partners with him and with one another in continuing his work of creation.

God put the first man and woman in the beautiful garden in Eden and shared his own friendship and life with them. They also had use of all the gifts of creation. The garden was a symbol that the biblical writer used to show the happiness that human beings had in the presence of God.

The biblical writer tells us about another symbolic event: God gave humans authority over all the animals by allowing them to name the animals. To the ancient Israelites, people had authority over those whom they named. So humans were called by God to be the caretakers of creation.

Of all of God's creatures, humans alone have the ability to care for creation and make it prosper. In fact, that is exactly what stewardship involves—authority and responsibility. A **steward** is a person who is given both the authority over what he or she cares for and the responsibility for seeing that it lives and grows.

Each of us is a steward of God's creation. By caring for creation, people show respect for the Creator.

Key Word

steward (p. 331)

We are all called to take care of creation every day. What specific things can we do to:

use water wisely _____

recycle _____

take care of pets _____

protect the environment _____

other _____

Plan specific times when you will do these things.

Evil entered the world through a human act.

In Chapter 3 of Genesis, the biblical writer uses a story to teach important truths about sin and suffering. This story tells of a very real truth—the choice of the human race to turn away from God and lose its close friendship with him.

As the story opens, the first man and woman were living in a beautiful garden in Eden. They were God's friends, and because of this they had harmony with God, each other, and the rest of creation. They were living in the original state of innocence, holiness, and justice for which God had created them.

The first humans were free to do all but one thing: they could *not* eat the fruit of the tree of the knowledge of good and bad. God told the man that if he ate from it, he would die.

This warning about the forbidden fruit symbolizes that friendship with God depends on complete trust in God and on following his will for us. It reminds us that, as created beings, we are limited and we must respect those limitations.

But we learn from the story that the first man and woman disobeyed God. A serpent spoke to the woman and said, "God knows well that the moment you eat of it [the fruit] your eyes will be opened and you will be like gods who know what is good and what is bad" (Genesis 3:5). She believed the serpent. So she picked some of the fruit and ate it. Then she offered some to the man, who also ate it.

This story is filled with symbols. The serpent represents the Devil, who tempted the woman to do evil. The fact that the woman believed the serpent reminds us of just how attractive evil can be. Eating the fruit symbolizes a choice. It shows that because of our free will, humans have the power to make choices that can lead to good or to evil.

As the story continues, the first man and woman realized the seriousness of their actions. They became frightened of God and hid from him. But God knew what they had done, and, as the story closes, God sent them out of the garden. They no longer had any right to be there. Of their own free will, humans had chosen to turn from God.

List some of the reasons that people make choices that lead them away from God and others.

_____

_____

_____

_____

_____

_____

_____

_____

All people suffer from the effects of Original Sin.

The story of the first human beings, whom we call Adam and Eve, shows how close the relationship between God and human beings originally was. It also shows that instead of respecting God's warning and trusting his words, human beings turned away from God. They selfishly did what *they* wanted, rather than what God commanded. In other words, they committed a sin. **Sin** is a thought, word, deed, or omission against God's law. This sin of the first humans took away their original innocence, holiness, and justice. They lost the harmony they felt with God, with each other, and with the rest of creation.

Because the first humans personally chose to turn from God, they committed personal sin. Their personal sin was the first sin and is called **Original Sin**. Original Sin weakened human nature and brought ignorance, suffering, and death into the world. This wounded human nature was passed on to the rest of humanity. Thus, we all suffer from the effects of Original Sin, though it is not a sin for which we are personally responsible.

Even after the first human beings turned away from God, God did not turn away from them. God did not abandon humanity. Instead God showed them his mercy.

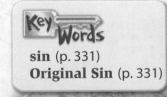

sin (p. 331)
Original Sin (p. 331)

In very symbolic language, the biblical writer tells us that God said a descendant of the first man and woman would save humanity. God promised that sin and evil would one day be overcome.

"He will strike at your head,
    while you strike at his heel." (Genesis 3:15)

So humanity was *not* completely lost. Human nature was wounded, but not destroyed. Humans were still a part of God's good creation, and God still loved them.

WE RESPOND

With a group discuss recent news stories that show that suffering is a part of human life. How can the people in these stories be comforted? Illustrate ways that you and your class can help people who are suffering in your own school and neighborhood.

As Catholics...

Our Lord and Savior Jesus Christ, as true God and true man, is free from all sin, including Original Sin. He died and rose to free us from sin. Because Mary was to be the Mother of the Son of God, she was blessed by God in a special way. Mary was free from Original Sin from the moment she was conceived, and she did not commit sin during her entire life. We call this truth the Immaculate Conception.

Mary, under the title of the Immaculate Conception, is the patroness of the United States. The whole Church celebrates the Feast of the Immaculate Conception on December 8. In the United States this feast is a holy day of obligation.

How does your parish celebrate this feast?

Pray
Learn
Celebrate
Share
Choose
Live

Show What *you* Know

Write a summary of the second creation story.
Use the **Key Words** in your summary.

_____

_____

_____

_____

_____

_____

_____

Celebrate!

Mary was free from Original Sin from the moment she was conceived. This truth is the Immaculate Conception.

As a parish, we gather together to celebrate the Immaculate Conception.

↳ **DISCIPLE CHALLENGE** When and how do we celebrate the Immaculate Conception?

_____

_____

DISCIPLE

Pray
Learn
Celebrate
Share
Choose
Live

More to Explore

Dangers such as pollution and climate change threaten the environment. The National Catholic Rural Life Conference (NCRLC) helps families in rural farm areas with these and other problems. The conference reminds us of our call to the stewardship of all creation. The NCRLC is concerned about scientific advances in growing food. Members speak out to make sure that Catholic social teachings guide us in making decisions about our environment. The NCRLC calls on all people to respect life, uphold human dignity, and show respect for creation.

DISCIPLE CHALLENGE

- Search the NCRLC Web site (www.ncrlc.com).
- Choose one of the programs or issues. Prepare to report on it to the class.
- Visit *Lives of the Saints* on www.webelieveweb.com to learn more about the NCRLC patron saints.

Question Corner

In the Book of Genesis, we learn God gave humanity "dominion over . . . all the living things that move on the earth" (Genesis 1: 28). *Dominion over* implies being a steward and having responsibility for living things. What are you responsible for?

_____

Make it Happen

Your local food bank needs volunteers and donations. Write one way you and your friends can help.

_____

_____

_____

Now, pass it on!

Take Home

Talk about the word *steward* with your family. Point out that all members of your family are stewards—each is given the authority over what he or she cares for and the responsibility for seeing that it lives and grows. Share some ways that each member of your family is a steward.

Write True or False for the following sentences.
Then change the false sentences to make them true.

1. __T__ In the stories of creation in the Book of Genesis, we find out that God's greatest creation was humanity.

_____

2. __T__ God calls each of us to be responsible for the earth and all the living things in it.

_____

3. __T__ Friendship with God depends on complete trust in him and on following his will for us.

_____

4. __F__ We are born with Original Sin and suffer from its effects because it is a sin for which we are personally responsible.

_____

Write the letter that best defines each term.

5. __D__ steward

6. __B__ sin

7. __C__ soul

8. __A__ Original Sin

a. the first sin that weakened human nature and brought ignorance, suffering, and death into the world

b. a thought, word, deed, or omission against God's law

c. the invisible spiritual reality that makes each of us human and that will never die

d. person who is given both the authority over what he or she cares for and the responsibility for seeing that it lives and grows

e. the original state of innocence, holiness, and justice for which humans were created

Write a paragraph to answer this question.

9–10. How did God respond when Adam and Eve sinned?

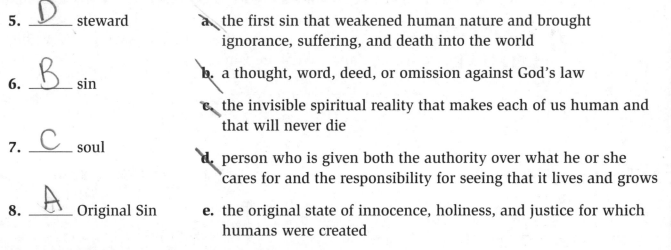

_____God banned Adam and Eve from his_____
garden, because they lyed to God.

_____

_____

WE GATHER

✝ **Leader:** Sit quietly and think of a beautiful place. It might be a mountaintop, a park, a deep canyon, or the ocean's edge. Choose a place that makes you feel happy and peaceful.

Now imagine Jesus standing with you in your special place.

- What do you say to Jesus?
- What does he say to you?
- What do you want to ask Jesus?
- What do you want to thank him for?

Have a short conversation together, as friend with friend. Now let us pray together.

Leader: Jesus, Son of the living God,

All: have mercy on us.
(Response to all petitions.)

Leader: Jesus, splendor of the Father,
Jesus, king of glory,
Jesus, dawn of justice,
Jesus, Son of the Virgin Mary,
Jesus, worthy of our love,
Jesus, prince of peace,
Jesus, all-powerful,
Jesus, God of peace,
Jesus, our refuge,
Jesus, Good Shepherd,
Jesus, crown of all saints.

Leader: Christ hear us.

All: Christ hear us.

Leader: Lord Jesus, hear our prayer.

All: Lord Jesus, hear our prayer. Amen.

☀ What are times when you need help?

WE BELIEVE
God promised to send a Savior.

We learn from the Old Testament that God would never stop loving people and forgiving them. Yet humanity could not undo the effects of Original Sin. Humanity needed God's help. So God promised to send a Savior. God's people believed that when the Savior came, he would fully restore their friendship with God.

The prophet Isaiah spoke to the people on God's behalf and reminded them of the way God wanted them to live. Isaiah told of someone who would come to free humanity from sin and restore their friendship with God. Isaiah described this person as the *Suffering Servant*.

"Through his suffering, my servant shall
    justify many,
  and their guilt he shall bear."
(Isaiah 53:11)

Christians believe that this Suffering Servant is God's own Son, Jesus Christ. Jesus is truly divine and truly human, and he fulfilled all that God promised. For our sake Jesus died on the cross and rose from the dead to save all people from sin and to bring us the hope of new life. As Saint Paul wrote, "For just as in Adam all die, so too in Christ shall all be brought to life" (1 Corinthians 15:22).

The New Testament contains four books about Jesus' life and teachings: the Gospels of Matthew, Mark, Luke, and John. The word *gospel* means "good news." The **Gospel** is the Good News about God at work in Jesus Christ.

In the Gospels we read of Jesus' work to bring hope to the poor and suffering, freedom to those who are persecuted, and healing to those who are sick. From the Gospels we learn that through his life, Death, and Resurrection, Jesus Christ makes it possible for all humanity to again share in God's life.

As Catholics...

We call our share in God's life and friendship *grace*, and we receive grace through the sacraments. A sacrament is an effective sign given to us by Jesus through which we share in God's life.

There are Seven Sacraments: Baptism, Confirmation, Eucharist, Penance and Reconciliation, Anointing of the Sick, Holy Orders, and Matrimony. Jesus instituted, or began, the sacraments so that his saving work would continue for all time.

The sacraments join Catholics all over the world with Christ and with one another.

How are the sacraments an important part of your life and the life of your family?

Gospel (p. 330)

With a partner discuss ways you show that you share in God's life and friendship. Draw or write about one way here.

The first human family struggled because of Original Sin.

In the fourth chapter of Genesis we find out about Adam and Eve's two sons. The older son Cain was a farmer. His younger brother, Abel, was a shepherd.

By all appearances this family was loving and happy. Then each brother made an offering to the Lord, but "the LORD looked with favor on Abel and his offering, but on Cain and his offering he did not" (Genesis 4:4–5).

The story does not explain why one offering was acceptable and the other was not. That was the biblical writer's way of indicating that we cannot always understand the ways of God and should not try to judge his ways. Yet Cain judged everything only from his own point of view. He felt that he had been treated unfairly, and he became very angry about it.

God told Cain that he could overcome evil, but Cain took his resentment out on his innocent brother. Cain killed Abel. Murder, one of the worst effects of Original Sin, had been committed.

God asked Cain where Abel was. Cain replied, "I do not know. Am I my brother's keeper?" (Genesis 4:9) God was deeply offended and said to Cain, "What have you done! Listen: Your brother's blood cries out to me from the soil! Therefore you shall be banned from the soil that opened its mouth to receive your brother's blood from your hand" (Genesis 4:10–11).

Cain realized that he was being sent away and would lose God's protection. He feared that he himself would now be killed. However, God put a mark on Cain to show that though he murdered Abel, Cain was protected by God. So even in this terrible circumstance God showed his great love for Cain.

The story of Cain and Abel can be understood on several levels. On one level it declares the sacredness of human life and prohibits murder. On another level it symbolizes the separation of human beings from one another. On a third level it is about accepting one's life and respecting one another. On a fourth level it is about the healing power of God's love.

Complete the chart.

Situations That Cause Anger or Resentment

_____

_____

_____

_____

_____

_____

_____

Ways We Can Overcome Anger or Resentment

_____

_____

_____

_____

_____

_____

_____

Pray for all families this week. Ask that they may solve their problems in a loving and caring way.

God made a covenant with Noah.

As the Book of Genesis continues, we learn that God is greatly displeased with human beings. They were not being faithful stewards of the world. But Noah, was a just man. *Just* comes from the word *justice*, which means

respecting the rights of others and giving them what is rightfully theirs.

Genesis 6:7—9:17

So to Noah, who was a just man, God said, "I have decided to put an end to all mortals on earth; the earth is full of lawlessness because of them. So I will destroy them and all life on earth" (Genesis 6:13). Then God commanded Noah to build a great ark and fill it with two of every living thing, male and female, along with his wife and family.

Then God sent forty days and nights of rain. God allowed the floodwaters to rise above the highest mountains. All life outside the ark was lost.

Eventually the floodwaters went down, and Noah, his family, and all the animals left the ark. In gratitude, Noah built an altar and offered God a sacrifice on it. God was pleased with this sacrifice and made a covenant, or agreement, with Noah. God promised that even if humanity failed him again, he would never send another flood to destroy life on earth. The symbol of this promise was a rainbow. God told Noah, "This is the sign of the covenant I have established between me and all mortal creatures that are on earth" (Genesis 9:17).

This story revealed an important religious truth: God's forgiveness and love, and humanity's goodness, can overcome all evil. Through Noah God made an everlasting covenant with all humanity. For that reason all people are called to friendship with God.

There is great meaning in the symbols found in the story of Noah. For the Church the flood water is a symbol of the waters of the Sacrament of Baptism. Through Baptism we are freed from Original Sin and all personal sins. Through Baptism God offers us his forgiveness and his love.

Noah and his family were brought through the flood to new life. Through the waters of Baptism we are brought to a new life in Christ. Through the waters of Baptism, God begins a covenant relationship with each Christian. Just as the world was washed and made clean by the flood, we are washed and made clean in the baptismal water.

Design a stained-glass window that reminds you of God's friendship with all people.

Tower of Babel, by Pieter the Elder Brueghel (1515–1569)

The unity of the human race was lost.

We now come to the very last event that the Book of Genesis records for the period called prehistory. In Genesis 11:1–9 we read the story of the tower of Babel. This story symbolizes the separation among different groups of people, humanity's loss of unity and the development of different languages.

We read that at first "the whole world spoke the same language, using the same words" (Genesis 11:1). This symbolizes that all human beings were related. Because they were able to communicate, they could truly act as God's stewards of the earth. Part of God's plan for completing the work of creation involved humanity's spread across the face of the earth. However, human beings feared this. So they decided to resist God's plan: They would all settle in one place and build a great tower to live in.

The tower that they tried to build looked very much like an ancient structure called a *ziggurat*. A ziggurat is made of a series of smaller and smaller brick platforms, one on top of the other. The biblical writer called the city and the tower that the humans built *Babel*, the Hebrew name for Babylon. Babylon was an ancient city with the most famous ziggurat of all.

In the story the tower was a symbol of human resistance to God's will. The people who were building it did not trust God. They preferred to do things their way.

God saw what human beings were doing and decided to stop them. He did this by confusing their language. As a result, humans could not work together. All the people could do was babble helplessly at one another. The unity of the human race had been lost.

People often disagree because they do not understand one another. This misunderstanding can lead to suspicion, mistrust, and even open hostility. This

began to happen to the human race after Babel. Humanity began to lose its unity and break up into rival groups.

As the story closes, the process of populating the earth continued as God had planned. Now, however, humans spoke many different languages and developed different ways of living and communicating. Today it is still necessary to respect these differences and to appreciate the dignity that all people possess.

What do you think this expression means: "They don't speak the same language"?

_____
_____
_____
_____
_____
_____
_____
_____

WE RESPOND

As a class produce a talk show. The topic of today's talk show is: Do the divisions symbolized by the story of the tower of Babel still affect our lives today? Why or why not?

63

Grade 6 Chapter 4

PROJECT

Pray
Learn
Celebrate
Share
Choose
Live

Show What *you* Know

Use the clues to find the  Key Word.

The word has six letters:

- The first letter can be found in *gnat*, but not in *antique*.
- The second letter can be found in *foal*, but not in *fable*.
- The third letter can be found in *psalm*, but not in *palm*.
- The fourth letter can be found in *poems*, but not in *some*.
- The fifth letter can be found in *pear*, but not in *party*.
- The sixth letter can be found in *lawn* but not in *wand*

The word is ____ ____ ____ ____ ____ ____.

List two things that you know about this word.

_____

_____

Fast Facts

Custom has it that Noah's ark was built more like a four-sided box than a ship, a good shape for a cargo vessel. It was made of gopherwood (an unidentified wood, not mentioned elsewhere in the Bible) and sealed with pitch (wood tar) to make it watertight. It had one door, which God closed when Noah, his family, and two of every living thing were safely aboard the ark. (See Genesis 7:16.)

DISCIPLE

More to Explore

Since 1920, the Catholic News Service has been letting people know what is going on in the world and in the Church. The professional journalists and photographers who work for the Catholic News Service write stories and take pictures that keep people informed about Catholic life today. The latest news is posted regularly at the service's Web site, www.catholicnews.com and is often printed in diocesan newspapers.

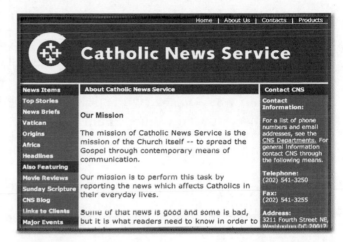

DISCIPLE CHALLENGE Why do you think the Catholic News Service is important?

_____

_____

Pray Today

Dear Lord,
Help me as I experience misunderstandings with my friends and family.
Give me patience as we work through disagreements.
Help me see things from the point of view of others.
Amen.

Make it Happen

It is necessary to respect the differences and appreciate the dignity that all people possess. What are some ways that you can teach this concept to someone younger than yourself?

_____

_____

_____ **Now, pass it on!**

Take Home

Share with your family that the word *gospel* means "good news." This week, urge your family to recognize people and events that share the Good News of Jesus Christ. List some here.

_____

_____

_____

_____

CHAPTER TEST

Circle the letter of the correct answer.

1. The _____ are the books of the Bible in which the Good News of Jesus' life and teachings are presented.

   a. covenants   **b.** Genesis   **c.** Gospels

2. Isaiah was a _____ who spoke to the people on God's behalf and reminded them of the way God wanted them to live.

   a. prophet   **b.** shepherd   **c.** farmer

3. The story of the Tower of Babel symbolizes the _____ among different groups of people.

   a. covenant   **b.** separation   **c.** love

4. God promised to send _____ who would restore humanity's friendship with God.

   a. Isaiah   **b.** Noah   **c.** a Savior

Short Answers

5. What did God do to help humanity after they turned away from him?

   God promised to send a Savior (Jesus)

6. The story of Cain and Abel can be understood on several levels. Write one.

   It symbolizes

7. What important religious truth is revealed in the story of Noah?

   God's forgiveness and love, and humanity's god goodness, can overcome any evil

8. In the story of the Tower of Babel, what does the tower symbolize?

   Human resistance to God's will

Write a paragraph to answer this question.

9–10. How did God keep his promise and restore his life and friendship to all humanity?

   _____

   _____

   _____

   _____

The Patriarchs: God Chooses a People

WE GATHER

✝ **Leader:** Loving God, your psalmist said, "Oh, that today you would hear his voice: Do not harden your hearts." (Psalm 95:7–8)

All: Help us to hear and follow your Word with open hearts. Amen.

Reader 1: For the times when we have deliberately chosen to do what we know is wrong.

All: Lord, have mercy.

Reader 2: For the times we have excluded others because they are not like us.

All: Lord, have mercy.

Reader 3: For the times we have used words to hurt and harm rather than to heal.

All: Lord, have mercy.

Reader 4: For the times we have walked by someone in need.

All: Lord, have mercy.

Leader: Loving God, we believe in you and place our trust in you. Help us strengthen our faith each day.

All: Amen.

☀ What do you know about your ancestors? How can you find out more about them?

St. Theresa's Fall Harvest Drive

WE BELIEVE
The patriarchs are our ancestors in faith.

In a new stage in God's relationship with humanity, God formed a people for himself. We call this formative period *The Age of the Patriarchs.*

A **patriarch** is a father, or founder, of a clan, a group of related families. The four Old Testament patriarchs are Abraham, Isaac, Jacob, and Joseph. Through them God chose a special family for himself. This family is the people of God. Sarah, Rebekah, Rachel, and Leah were important women in God's family. They are called matriarchs. These men and women lived from approximately 1900 B.C. to about 1650 B.C. Their story is told in Chapters 12—50 of the Book of Genesis.

The families of these Old Testament patriarchs and matriarchs lived in tents and made their living primarily by raising flocks of sheep and goats. Their life centered on their families and the clan. They roamed the unoccupied territory between the towns and villages of Canaan and the desert. **Canaan** was an area in western Palestine that included most of present-day Israel.

During the period of the patriarchs, Canaan was made up of small independent city-states. A king ruled each city-state. Each city-state was made up of a walled city and the surrounding countryside.

The inhabitants of Canaan, or Canaanites, had the same background as the patriarchs and their families. They all spoke a similar language. That is why they treated one another as distant cousins rather than as complete strangers.

The families of the patriarchs and matriarchs are our ancestors in faith. **Faith** is a gift from God that enables us to believe in him and accept all that he has revealed.

"Faith is the realization of what is hoped for and evidence of things not seen." (Hebrews 11:1). Through the trusting relationship of faith, the patriarchs and their families learned what it meant to be a part of God's family. They lived their lives trying to follow God's commands and going where God led them.These ancestors in faith are a good example of reliance on God during our own journey through life. Through the gift of faith we can begin to see our lives and the world around us as God sees them. We can live the way God wants us to live, too.

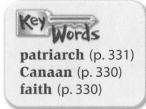

Key Words
patriarch (p. 331)
Canaan (p. 330)
faith (p. 330)

One day you will be an ancestor in faith. How would you like to be remembered by future generations?

_____

_____

_____

_____

_____

_____

God chose Abraham to be the father of his people.

The Book of Genesis describes how God decided to form a people for himself.

📖 Genesis 12:1–7

God looked about him and called Abram. God said, "Go forth from the land of your kinsfolk and from your father's house to a land that I will show you" (Genesis 12:1). This land was the land of Canaan, which God promised to give to Abram and his descendants forever.

As soon as Abram heard God's call, he and his wife, Sarai, gathered their family and property and started out on the long journey to Canaan.

In Abram God chose a very unlikely person to begin his people. Abram was seventy-five years old; he was neither famous nor powerful; and, his wife, Sarai, could not have children.

When God spoke to him, Abram did not argue with God. Rather, Abram had great faith, and trusted completely in God's will. In fact, Abram is our most important Old Testament model of faith.

When Abram and Sarai arrived in Canaan, God made a covenant with Abram. God said, "I am God the Almighty. Walk in my presence and be blameless. Between you and me I will establish my covenant, and I will multiply you exceedingly" (Genesis 17:1–2). By this agreement Abram and his descendants would serve God and follow his ways, and God would give Abram a son and make "a great nation" of him (Genesis 12:2). To indicate that they were beginning a new life as a new people, God changed Abram's name to Abraham and Sarai's name to Sarah.

As predicted, Isaac, Abraham and Sarah's long-awaited son, was finally born. When Isaac was a young boy, Abraham's faith was tested by God.

📖 Genesis 22:2–18

God said to Abraham,

"Take your son Isaac, your only one, whom you love, and go to the land of Moriah. There you shall offer him up as a holocaust on a height that I will point out to you" (Genesis 22:2).

Abraham did what God asked. But as he was about to sacrifice Isaac to God, a messenger from God called to him, "Do not do the least thing to him. I know now how devoted you are to God, since you did not withhold from me your own beloved son" (Genesis 22:12).

The Church sees a New Testament parallel in this story: God the Father offered his only Son, Jesus Christ, to save us.

Do you think that like Abraham you could trust in God if he told you to do something very difficult? Why or why not?

Write a prayer asking God to help you trust him in difficult times.

As Catholics...

The word *angel* comes from the Greek word meaning "messenger." Angels were created by God as pure spirits with no physical bodies. All through the Bible, we find angels carrying God's messages to his people. We honor the angels today, and we benefit from their powerful help. Saint Basil wrote, "Beside each believer stands an angel as protector and shepherd leading him to life."

This week remember to ask your angel for the help that you need in your life.

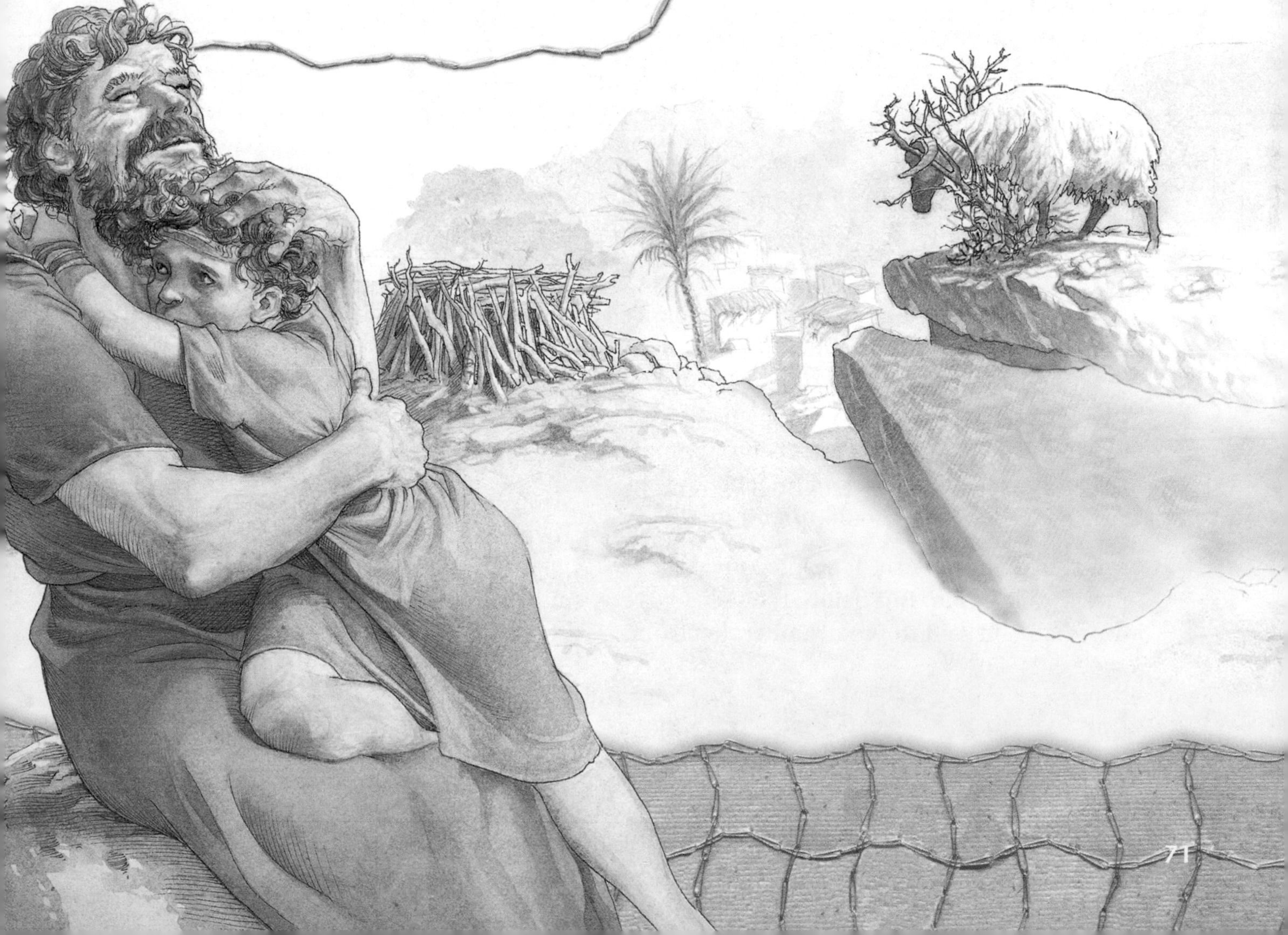

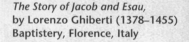

The Story of Jacob and Esau,
by Lorenzo Ghiberti (1378–1455)
Baptistery, Florence, Italy

God's people became known as the Israelites.

When Abraham died, his son, Isaac, inherited his father's position as patriarch of the family. Isaac married a woman named Rebekah, with whom he had twin sons: Esau and Jacob. The birth of twin sons caused a problem: Which son would someday have Isaac's position in the family? The position could not be divided. Only one of the twins could inherit it.

Esau was the first born. It seemed his right to inherit Isaac's role. But before the twins were born, God had said to their mother, Rebekah,

"Two nations are in your womb,
  two peoples are quarreling while still
    within you;
But one shall surpass the other,
  and the older shall serve the younger"
(Genesis 25:23).

However, to inherit Isaac's position Jacob must overturn the man-made rules of inheritance. Thus, the story of Jacob is a story of conflict.

The choice of Jacob as Abraham's successor was surprising. Jacob grew up to be something of a trickster. We get our first hint of this side of Jacob's character in Genesis 25:27–34 when he tricked Esau into selling him his birthright for a bowl of lentil stew. A birthright is the child's natural right to inherit the father's property.

As we read in Genesis 27:1–46 this was not the end of Jacob's tricks. With his mother's help Jacob pretended to be Esau. He tricked his elderly and blind father into giving him the blessing that Esau had the right to. When his father Isaac discovered what had happened, he was outraged. And Esau wanted to kill his brother, Jacob. So Rebekah told Jacob to flee to the land of Haran.

It is clear that Jacob possessed the one quality that was crucial to living out the covenant. This quality was determination, or perseverance. Jacob never gave up.

On his way to Haran, Jacob had a dream in which he saw a great staircase reaching to Heaven. In the dream God told Jacob what he told Abraham, "I, the LORD, am the God of your forefather Abraham and the God of Isaac; the land on which you are lying I will give to you and your descendants. These shall be as plentiful as the dust of the earth. . . . Know that I am with you; I will protect you wherever you go, and bring you back to this land. I will never leave you until I have done what I promised you" (Genesis 28:13–15).

With these words, God assured Jacob that he would inherit Canaan and that God would always protect him.

In Haran, Jacob prospered, married, had many children, and grew very rich. This was the biblical writer's way of telling us that God's people were blessed. After

twenty years Jacob decided to return to Canaan, where he was finally reconciled to his brother and father.

In Genesis 35:9–15 we can read that God renewed the covenant with Jacob. He also changed Jacob's name to Israel. This was the symbolic way to show that God's people had grown to the point that they could actually be distinguished by name. God's people were now called the people of Israel, or the Israelites.

Imagine you are an advice columnist. Answer this e-mail.

✉ ▼ / 𝒫 🖫 ▼	What should I do?	_ 🗗 ✕

From: Esau

Subject: What should I do?

Hi! My name is Esau. I'm having problems with my family. My brother and I haven't spoken in 20 years because he played a trick on my father and on me. I hear that he wants to make up and is on his way back home.

Can you help me? What should I say and do?

Esau

✉ ▼ / 𝒫 🖫 ▼	Re: What should I do?	_ 🗗 ✕

From:

Subject: Re: What should I do?

73

God cared for the Israelites.

The last of the Old Testament patriarchs is Joseph. His story is told in Genesis 37:1—50:26. Joseph's story is about the way that God's will is achieved. In Joseph's case, God's plan was to provide a temporary home for his people.

Providence is God's plan for and protection of all creation. Through providence God leads his creation toward the perfection for which it was made. In the story of Joseph, providence was symbolized by the fulfillment of dreams. Joseph's only contact with God is through dreams which indicated God's plan.

Genesis 37:3–28; 39:1–23; 40:1—46:30

Joseph and his brothers were not on friendly terms. Joseph was the son of Rachel and Jacob, and was the favorite of Jacob's twelve sons. Jacob had given Joseph a special long robe such as a king might wear. The other brothers hated Joseph because their father, Jacob, loved him so much.

Joseph had dreams that predicted that he would have authority over his family. These dreams upset Joseph's brothers. So one day they sold Joseph as a slave to a passing caravan of merchants. The merchants sold Joseph to the chief steward of the **pharaoh**, the king of Egypt.

At first Joseph did well, but eventually he was thrown into prison on false charges. In prison Joseph discovered his ability to interpret dreams. This skill brought him to the attention of the pharaoh, who had been disturbed by strange dreams.

Twelve Sons of Jacob

1. Reuben
2. Simeon
3. Levi
4. Judah
5. Dan
6. Naphtali
7. Gad
8. Asher
9. Issachar
10. Zebulun
11. Joseph
12. Benjamin

Key Words
providence (p. 331)
pharaoh (p. 331)

Joseph told the pharaoh that his dreams meant that a period of great abundance would be followed by a time of terrible famine. The pharaoh was delighted by the explanation of his dreams, and put Joseph in charge of the management of his kingdom. Joseph prepared Egypt for the famine.

When the famine arrived, Jacob and his family in Canaan suffered greatly from hunger. Hearing that there was food in Egypt, Joseph's brothers traveled there to buy grain. This brought them face-to-face with Joseph. They did not recognize Joseph at first and bowed down to him when he entered the room. So Joseph's dreams had come true. Joseph now had authority over his family.

Joseph was eventually reconciled to his brothers. He invited his whole family to move to Egypt. His father, Jacob, accepted the invitation, and made the long journey to Egypt. God's purpose had been fulfilled. God's people found a temporary home in Egypt.

WE RESPOND

Write about a time when God acted in your life in an unexpected way. Share your story with a partner.

Thank God for his care and providence.

PROJECT

Show What *you* Know

Unscramble the letters of the Key Words. Then put the numbered letters in the boxes to find out who Abraham is.

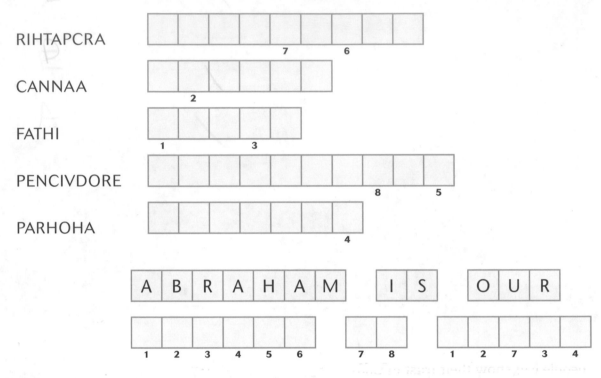

RIHTAPCRA

						7		6	

CANNAA

		2			

FATHI

1		3		

PENCIVDORE

						8		5	

PARHOHA

				4	

A	B	R	A	H	A	M		I	S		O	U	R

1	2	3	4	5	6		7	8		1	2	7	3	4

Pray Today

Blessings are a large part of our daily prayer. This is a custom we received from and share with the Jewish People. There are blessings for meals, families, children, homes, animals, workplaces, times of joy, and times of sorrow, and so on. Share this blessing and pray it with your family:

May the Lord bless and keep you.
May the Lord's face shine upon you,
And be gracious to you.
May the Lord look upon you,
And give you peace.

(add your own family verse)

_____

Amen.

DISCIPLE

Pray
Learn
Celebrate
Share
Choose
Live

Fast Facts

Joseph and the Amazing Technicolor Dreamcoat is a musical written by the team of Andrew Lloyd Webber and Tim Rice. Loosely based on the story of Joseph in the Bible, this musical was first presented on Broadway in 1982. Its family-friendly storyline, universal themes, and catchy music have made it a continued success. In addition, more than 20,000 schools and amateur theatre groups have successfully put on productions of this musical.

Reality Check

What are some situations in which people can show their trust in God?

Now, pass it on!

What Would you do?

What advice would you give to a friend that has a "difficult" relationship with a sibling?

_____

_____

_____

Take Home

This week, encourage your family members to go where God leads them. Ask God to lead you and your family to the people and places where your love and care are needed.

Write the letter that best defines each term.

1. __B__ faith

2. __E__ providence

3. __P__ patriarch

4. __A__ Canaan

a. an area in western Palestine that included most of present-day Israel

b. a gift from God that enables us to believe in him and accept all that he has revealed

c. the natural right to inherit the father's property

d. a father, or founder, of a clan, a group of related families

e. God's plan for and protection of all creation

Short Answers

5. Who are the patriarchs of the Old Testament?

   Joseph, Isaac, Abraham, Jacob

6. How is providence symbolized in the story of Joseph?

   by the fulfillment of dreams

7. What quality did Jacob have that enabled him to live out the covenant?

   ~~As long Abraham to sacrifice Isaac to~~

8. How was Abraham's faith tested?

   Abraham had to sacrifice Isaac to God Moriah to sacrifice Abrahams only son not gin

Write a paragraph to answer this question.

9–10. What does the story of each patriarch show about our relationship with God?

_____

_____

_____

_____

"Rejoice in the Lord always.
I shall say it again: rejoice!"

Philippians 4:4

SEASONAL

CHAPTER 6

This chapter presents an overview of the
Liturgical Year.

Throughout the liturgical year we celebrate the entire mystery of Christ.

WE GATHER

✝ *Lord, you create all things to give you glory.*

What are some days of the year that are very important to you? Why? How do you show others that these days and times are special to you?

WE BELIEVE

As the Church we have special days and times of the year that are very important to us. One special way we remember these times is in the celebration of the liturgy. The liturgy is the official public prayer of the Church. It includes the celebration of the Eucharist, or Mass, and the other sacraments. The liturgy also includes the Liturgy of the Hours, a prayer, parts of which the Church prays at various times during the day and night.

In the liturgy throughout the year, we remember and rejoice in the saving actions of Jesus Christ. So we call the Church year the *liturgical year*. During the liturgical year we recall and celebrate the whole mystery of Christ. We celebrate the birth of the Son of God, his younger years, his public ministry, his suffering, Death, Resurrection, and Ascension into Heaven. During this year we also venerate, or show devotion to, Mary, the Mother of God, and all the saints.

Advent

Christmas

Ordinary Time

Lent

Triduum

Easter

Ordinary Time

Advent   The season of Advent begins the liturgical year in late November or early December. Advent is a time of joyful preparation for the coming of Christ. We look forward to Christ's second coming at the end of time. We celebrate that Christ comes into our lives every day. We await Christmas, the celebration of the first coming of the Son of God.

Christmas   The Christmas season begins on Christmas Day with the celebration of the birth of the Son of God. During this entire season we celebrate that God is with us always.

Lent   The season of Lent begins on Ash Wednesday. Lent is the special time when we remember that Jesus suffered, died, and rose to new life to restore our relationship with God. During Lent we work to grow closer to Jesus and one another through prayer, fasting, and penance. We pray for and support all who are preparing for the Sacraments of Christian Initiation. We prepare for the Easter Triduum.

Triduum   The Easter Triduum is the Church's greatest and most important celebration. The word *triduum* means "three days." During these three days, from Holy Thursday evening until Easter Sunday evening, we remember and celebrate Jesus' suffering, Death, and Resurrection in a very special way.

Easter   The season of Easter begins on Easter Sunday evening and continues until Pentecost Sunday. During this season we rejoice in Jesus' Resurrection and in the new life we have in Jesus Christ.

Ordinary Time   The season of Ordinary Time is celebrated in two parts: the first part is between Christmas and Lent, and the second part is between Easter and Advent. During this time we celebrate the life and teachings of Jesus Christ and learn what it means to live as his disciples. On the last Sunday of Ordinary Time, also the last Sunday of the liturgical year, we celebrate the Feast of Christ the King.

The calendar Our calendar of years, months, and days depends upon elements of nature, like the sun and the moon. Many of our liturgical feasts also reflect the cycle of nature.

Our liturgical year is constructed around the dates of the Easter Triduum, which depend each year on the spring equinox and the rising of the full moon. The spring equinox is the day the sun crosses the equator, making day and night of equal length everywhere. Easter Sunday follows the full moon after the spring equinox. This fact alone is a beautiful proclamation of the Resurrection of Christ, whose rising brings light to our darkness.

Astronomers can calculate the date of the spring equinox. They use formulas to do this for years into the future. Looking at their calculations we find that the date of Easter Sunday is always between March 22 and April 25.

Using the date for Easter Sunday, we can construct the liturgical calendar for each year. We can work backward six weeks to determine the beginning of Lent, and forward seven weeks to find the date of Pentecost.

WE RESPOND

The readings we hear, the songs we sing, the colors we see, and the ways we worship, help us to celebrate each liturgical season.

In groups describe some of the ways your parish celebrates each of these seasons of the liturgical year.

Advent

_____

_____

Christmas

_____

_____

Lent

_____

_____

Triduum

_____

_____

Easter

_____

_____

Ordinary Time

_____

_____

✙ We Respond in Prayer

Leader: Give praise to God, who is rich in mercy and who has favored us in wonderful ways. Blessed be God for ever.

All: Blessed be God for ever.

Leader: Saint Paul urges us to give thanks to God always through Christ, for in him, God has given us everything.

Reader: A reading from the Letter of Saint Paul to the Philippians

"Rejoice in the Lord always. I shall say it again: rejoice! Your kindness should be known to all. The Lord is near. Have no anxiety at all, but in everything, by prayer and petition, with thanksgiving, make your requests known to God."
(Philippians 4:4–6)

The word of the Lord.

All: Thanks be to God.

Leader: Let us thank God for our blessings and offer our needs to him.

All: Hear us, O Lord.

🎵 Rejoice in the Lord Always

Round 1

Rejoice in the Lord always,
again I say, rejoice!
Rejoice in the Lord always,
again I say, rejoice!

Round 2

Rejoice! Rejoice! Again I say, rejoice!
Rejoice! Rejoice! Again I say, rejoice!

Pray Learn Celebrate Share Choose Live

PROJECT DISCIPLE

Celebrate! Design a Web page that explains the liturgical year.

What's the Word?

*"There is an appointed time for everything, ...
A time to be born, and a time to die;
a time to plant, and a time to uproot the plant."*
(Ecclesiastes 3:1–2)

How does the Church use "appointed times" to recall and celebrate the whole mystery of Christ?

_____

_____

Pray Today

Dear God, Help me to make the most of the seasons of the Church year. In this liturgical year I will recall and celebrate the mystery of Christ. Amen.

Take Home

Plan a family project: make a liturgical calendar for the upcoming liturgical year. Include labels for holy days, liturgical colors and seasons, feasts, and family dates on the calendar. Be creative! Display the completed calendar in a prominent place.

"This is the day the LORD has made;
let us rejoice in it and be glad."

Psalm 118:24

SEASONAL

CHAPTER 7

**This chapter helps us to understand
the season of Ordinary Time.**

During the season of Ordinary Time, we celebrate the life and teachings of Jesus Christ.

WE GATHER

✝ *Jesus, help us to keep Sunday holy.*

What is your attitude toward Sunday? Do you look forward to it? Why or why not? How is it the same as other days of the week? How is it different?

WE BELIEVE

Ordinary Time is a season of life and hope. We learn what it means to live as Christ's disciples, and we grow as members of the Church. The color green, which we use during this season, reminds us of the life and hope that come from Christ.

Other seasons during the liturgical year focus on a particular event or period in Jesus' life. During the season of Ordinary Time, we celebrate all that Christ does for us through his birth, life, Death, Resurrection, and Ascension. We recall the life of Jesus Christ and focus on his teachings in a special way.

The season of Ordinary Time lasts thirty three to thirty four weeks. It is called Ordinary Time because the weeks are "ordered," or named in number order. For example, the first week in Ordinary Time is followed by the second week in Ordinary Time, and so on.

We celebrate Ordinary Time twice during the liturgical year. We celebrate first for a short time between the seasons of Christmas and Lent. The first part of Ordinary Time begins in early January and lasts until the Tuesday before Ash Wednesday. The second part of Ordinary Time is between the seasons of Easter and Advent. So it begins in late May or June after Pentecost Sunday, which ends the Easter season, and lasts several months until the evening before the first Sunday of Advent in late November or early December.

The Lord's Day   In the Jewish calendar, Saturday was and still is the Sabbath, the day of rest set apart to honor God in a special way. The Sabbath is a special day to praise God for giving us his creation and for acting in the lives of his people. Saturday is the last day of the week, and the Jewish People rest as God rested on the seventh day after completing his creation. It is Jewish tradition to observe that Sabbath from sundown on Friday to sundown on Saturday.

The early Christians followed many of the Jewish customs of prayer and worship. They prayed the psalms and they kept the Sabbath. Gradually, because Jesus Christ rose on a Sunday, Sunday became the Christian Sabbath. Because Christ rose on a Sunday, the Christians called it "the Lord's Day." On this day they gathered to recall Christ's Death and Resurrection by celebrating the Eucharist.

Today the Church keeps Sunday as our first holy day. We keep the Lord's Day holy by participating in the celebration of the Eucharist, by resting from work and enjoying our families, by remembering our relationship with God and by serving the needs of the community.

Sunday is the most important day to gather with our parishes for the celebration of the Eucharist, the Mass. In the Mass, we

- praise and thank God for his many gifts

- listen to God's Word

- remember Jesus' life, Death, and Resurrection and celebrate Jesus' gift of himself in the Eucharist

- receive the Body and Blood of Christ in Holy Communion

- are joined more closely to Christ and one another in the Church

- are sent out to share Jesus' love, serve others, and work for justice and peace.

In observing the Lord's Day we follow the Jewish custom of celebrating from sundown to sundown. So we begin our celebration on Saturday evening and complete it on Sunday evening. This is why some people participate in the Sunday Mass on Saturday evening.

Receiving the Eucharist

A Procession On the Feast of the Body and Blood of Christ, we celebrate the presence of Jesus Christ with us in the Eucharist in a special way. Many parishes have a procession in honor of Christ's presence in the Eucharist, the Blessed Sacrament. The priest carries the Blessed Sacrament in a special holder called a monstrance. People carry banners and flowers and worship together as they process, or walk, through the city streets or around the area of the parish. In some places flowers are strewn on the streets as the community processes with the Blessed Sacrament. In the church a carpet made of flowers is sometimes laid in the center aisle as a sign of respect and reverence to Jesus in the Blessed Sacrament.

Sundays during Ordinary Time Sundays are the foundation of our liturgical year, and we use them to mark the passing of the weeks of Ordinary Time and the other seasons. Sunday's importance comes from the fact that Jesus' Resurrection was on a Sunday.

During Ordinary Time there are three very important Sundays.

- Trinity Sunday, the first Sunday after Pentecost, is the first Sunday in the second part of Ordinary Time. On this Sunday we celebrate in a special way our belief in the Blessed Trinity: God the Father, God the Son, and God the Holy Spirit.

- The Body and Blood of Christ is the Sunday after Trinity Sunday. This is sometimes called "Corpus Christi Sunday" because the term *Body of Christ* comes from these two Latin words.

- Christ the King is the last Sunday in Ordinary Time. On this day we rejoice that Christ is the King of the universe. He saves us from evil and brings us new life. Through him the Kingdom of God has begun on earth.

WE RESPOND

In groups list some ways that you celebrate the Lord's Day.

_____

_____

_____

_____

_____

_____

Have the rest of the class guess what you listed by acting out some of the ways.

✝ We Respond in Prayer

Leader: Lord our God, we bless you. As we come together we ask you in your kindness to fill us with the knowledge of your will so that, pleasing you in all things, we may grow in every good work.

We ask this through Christ our Lord.

All: Amen.

Reader: A reading from the holy Gospel according to Matthew

All: Glory to you, O Lord.

Reader: "You are the light of the world. A city set on a mountain cannot be hidden. Nor do they light a lamp and then put it under a bushel basket; it is set on a lampstand, where it gives light to all in the house. Just so, your light must shine before others, that they may see your good deeds and glorify your heavenly Father." (Matthew 5:14–16)

The Gospel of the Lord.

All: Praise to you, Lord Jesus Christ.

♫ This Little Light of Mine

This little light of mine,
I'm gonna let it shine. (Repeat 3 times)
Let it shine, let it shine, let it shine.

Ev'rywhere I go,
I'm gonna let it shine. (Repeat 3 times)
Let it shine, let it shine, let it shine.

Jesus gave it to me;
I'm gonna let it shine. (Repeat 3 times)
Let it shine, let it shine, let it shine.

Pray Learn Celebrate Share Choose Live

PROJECT DISCIPLE

Picture This

The Chi-Rho symbol is usually associated with the liturgical season of Ordinary Time. It is formed by Greek letters χ(Chi) and ρ(Rho). These are the first two letters in the Greek word *Christ*. Draw the Chi-Rho symbol in the space below. (For reference see the bottom of page 85.)

Celebrate!

Write a "top ten" list about Ordinary Time.
1. will be the most *extraordinary*!

10. _____   5. _____

9. _____   4. _____

8. _____   3. _____

7. _____   2. _____

6. _____   1. _____

Fast Facts

During Ordinary Time the Church proclaims the Gospels in a three-year Sunday cycle. Each cycle highlights one of these Gospels—(Year A) Matthew, (Year B) Mark, and (Year C) Luke.

Take Home

The Church celebrates Sunday, the Lord's Day, as a holy day. As a family, we can keep the Lord's Day holy by

_____

_____

_____.

UNIT TEST

**Write True or False for the following sentences.
Then change the false sentences to make them true.**

1. _____ Tradition is the Revelation of the Good News of Jesus Christ as lived out in the Church, past and present.

   _____

2. _____ An agreement between God and his people is called grace.

   _____

3. _____ The special guidance that the Holy Spirit gave to the human writers of the Bible is called Divine Inspiration.

   _____

4. _____ Every human being has an invisible spiritual reality that will never die. This breath of life from God refers to the body.

   _____

5. _____ In the story of Joseph, God's plan for and protection of all creation, which we call providence, is symbolized by the fulfillment of dreams.

   _____

6. _____ The prophet Isaac described a person as the Suffering Servant who would come to free us from sin.

   _____

7. _____ The flood is the sign God gave to Noah to symbolize the covenant between God and all mortal creatures on earth.

   _____

8. _____ The four patriarchs of the Old Testament are Abraham, Isaac, Jacob, and Joseph.

   _____

Fill in the circle beside the correct answer.

9. God's making himself known to us is called _____.

   ○ personal sin   ○ Divine Revelation   ○ free will

continued on next page   91

10. Evil entered the world through a human act that we call _____.

○ Original Sin   ○ Genesis   ○ suffering

11. The first book of the Bible is called *Genesis,* a word meaning _____.

○ "Scripture"   ○ "beginning"   ○ "covenant"

12. A _____ is a person who has both the authority over what he or she cares for and the responsibility for seeing that it lives and grows.

○ patriarch   ○ prophet   ○ steward

13. Among the _____, or characteristics, of God are that he is eternal, all-knowing, and ever-present.

○ attributes   ○ symbols   ○ genealogies

14. To fully restore the friendship with God that was broken by the first humans' disobedience, God promised to send a _____.

○ prophet   ○ Savior   ○ covenant

15. God renewed his covenant with Jacob, and changed that patriarch's name to _____.

○ Israel   ○ Isaac   ○ Abram

16. In the Old Testament story of _____, the Church sees a parallel to God the Father's offering his only Son, Jesus Christ, to save us.

○ Esau and Jacob   ○ Cain and Abel   ○ Abraham and Isaac

Write a paragraph to answer each question.

17–18. Among all the creatures made by God to dwell on earth, humans alone are created with free will. What does this mean and why is it important?

_____

_____

19–20. The patriarchs of the Old Testament are our ancestors in faith. They freely said yes to God with all their hearts. How can we follow their example?

_____

_____

Building the Covenant Nation

UNIT 2

Seasonal Chapters

In Unit 2 your child will grow as a disciple of Jesus by:

- learning about the enslavement of the Israelites, and God's choice of Moses to lead the people to freedom
- understanding God's guidance of his people as he gave them his law and led them toward the promised land
- appreciating God's people who settled in Canaan, and the stories of Samson and Ruth
- recognizing God's faithfulness to his people, and his guidance of their leaders, Samuel and David
- praying for wisdom as Solomon did, and praying with the psalms.

More to Explore

Visuals can assist with learning. There are DVDs and books that capture some of the biblical events that are in this unit. There are also Internet sites where you can find images of the pyramids or works of art depicting Moses, David, and Goliath. Look for one of these resources to enhance your family's experience of this unit.

Show That You Care

God led his people from slavery to freedom. As people of faith we are to help people who are oppressed or treated unjustly. Talk with your child about the minor, but still painful, "oppressions" that can happen every day, in school or the community. Are there new students who are ignored? Are younger children teased by older students? Do you see children or teachers or crossing guards who are rejected and made fun of? What might your family do to help?

Reality Check

"The importance of the family for the life and well-being of society entails a particular responsibility for society to support and strengthen marriage and the family."
(*Catechism of the Catholic Church*, 2210)

Picture This

Turn to the timeline on pages 96–97 in your child's text. What names and events do you recognize? Ask each family member to share what he or she knows about one of the events or people on the timeline. Have each member identify one person or event to learn more about. Give your 6th grader the responsibility of finding out and sharing what the family wants to know.

Celebrate!

This unit highlights some of the leaders God chose for his people: Moses, Joshua, Deborah, Samson, Samuel, Saul, David, Solomon. Who are the people that lead you as Catholics today? How does their leadership help your family to be better disciples? Pray for those leaders; send a card or an e-mail to thank them and encourage them.

Take Home

Be ready for this unit's Take Home:

Chapter 8: Working to protect human rights

Chapter 9: Praying a psalm together

Chapter 10: Serving the Lord

Chapter 11: Writing a prayer of blessing

Chapter 12: Appreciating God's gift of wisdom

An Enslaved People

WE GATHER

✝ **Leader:** For followers of Christ, freedom is a gift of love and goodness, and comes from Christ. Let us pray for all those who are not free, who are enslaved, in our world today.

Reader 1: "For freedom Christ set us free; so stand firm and do not submit again to the yoke of slavery." (Galatians 5:1)

Reader 2: For all who are enslaved by the habit of sin and selfishness, let us pray:

All: Lord Jesus Christ, set them free.
(This is the response to each petition.)

Reader 3: For all who are enslaved by unsafe working conditions and low pay, let us pray:

Reader 4: For all who are enslaved by addiction, let us pray:

Reader 5: For all who are enslaved by disease and chronic illness, let us pray:

Reader 6: For all who are enslaved by poverty and hunger, let us pray:

Reader 7: For all who are unjustly denied their freedom, let us pray.

☀ In what ways are you free to do and say things? Do people in all parts of the world have these same freedoms?

♫ **Go Down, Moses**

When Israel was in Egypt's land,
Let my people go;
Oppressed so hard they could not stand,
Let my people go.

Refrain:
Go down, Moses,
Way down in Egypt's land;
Tell old Pharaoh: Let my people go.

Oh, let us all from bondage flee,
Let my people go;
And let us all in Christ be free,
Let my people go. (Refrain)

95

Israelites grow and prosper in Egypt

Moses is born and raised by pharaoh's daughter

God reveals himself to Moses

Oppression of the Israelites increases

The first Passover: God leads the Israelites out of Egypt

God speaks with Moses on Mt. Sinai/ Israel is a holy nation

Israelites journey for many years

Pharaoh begins oppression of Israelites

Moses flees Egypt

Moses returns to Egypt to lead the Israelites

Egypt suffers many plagues

Miriam leads rejoicing

Moses dies

God gives Moses the Ten Commandments

Timeline for Chapters 8–12

WE BELIEVE

Egypt became the home of the Israelites.

God led the family of Jacob, or as God had named him, Israel, into Egypt. All twelve of Israel's sons, including Joseph, were reunited. In Egypt Jacob's family was saved from famine and protected from hardships. God had provided for his people through Joseph.

Joseph told the pharaoh, "My father and my brothers have come from the land of Canaan, with their flocks and herds and everything else they own; and they are now in the region of Goshen" (Genesis 47:1). The pharaoh told Joseph that they could settle there. He said, "the land of Egypt is at your disposal" (Genesis 47:6).

So Jacob's family became honored guests in Egypt. They were given the best land in Goshen, a fertile area in northern Egypt. At the time Egypt was divided into two kingdoms. The southern part of the country was ruled by Egyptian kings. A separate kingdom in northern Egypt was ruled by people who came from regions to the east of Egypt.

Change in Egypt   In Goshen, in northern Egypt, Jacob's family prospered and God's people grew in number. At first they lived there in safety and comfort. But in time the Egyptians gained control of the northern

kingdom. Two Egyptian kings united Egypt. Egypt entered a period of great wealth and power. This period, called the New Kingdom, lasted for hundreds of years.

As time passed, Joseph and his generation died. A new pharaoh came into power. He did not know of Joseph and did not look upon the Israelites as honored guests. In fact, he feared them, saying, "Look how numerous and powerful the Israelite people are growing. . . in time of war they too may join our enemies to fight against us, and so leave our country" (Exodus 1:9–10).

In the Book of Exodus, the second book of the Bible, we find out that eventually the Egyptians made the Israelites their slaves. The pharaoh forced them to build monuments, and to work long hours in the fields. The Israelites were no longer free to worship the one true God and to follow his laws. And the lives of the Israelites became so unbearable that they cried out to God to be rescued from Egypt.

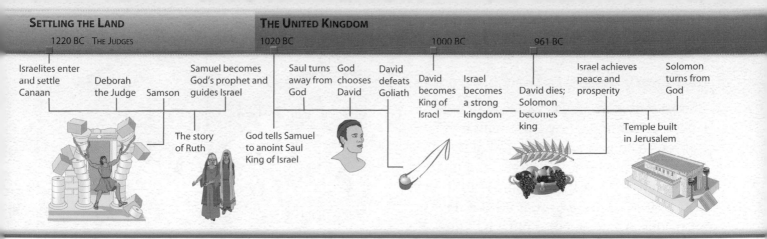

Israelites enter and settle Canaan

Deborah the Judge

Samson

The story of Ruth

Samuel becomes God's prophet and guides Israel

God tells Samuel to anoint Saul King of Israel

Saul turns away from God

God chooses David

David defeats Goliath

David becomes King of Israel

Israel becomes a strong kingdom

David dies; Solomon becomes king

Israel achieves peace and prosperity

Temple built in Jerusalem

Solomon turns from God

In the Book of Exodus we also read of the terrible suffering of the Israelites as slaves of the pharaoh. Yet we learn that God carried out his plan to bring his people back to Canaan. **Exodus** is the biblical word describing the Israelites' departure from slavery to freedom.

Key Word
exodus (p. 330)

Today there are people who need to be rescued from slavery, poverty, homelessness, and hunger.

List some other things from which people need to be rescued.

_____

_____

_____

_____

As Catholics...

Slavery devalues human dignity and takes away freedom. Most countries protect people from slavery and from forced labor. However, the need to protect the rights of workers remains.

The Church teaches us that the opportunity to be employed, to have safe working conditions, and to earn a fair wage are issues of justice. The Church speaks out against any system, private organization, or government that focuses on making a profit at the expense of human dignity and freedom.

What can you do to respect the dignity of workers?

97

God chose Moses to lead his people.

The Israelites were also called Hebrews, since their language was known as Hebrew. The pharaoh noticed that despite all the difficulties in their lives, the number of Hebrews was still growing. He told some of the Hebrew women that all the newly born sons of the Israelites must be killed. But these women did not listen to the pharaoh. So the pharaoh gave a new command: "Throw into the river every boy that is born to the Hebrews" (Exodus 1:22).

To save her son, one woman made a basket out of reeds from the river. She coated it with tar to prevent it from sinking and then put her son in it. She placed the basket in the shallow water near one of the riverbanks. The pharaoh's daughter found the child and took him home with her. She named the child Moses and raised him as an Egyptian.

Life in Midian   When Moses was an adult, he often visited his fellow Hebrews. One day he saw a Hebrew slave being beaten by an Egyptian, and got so angry that he killed the Egyptian. Moses had to run away to the desert region of Midian because now the pharaoh wanted Moses put to death. Moses settled there and lived the life of a shepherd. He married a woman named Zipporah and they had children.

One day while Moses was tending his flocks, God appeared to him in a burning bush. The fire was flaming from the bush but not destroying it. God called out to Moses from the bush and Moses answered, "Here I am" (Exodus 3:4). God told Moses that he wanted him to return to Egypt and lead the Hebrews out of slavery. Moses asked God how he would be able to do this, and God told Moses that he would be with him.

Moses asked God what he should say when the Israelites asked him who sent him to them. "God replied, 'I am who am.' Then he added, 'This is what you shall tell the Israelites: I AM sent me to you'" (Exodus 3:14).

This name that God gave was the source of the word *Yahweh.* "I AM" was a name that described God as ever-present to his people. This name was so holy that out of reverence the Israelites did not even speak it. Instead they used the title *Adonai,* which means "my Lord."

Again God spoke to Moses. "Go and assemble the elders of the Israelites, and tell them: The LORD, the God of your fathers, the God of Abraham, Isaac and Jacob, has appeared to me and said: I am concerned about you and about the way you are being treated in Egypt; so I have decided to lead you up out of the misery of Egypt into the land of the Canaanites, . . . a land flowing with milk and honey" (Exodus 3:16–17). Moses did as God commanded.

Write and illustrate a prayer that expresses gratitude for the many ways God shows love and care for all people.

God helped his people.

After Moses returned to Egypt, Aaron, his brother, helped him to explain God's message to the Israelites. Gradually, Moses gained the support of the people.

Moses and Aaron met with the pharaoh. They said, "Thus says the LORD, the God of Israel: Let my people go, that they may celebrate a feast to me in the desert" (Exodus 5:1). The pharaoh refused. Worse still, the pharaoh now would not give the Israelite slaves the materials they needed for their work.

It became impossible for the Israelites to complete their required work. They blamed Moses for this hardship. Moses told God how the people were suffering, and God replied, "Now you shall see what I will do to Pharaoh . . . compelled by my outstretched arm, he will drive them from his land" (Exodus 6:1).

God knew that it would be difficult to convince the pharaoh to let the Israelites leave Egypt. So God said to Moses, "I will lay my hand on Egypt and by great acts of judgment I will bring the hosts of my people, the Israelites, out of the land of Egypt, so that the Egyptians may learn that I am the LORD" (Exodus 7:4–5). These "great acts of judgment" that God speaks of were the plagues. During biblical times, a major disaster or catastrophe was considered a plague.

The Plagues Moses and Aaron went to the pharaoh to demand freedom for the Israelites. They showed the pharaoh a sign of God's power. The pharaoh and the Egyptians disregarded this sign. A great struggle then began between God and the pharaoh. The ten plagues, the catastrophies that the Egyptians had to endure, symbolize this struggle.

Egyptian clay figure (14th Century BC) highlights the terrible destruction of the plague of the frogs.

THE TEN PLAGUES

the river of blood	Exodus 7:17
frogs	Exodus 7:27–28
gnats	Exodus 8:12
flies	Exodus 8:16–17
disease	Exodus 9:1–3
boils	Exodus 9:8–9
hail	Exodus 9:18–19
locusts	Exodus 10:4–5
darkness	Exodus 10:21
death of first born	Exodus 11:4–5

When the Israelites saw the effects of the plagues on the Egyptians, they knew that God was protecting them. Their faith in God was strengthened.

Through Moses God continually called the Pharoah to listen to him. However, the pharaoh did not listen to God's warnings and refused to free the Israelites from slavery. Because of his actions the pharaoh was responsible for the suffering of the Egyptian people.

At the end of the ninth plague, the pharaoh seemed to give in to Moses' requests. But again the pharaoh changed his mind. Then the Lord told Moses, "One more plague will I bring upon Pharaoh and upon Egypt. After that he will let you depart. In fact, he will not merely let you go; he will drive you away" (Exodus 11:1).

What were some of the reasons why the Pharoah wanted to keep the Israelites in Egypt?

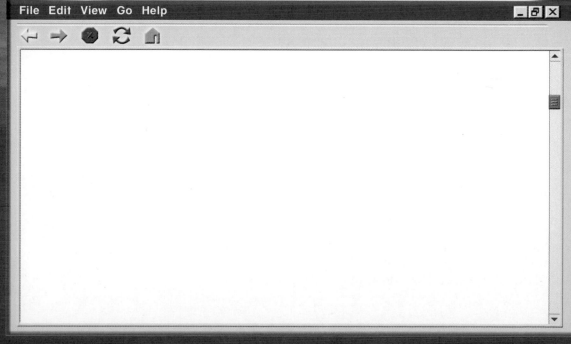 Imagine that you have been asked to design a banner advertisement for a Web site devoted to people throughout the world whose freedoms are being denied. Design a banner ad that will make people want to visit the Web site and assist in the work of freedom for all.

God guided his people to freedom.

When Moses left the pharaoh after the ninth plague, God told him to have every Israelite family prepare for their escape from Egypt. They were to kill a lamb and mark the doorframes of their houses with its blood. This would be a sign that the people inside the house were Israelites, not Egyptians.

Then, the Israelites were to remain inside their houses. They were to cook the lambs and eat them with bitter herbs and unleavened bread. Unleavened bread, made without yeast, does not need to rise and so takes less time to prepare. It symbolized the Israelites' rush to escape.

The Israelites obeyed God's instructions. At midnight God passed over all of Egypt, taking the lives of every firstborn Egyptian, including the son of the pharaoh. Only the Israelites and their animals were spared. This event was called the **Passover**, since God passed over, or spared, his people.

Every year during the feast of Passover Jews follow God's command and remember this special night. They celebrate a seder by eating the same meal that their ancestors ate on the first Passover. By celebrating this feast, Jews recall how God spared the lives of their ancestors and brought them out of slavery in Egypt.

Leaving Egypt Horrified by what had happened, the pharaoh summoned Moses and Aaron. He told them to take the Israelites out of Egypt immediately. Moses and the Israelites left quickly. The Exodus was finally underway.

Moses led the Israelites toward the Red Sea, the water that separated Egypt from the Arabian Peninsula. During their escape, "The LORD preceded them, in the daytime by means of a column of cloud to show them the way, and at night by means of a column of fire to give them light" (Exodus 13:21).

As soon as the Israelites were gone, the pharaoh changed his mind and sent his army to recapture them. By this time, the Israelites were at the Red Sea, and God again caused a wonder that saved his people.

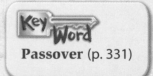
Passover (p. 331)

The Egyptian army closed in on the Israelites. God parted the Red Sea, and the Israelites escaped over the dry path God had made through it. But when the Egyptians tried to follow, the waters closed over them, and they drowned.

In this way God brought his people from slavery into freedom. It was the great turning point in the history of God's relationship with his people. As in the story of Noah, God used water to save the people. For the Israelites the salvation of the nation came about as they passed through the waters of the Red Sea. As Christians the waters of the Red Sea symbolize the saving waters of our own Baptism.

In what ways is the symbol of water used in Baptism?

_____

_____

_____

_____

_____

_____

WE RESPOND

🎵 **Be Not Afraid**

Refrain:
> Be not afraid.
> I go before you always.
> Come, follow me,
> and I will give you rest.

> If you pass through raging waters
>   in the sea,
>   you shall not drown.
> If you walk amid the burning flames,
>   you shall not be harmed.
> If you stand before the pow'r of hell
>   and death is at your side,
>   know that I am with you through it all.

(Refrain)

Show What *you* Know

The Passover and the Exodus were two events that occurred when Jacob's descendants were enslaved in Egypt. Complete the chart to describe the sequence of these events.

What's *the* Word?

"*Moses and Aaron went to Pharaoh and said, 'Thus says the L*ORD*, the God of Israel: Let my people go, that they may celebrate a feast to me in the desert.' Pharaoh answered, 'Who is the Lord, that I should heed his plea to let Israel go? I do not know the Lord; even if I did, I would not let Israel go.'*" (Exodus 5:1–2)

• Underline the phrase that describes why God wants "Israel" to be set free.

• Why does Pharaoh refuse to let "Israel" go?

_____

DISCIPLE

Pray
Learn
Celebrate
Share
Choose
Live

Saint Stories

Pierre Toussaint, born in Haiti in 1778, was a slave. He came to New York with the Catholic couple who owned him. They taught him to read and write, which was unusual at the time. They allowed him to become a hairdresser. Pierre encouraged his clients to pray, to trust in God, and to live according to the Gospel. Pierre eventually purchased his freedom. He married a Haitian woman. Together they helped the poor and worked to free slaves. They founded one of the first orphanages and the first Catholic school for children of color. Pierre Toussaint died in 1853. In 1996 Blessed Pope John Paul II recognized Pierre Toussaint as having lived an outstanding Christian life. The pope declared him Venerable Pierre Toussaint—a step on Pierre's road to becoming a canonized saint.

↳ DISCIPLE CHALLENGE

- Underline the sentence that describes how Pierre used his profession to spread the Gospel.
- What pope recognized that Pierre Toussaint had lived an outstanding Christian life?

_____

Visit *Lives of the Saints* on **www.webelieveweb.com** to learn about more saints and holy people.

Fast Facts

The term *jubilee* refers to a year-long period observed by Jewish People of ancient times. Every fifty years Jewish slaves were freed, debts were forgiven, and lands were returned to original owners.
(See Leviticus 25:8–55.)

Take Home

Initiate family computer time. Together, visit a news Web site to learn about people in the world being oppressed or enslaved. Consider how your family can support the work of agencies and organizations that work to restore and protect human rights.

Complete the following.

1. When Israel's family first entered Egypt, they were treated as honored guests and given

   The Best land in Goshen

2. The child Moses was saved from

   Death by drowning / slavery

3. While Moses was living in Midian and tending his flocks,

   God appered to him in a burning bush

4. The pharaoh would not let the Israelites leave Egypt, so God

   The pleauges

Write True or False for the following sentences.
Then change the false sentences to make them true.

5. ___*F*___ Goshen was the period of tremendous wealth and power of Egypt.

   The new kingdom

6. ___*F*___ The Israelites suffered terribly as slaves of the pharaoh.

   To Mosus

7. ___*T*___ God revealed his name to the pharaoh.

8. ___*F*___ After the Passover the Israelites were able to escape from the pharaoh's army.

Write a paragraph to answer this question.

9–10. Why did God free the Israelites from slavery in Egypt?

A Free People

WE GATHER

✝ **Leader:** Like the Israelites, we are on a journey with God. Along the way, there are difficulties, obstacles, and hardships that test our faith and courage. But we follow Jesus, who tells us, "Do not be afraid" (Matthew 14:27).

Side 1: "Send your light and fidelity, that they may be my guide

Side 2: And bring me to your holy mountain, to the place of your dwelling,

Side 1: That I may come to the altar of God, to God, my joy, my delight."

(Psalm 43:3–4)

Side 2: Glory to the Father, and to the Son, and to the Holy Spirit.

All: As it was in the beginning, is now, and will be for ever. Amen.

♫ **Be Not Afraid**

You shall cross the barren desert,
  but you shall not die of thirst.
You shall wander far in safety,
  though you do not know the way.
You shall speak your words in foreign
  lands and all will understand.
You shall see the face of God and live.

Refrain:
Be not afraid.
I go before you always.
Come, follow me,
and I will give you rest.

☀ Can you remember a very long trip you took with your family? Describe some of the events that might have happened along the way.

107

WE BELIEVE

Moses led God's people through the wilderness.

The Israelites had escaped from Egypt and were beginning their journey to the land of Canaan. Moses and the Israelites sang a song of praise to God. Miriam, the sister of Moses and Aaron, took a tambourine and led a dance of victory. She sang,

"Sing to the LORD, for he is gloriously
     triumphant;
  horse and chariot he has cast into the sea"
(Exodus 15:21).

As is mainly told in Chapters 16—18 of the Book of Exodus, the Israelites spent many years in the wilderness. It was during this period that the Israelites made the transition from being slaves under the pharaoh to living as a free people in service of God.

Toward Mount Sinai   God was with his people during their time in the wilderness. With God's help Moses led the Israelites toward **Mount Sinai**, a mountain peak in the southern part of the Sinai Peninsula. During this journey God tested his people's faithfulness. As we saw in the story of Abraham, God asked his people to show their faith and trust in him. Though some things might not seem reasonable when the people followed God's will, they saw the wisdom of his plan for them.

The Israelites, however, did not always follow God's will for them. They grumbled against Moses for the hardships of this journey and sometimes even doubted God. Yet God demonstrated his faithfulness to his people and worked many miracles. A **miracle** is an extraordinary event that is beyond human power and brought about by God.

For instance, when the people complained that they had no food, God sent small birds called quail. All through their journey God also provided a bread-like substance called **manna**. This manna, a sweet food that tasted like honey, fell from the desert shrubs. And when the Israelites grumbled that they had no water, God told Moses to strike a certain rock and water miraculously gushed out. In all of these ways, God made sure his people had what they needed to live and to follow his plan for them. And throughout history God has continued to care for the needs of his people.

We, too, are called by God to follow his plan for us. We may not cross seas and deserts but we do need God's love and guidance on our journey through this life. Just like the Israelites in the desert, we, too, need to trust in God and to believe in his love for us.

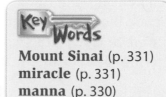

Key Words
Mount Sinai (p. 331)
miracle (p. 331)
manna (p. 330)

The rugged mountain landscape of Mount Sinai, Egypt

Write the lyrics to your own song or poem praising God for something he has done for you.

God gave his people the law.

When the Israelites arrived at Mount Sinai, Moses went up to the mountain to pray to God. There God reminded Moses that the Israelites were God's people. Because of this covenant relationship, the Israelite people were consecrated to God in a special way. All of them were to take part in worshiping God and offering sacrifice to him.

When Moses told the Israelites what God had said, they answered together, "Everything the LORD has said, we will do" (Exodus 19:8). On the third day of their stay at Mount Sinai, God made his presence known through thunder, lightning, and the sound of trumpets.

Then God called Moses back to the top of the mountain. There God gave the Ten Commandments to Moses. The **Ten Commandments** are the laws of God's covenant. If God's people would live by the Ten Commandments, they would keep their covenant relationship with God. He would be their God, and they would be his people. We can find the commandments in Exodus, Chapter 20. God also gave Moses other laws to help the people, and these are recorded in the Book of Leviticus.

Growing up in a Jewish family, Jesus learned the commandments. He lived by God's laws, and as disciples of Christ, we follow the Ten Commandments too.

Key Word

Ten Commandments
(p. 331)

THE TEN COMMANDMENTS

1. I am the LORD your God: you shall not have strange gods before me.
2. You shall not take the name of the LORD your God in vain.
3. Remember to keep holy the LORD 's Day.
4. Honor your father and your mother.
5. You shall not kill.
6. You shall not commit adultery.
7. You shall not steal.
8. You shall not bear false witness against your neighbor.
9. You shall not covet your neighbor's wife.
10. You shall not covet your neighbor's goods.

Write a few ways that you can show your love for God and others by following the Ten Commandments.

_____

_____

_____

_____

Sealing the Covenant Moses shared with the people all the laws that God had given him. The Israelites agreed to follow these laws. So Moses wrote the laws down. He then set up a stone altar with twelve pillars. The pillars represented the twelve tribes of Israel, the descendants of the twelve sons of Jacob.

Moses then sealed the covenant by sacrificing some young bulls as a peace offering to God. Moses sprinkled some of the blood from the bulls, saying "This is the blood of the covenant which the LORD has made with you in accordance with all these words of his" (Exodus 24:8).

The New Covenant According to Christian interpretation, the twelve pillars of the stone altar also symbolize the twelve Apostles, the men with whom Jesus shared his ministry in a special way. Jesus Christ would send them out to spread the Good News that he was the Son of God, sent to save all people.

Before his Death Jesus was with his Apostles and some disciples celebrating the Passover meal. At this meal, which Christians call the Last Supper, Jesus said, "This cup is the new covenant in my blood, which will be shed for you" (Luke 22:20).

Jesus Christ offered his own life to save us and to free us from sin. So the *new* covenant between God and his people has been sealed with Jesus' blood. Through this new covenant it is possible for us to share in God's life and friendship. We celebrate the new covenant at each celebration of the Eucharist.

The people built God a dwelling place.

While Moses was on Mount Sinai, God gave him two tablets on which the Ten Commandments were written. God reminded Moses that the Israelites were not to worship false gods. God gave Moses instructions on the ways the people should worship the one true God. These instructions included plans to make different things that the Israelites needed to use in their worship.

Since Moses had been on the mountain for a very long time, the Israelites became restless. They went to Aaron and said, "Come, make us a god who will be our leader; as for the man Moses who brought us out of the land of Egypt, we do not know what has happened to him" (Exodus 32:1). So they constructed a statue of a calf out of their gold jewelry. When it was finished, they began to worship it as if it were a god.

When Moses came down and saw the people celebrating around the calf, he was angry. He threw down the tablets and they broke. The people had gone against God's commandment by building an idol. Moses then punished those who were unfaithful to God and begged God to forgive the people.

God called Moses to the mountain one last time. And when Moses returned from the mountain he had two new tablets of the commandments.

When people let other people and things take the place of God, we say they are worshiping a false god. What are some of the false gods in today's world?

_____

_____

_____

_____

_____

_____

_____

As Catholics...

In our churches, the tabernacle is a beautifully crafted box in which the Blessed Sacrament, or the Eucharist, is reserved for distribution to those who are sick, and also for adoration. *Tabernacle* comes from the Latin word for "tent." In the Blessed Sacrament Christ is really and truly present.

So we show reverence and worship for Jesus, the Son of God.

Visit your parish and spend some time in prayer before the Blessed Sacrament.

Artist's interpretation of the way the ark of the covenant might have looked.

The Dwelling Place

Building the Dwelling Place Then as God had instructed, the Israelites began making the "dwelling place" for God. They contributed their personal belongings, and made

- a meeting tent, God's dwelling place, which served as a movable place of worship

- the **ark of the covenant**, a wooden box in which the tablets of the Ten Commandments were kept

- several altars

- various pieces of furniture needed for worship

- vestments for the priests.

And on the first day of the first month, almost a year after the Israelites had left Egypt, God entered this "dwelling place." The biblical writer symbolized the presence of God by the thunder and lightning that appeared over the tent.

God no longer seemed far away. The Israelites realized that God was always with them, and they were comforted by the visible reminder of his presence.

Key Word

ark of the covenant
(p. 330)

When or where do you feel God's presence most strongly?

_____

_____

_____

_____

_____

_____

_____

God led his people toward the promised land.

The journey of the Israelites to the promised land of Canaan is said to have taken forty years. The story of this journey is mainly told in the Book of Numbers. The Hebrew name for this book means "in the desert." The English meaning refers to two censuses, or head counts of all the people, that took place during the journey.

On their journey God made his presence known by the huge cloud that hung over the meeting tent during the day. At night the cloud became fiery, so that the Israelites could see it. When the cloud moved, they followed it. When it did not move, the Israelites remained where they were. The guiding cloud symbolized that God himself was directing their journey.

On the Plains of Moab   God used the experience in the desert to help his people grow to be more loving and faithful. The Israelites faced many difficult situations during their journey. From these they learned more about God and about themselves. Finally the Israelites arrived on the plains of Moab, east of Canaan. Here they met a prophet named Balaam, who predicted the greatness of Israel in the centuries to come.

"I see him, though not now;
    I behold him, though not near:
A star shall advance from Jacob,
    and a staff shall rise from Israel"
(Numbers 24:17).

Though the Israelites had not yet entered Canaan, the time was coming for Moses, who was a very old man, to die. So Moses asked God, "May the LORD, the God of the spirits of all mankind, set over the community a man who shall act as their leader in all things, to guide them in all their actions; that the LORD's community may not be like sheep without a shepherd" (Numbers 27:16–17).

God told Moses to lay his hand on Joshua, one of his trusted generals, and commission him to lead God's people into Canaan. God's promise would be fulfilled.

WE RESPOND

Look back at page 114. Highlight the ways God acted in the lives of the Israelites.

Look back at your own life. What are some of the ways God has acted in your life?

_____

_____

_____

_____

_____

_____

Pray Learn Celebrate Share Choose Live

PROJECT

Show What *you* Know

Design a "desktop wallpaper" summarizing the Israelites' journey through the wilderness. Include **Key Words** and captions in your design.

What's *the* Word?

"[Jesus] took Peter, John, and James and went up to the mountain to pray. While [Jesus] was praying his face changed in appearance and his clothing became dazzling white. And behold, two men were conversing with him, Moses and Elijah, who appeared in glory and spoke of his exodus that he was going to accomplish in Jerusalem." (Luke 9:28–31)

- Underline the phrase that describes Jesus.
  (Note: This description tells of the Transfiguration of Jesus.)

- Circle what Moses and Elijah were speaking about.
  (Note: Jesus' exodus was his suffering, Death, Resurrection, and Ascension.)

DISCIPLE

Pray
Learn
Celebrate
Share
Choose
Live

Celebrate!

Catholics inherited some customs of worship from the Jewish People. One custom was the use of music and songs. Moses' sister Miriam played a tambourine with joy when the people gained their freedom. The Jewish People often praised God with pipes and cymbals, trumpets and horns, lyres and harps. As Catholics, we celebrate with these instruments and many others. Organs, pianos, drums, and guitars—all can help us to "Sing to the LORD a new song" (Psalm 149:1).

DISCIPLE CHALLENGE Create a playlist of songs to praise God.

8:26 PM

PLAYLIST

Fast Facts

Moses is mentioned in the New Testament, more than any other Old Testament person. References to him are found in the Gospels of Matthew, Mark, Luke, and John; in the Acts of the Apostles; these Epistles: Romans, 1 Corinthians, 2 Corinthians, 2 Timothy, Hebrews, and Jude; and in the Book of Revelation.

Take Home

Share these verses from Psalm 119 with your family.

"LORD, teach me the way of your laws;
    I shall observe them with care.
Give me insight to observe your teaching,
    to keep it with all my heart.
Lead me in the path of your commands,
    for that is my delight."

(Psalm 119:33–35)

CHAPTER TEST

Write the letter that best defines each term.

1. ___B___ miracle

2. ___D___ manna

3. ___A___ Ten Commandments

4. ___C___ ark of the covenant

a. the laws of God's covenant given to Moses on Mount Sinai

b. an extraordinary event that is beyond human power and brought about by God

c. a wooden box in which the tablets of the Ten Commandments were kept

d. sweet bread-like food that God provided for the Israelites in the desert

e. a meeting tent that served as a movable place of worship

Short Answers

5. How did God demonstrate his faithfulness to his people on their journey to Mount Sinai?

   Provided food and water

6. Why did the people need the Ten Commandments?

   To keep our covinent with God

7. List three things that the Israelites made for the "dwelling place" of God.

   Tent, ark of the covenant, clothes for priest

8. How was God's presence made known to his people during their journey to the promised land?

   _____

Write a paragraph to answer this question.

9–10. What does the story of the journey of God's people to the promised land tell us about our relationship with God?

_____

_____

_____

_____

A Conquering People

10

WE GATHER

✝ **Leader:** Blessed be our God who has shown his people great love. Blessed be God for ever.

Reader 1: "'Give thanks to the LORD who is good,
   whose love endures forever!'
Let that be the prayer of the LORD's redeemed,
   those redeemed from the hand of the foe,
Those gathered from foreign lands,
   from east and west, from north and south."

Reader 2: "Some had lost their way in a barren desert;
   found no path toward a city to live in.
They were hungry and thirsty;
   their life was ebbing away."

Reader 3: "In their distress they cried to the LORD,
   who rescued them in their peril,
Guided them by a direct path
   so they reached a city to live in."

Reader 4: "Let them thank the LORD for such kindness,
   such wondrous deeds for mere mortals.
For he satisfied the thirsty,
   filled the hungry with good things."

(Psalm 107:1–9)

Leader: Let us pray that all places be true cities of God.

🎵 **City of God**

O comfort my people; make gentle your words.
Proclaim to my city the day of her birth.

Refrain:
Let us build the city of God.
May our tears be turned into dancing!
For the Lord, our light and our love,
has turned the night into day!

☀ Name one important truth you have learned lately. How did you learn it?

119

WE BELIEVE
God's people conquered Canaan.

The theme of the Book of Deuteronomy is that God's people must love God and be obedient to him. In Deuteronomy we read that Moses told the people: "Hear, O Israel! The LORD is our God, the LORD alone! Therefore, you shall love the LORD, your God, with all your heart, and with all your soul, and with all your strength" (Deuteronomy 6:4–5). These words of Moses became an important prayer which is known as the *Shema*.

Moses told the Israelites, "Take to heart these words which I enjoin on you today. Drill them into your children. Speak of them at home and abroad, whether you are busy or at rest" (Deuteronomy 6:6–7). The Israelites followed Moses' instructions. Through the ages, the Jewish People have made this prayer a part of their everyday lives. God's covenant relationship with the Jewish People remains strong today.

Bringing the People into Canaan As the Book of Deuteronomy ends, we learn that Moses saw the promised land from a mountain top but did not live to enter it. Then in the Book of Joshua we read that God said to Joshua, "My servant Moses is dead. So prepare to cross the Jordan here, with all the people, into the land I will give the Israelites . . . the LORD, your God, is with you wherever you go" (Joshua 1:2, 9).

Ancient ram's horn

In the Book of Joshua the details of the Israelites' entry into the promised land are greatly simplified. The account of the conquest and entry is not a day-by-day description, but rather the biblical writer's interpretation of the religious significance of events.

In the Book of Joshua, we find one very famous event in the conquest of Canaan—the fall of Jericho. Jericho was a well-known city in the center of Canaan. Here is the story of the fall of Jericho.

📖 Joshua 6:1–20

God told Joshua not to attack the city directly but to march around it with his troops. Joshua had his troops do all that God commanded him. They carried the ark of the covenant before them. Seven priests using rams' horns as trumpets led the march. Joshua and his troops did this for six days. On the seventh day they marched around the city seven times. Then the priests blew their horns, and the Israelites shouted loudly. And the walls of Jericho fell down! Then Joshua and the Israelites took over the city of Jericho.

The Israelites conquered this city because they followed the plan of God. Even though Joshua was the military leader, it was God who was the real hero in the capture of Jericho. The biblical writer used this story to show that the Israelites believed that God was with them in every part of their lives.

The Book of Joshua emphasizes that God is with his people. Write and illustrate a story that will tell others that God is with them in every part of their lives. Plan your story here.

God's people settled in Canaan.

After the Israelites conquered Canaan, the land was distributed among the twelve tribes of Israel, the descendants of the twelve sons of Jacob, or Israel. The land was parceled out to each tribe by the ancient practice of casting lots. Lots were coins, sets of specially marked stones, or sticks wrapped in paper. Rules which stated what the lots or the various positions of the lots would represent were agreed upon. The outcome of the lots was believed to be an expression of God's will. The biblical writer used the casting of lots to show us that God alone was responsible for the distribution of the land. The land was a gift from God.

Once the land had been distributed, the tribes gathered to thank God for the great blessings he had bestowed on them and to renew their covenant with him. The Israelites then began to settle in Canaan. The story of their settlement can be found in the Book of Judges. This book also records the accounts of Israel's judges, men and women sent by God to help the Israelites. A judge was not an officer of the court. He or she was often a military leader who defeated the enemy and ruled the land as God directed. During the time of the Judges, the Israelites continually turned from God and needed help to be faithful.

Deborah, the Judge   One of the great judges described in the Old Testament was Deborah. God chose Deborah to remind the Israelites to keep the covenant. She settled legal disputes and offered advice to the people. "She used to sit under Deborah's palm tree . . . and there the Israelites came up to her for judgment." (Judges 4:5)

During Deborah's lifetime the Israelites once again began to worship false gods. Because of this failure, Israelite territory was taken over by a Canaanite king and his general. So Deborah ordered the Israelite commander Barak to call his troops together at Mount Tabor. She told him that God would give the Israelites a great victory there.

Barak doubted Deborah, but she insisted. Barak told Deborah that he would follow her order as long as she accompanied him and his army to Mount Tabor. Thus, Deborah went with Barak and the army to meet the Canaanites at Mount Tabor. God sent a great thunderstorm that caused the chariots of the Canaanites to get stuck in the mud, and they were defeated. Through God's actions and Deborah's faith, the land was again free of enemies. Deborah prayed a great hymn, a canticle, in praise of God. Here is its ending:

"May all your enemies perish thus, O Lord!
but your friends be as the sun rising in
its might!" (Judges 5:31).

Bible engraving of Deborah, by Gustave Dore, France

There are people in our lives who help us to stay focused on loving God and one another. Name some of these people in your life. What do they do to help you?

_____

_____

_____

_____

Samson was the most famous judge.

The Israelites again turned from God and some of them came under the rule of their enemies, the Philistines. So God sent another judge to his people. This judge was the only one whose birth was foretold in a very extraordinary way.

An angel of the Lord appeared to a woman in Zorah and said, "Though you are barren and have had no children, yet you will conceive and bear a son . . . no razor shall touch his head, for this boy is to be consecrated to God from the womb. It is he who will begin the deliverance of Israel from the power of the Philistines" (Judges 13:3, 5).

When the baby was born he was given the name Samson and the spirit of the Lord was with Samson. He was blessed by God with great strength. Throughout his life Samson was a **Nazirite**, a person consecrated to God. As a Nazirite Samson was to keep special promises, or vows. He was not to drink wine or strong drink, touch anyone or anything that had died, or cut or shave his hair. And as long as Samson kept his vows, God continued to make him strong.

Samson married a Philistine woman, but the Philistines mistreated him and his wife. So a very personal struggle began between Samson and the Philistines. The Philistines went so far as to kill Samson's wife and her family. Samson was enraged by this and took revenge on the Philistines. They began to fear Samson's strength and wanted to capture him.

Samson and Delilah   Samson fell in love with another Philistine woman, Delilah. The Philistine leaders paid Delilah to find out the secret of Samson's great strength. At first Samson lied. This made Delilah very angry. Afraid of losing her, Samson told Delilah that God gave him strength as long as he kept his Nazirite vows. So while Samson was asleep, Delilah had a man shave off Samson's hair. Then she called in the waiting Philistines who blinded Samson. They then took Samson to a prison, kept him chained, and forced him to turn a great stone that ground grain.

While in prison, Samson's hair grew back. One day the Philistines brought Samson into the temple while they were having a religious festival. They placed him between two temple columns. There Samson prayed and asked God to give him his strength once again. Samson pushed down the columns that were holding up the temple. They fell killing Samson and everyone else in the temple.

The story of Samson symbolized the Israelite nation of his time. Samson's birth, like the birth of Israel, was the result of God's guiding hand. Samson was dedicated to God, and God was with him, just as God was with the Israelites. Yet Samson forgot about his vows to God. He used his strength to take revenge on those who had personally hurt him. But God turned Samson's defeat into the beginning of the downfall of the Philistines. God again allowed the Israelites to be victorious against those who tried to defeat them.

As Catholics...

Vows are serious promises that people make to God or to each other. During the Sacrament of Matrimony a man and a woman promise to love and honor each other. Similarly, women and men in religious life take vows of chastity, poverty, and obedience. In both cases, the vows help those who make them focus on living lives dedicated to God and others.

Do you know anyone who has taken vows?

Nazirite (p. 331)

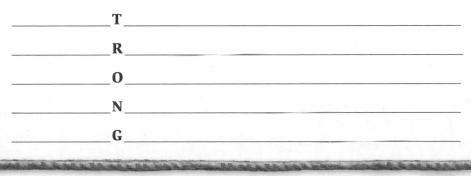

Being strong is more than having physical strength. God makes us strong by sharing his life and love with us. What are some ways God does this in our lives?

Write a sentence using each letter of the word *strong* to tell how God shares his life and love with us.

In the **Sacraments** God shares his life and love with us.

_____ **T** _____

_____ **R** _____

_____ **O** _____

_____ **N** _____

_____ **G** _____

Ruth lived a life of self-sacrifice.

The Book of Ruth, one of the Bible's most beautiful short stories, shows God's presence in the events of daily life. The story of Ruth teaches us that even in difficult times people can faithfully live out the covenant. They can follow God's will for them.

The story begins in a time of famine in Israel. An Israelite named Elimelech, his wife Naomi, and their two sons needed to find food. So they traveled eastward from Bethlehem of Judah and crossed the Jordan River into Moab. There people did not believe in the one true God, but Elimelech's family settled in Moab because they were able to find food.

Sometime after that, Elimelech died, and each of his sons married a Moabite woman. Then the two sons also died. This left Naomi and her daughters-in-law, Orpah and Ruth, sad and in financial trouble. Naomi had no relatives in Moab who could help them.

When she decided to go back to her homeland, Naomi told her daughters-in-law that they should go back to their own mothers' houses. But Ruth refused to leave her mother-in-law. She said, "Do not ask me to abandon or forsake you! for wherever you go I will go, wherever you lodge I will lodge, your people shall be my people, and your God my God" (Ruth 1:16). Ruth's loyalty and her acceptance of the God of Israel impressed Naomi. The two women went together to Bethlehem.

When it was time for the harvest, Ruth went into a field to gather up grain left behind from the harvest. People without money were allowed to do this. Boaz, who owned the field, was a relative of Naomi's deceased husband, and he had been told about Ruth's devotion to Naomi. So Boaz told his servants to help and protect Ruth.

When Naomi heard this, she hoped that Boaz, as her relative by marriage, would claim some land that she was selling. If he did, then by the law of the Israelites, Boaz would also have the responsibility of taking Ruth as his wife.

Boaz did claim the land and married Ruth. God blessed Boaz and Ruth with a son, who was given the name Obed. "He was the father of Jesse, the father of David" (Ruth 4:17).

In the story of Ruth, the biblical writer shows us that sadness can be turned into joy. We learn that when we bring God's love to one another, God's will is accomplished by our actions. Like Naomi, Ruth, and Boaz, we are called to be part of God's plan by living lives of faithfulness and kindness.

WE RESPOND

God is always faithful to us. He asks us to be faithful, too.

Imagine that you have been asked to write a song about faithfulness. What would you name your song? What lyrics would you include? Write them here.

Pray Learn Celebrate Share Choose Live

PROJECT

Show What *you* Know

Use the clues to complete the chart.

Clue	Your Answer
wife of Elimelech and mother-in-law of Orpah and Ruth	
appeared to Samson's mother	
home of Samson's parents	
the people who conquered Canaan	
refused to leave her mother-in-law	
the twelve tribes were descendants of his twelve sons	
"weapons" used to conquer Jericho	
Naomi's husband	

↳ DISCIPLE CHALLENGE

• Now, circle the first letter of each answer. Use the circled letters to write

the Key Word : ____ ____ ____ ____ ____ ____ ____ ____

• How does this Key Word relate to the story of Samson?

_____

Make *it* Happen

Be part of God's plan by living a life of faithfulness and kindness. This week, I will be part of God's plan by

_____

_____

Now, pass it on!

Fast Facts

Ruth was the great-grandmother of David. Her son Obed was the father of Jesse, who was the father of David. Therefore, Ruth was an ancestor of Jesus.

Naomi and Ruth, Malach Zeldis

DISCIPLE

Pray
Learn
Celebrate
Share
Choose
Live

Saint Stories

Catherine was born in 1347 in Siena, Italy. From a very young age, she lived a life of prayer focused on Christ. Gradually, people began to realize that she had the gift of good judgment. People went to her when they had disputes within their families or among their neighbors. Catherine was concerned about current events and politics, and helped the Church as much as she could. She visited kings and queens and asked them to avoid war. While in Rome working for peace within the Church, Catherine died at the age of thirty-three. She was later canonized a saint and is known as Saint Catherine of Siena.

↳ DISCIPLE CHALLENGE

• Underline the sentence that describes how Catherine lived her life.

  Visit *Lives of the Saints* on **www.webelieveweb.com** to answer these questions about Saint Catherine of Siena:

• What did Catherine encourage people to do?

  _____

• When is her feast day?

  _____

Reality Check

Like the biblical characters presented in this chapter, we all have unique qualities, or "strengths." List five of your "strengths."

_____

_____

_____

↳ DISCIPLE CHALLENGE Look over your list. How can you use these strengths to help others?

Take Home

Joshua led the Israelites to the Promised Land. Before Joshua died, he called the Israelites to remember their covenant with God:

"As for me and my household we will serve the LORD" (Joshua 24:15).

As a family, talk about ways you can serve the Lord this week.

CHAPTER TEST

Write True or False for the following sentences.
Then change the false sentences to make them true.

1. __F__ The Israelites conquered the city of Jericho with special machines.

_____

2. __T__ The land of Canaan was distributed to the twelve tribes of Israel by casting lots.

_____

3. __F__ Delilah was chosen by God to remind the Israelites to keep God's covenant, settle legal disputes, and offer other advice.

_____

4. __F__ During the times of the judges, the Israelites stayed faithful to the one true God.

_____

Circle the letter of the correct answer.

5. The Book of _____ teaches that in difficult times people can live out the covenant.

   a. Deborah   **b.** Naomi   **c.** Ruth

6. A _____ was a person consecrated to God who promised vows.

   a. Nazirite   **b.** Philistine   **c.** Moabite

7. The Book of _____ emphasizes God's role in the people's entry into the promised land.

   a. Joshua   **b.** Ruth   **c.** Judges

8. God blessed Samson with great _____.

   a. wisdom   **b.** strength   **c.** hair

Write a paragraph to answer this question.

9–10. How does the story of Samson symbolize the Israelite nation of his time?

_____

_____

_____

_____

A Royal People

11

WE GATHER

✝ **Leader:** Jesus, you are the Good Shepherd. Help us to follow you in all that we say and do. Be with us as we pray.

Reader 1: "The LORD is my shepherd; there is nothing I lack. In green pastures you let me graze; to safe waters you lead me; you restore my strength."

All: Jesus, Good Shepherd, lead us in paths of peace.

Reader 2: "You guide me along the right path for the sake of your name. Even when I walk through a dark valley, I fear no harm for you are at my side; your rod and your staff give me courage."

All: Jesus, Good Shepherd, keep us from darkness and evil.

Reader 3: "You set a table before me as my enemies watch; You anoint my head with oil; my cup overflows."

All: Jesus, Good Shepherd, thank you for your Bread of Life.

Reader 4: "Only goodness and love will pursue me all the days of my life; I will dwell in the house of the LORD for years to come."
(Psalm 23:1–6)

All: Jesus, Good Shepherd, show us your goodness and love!

☀ Have you ever felt called to do something? What was it?

♫ The King of Love My Shepherd Is

The King of love my shepherd is,
Whose goodness fails me never;
I nothing lack if I am his,
And he is mine forever.

Where streams of living water flow
With gentle care he leads me,
And where the verdant pastures grow,
With heav'nly food he feeds me.

WE BELIEVE
God called Samuel to serve him.

The Bible contains many literary forms, or types of writing, used to retell events that help us know and encounter God. Historical writing gives an account of historical events or periods in history. The First and Second Books of Samuel, along with some other books in the Bible, represent Scripture's historical books. (See chart, page 27.)

As the First Book of Samuel opens, we read about Hannah and her prayer for a child. She promised God that if he blessed her with a son, she would dedicate the child to him. Hannah did have a son. She called him Samuel and dedicated him to God's service. Samuel grew up at the shrine of Shiloh under the watchful eye of an old priest named Eli.

When Samuel was still very young, God called to him while he was sleeping. At first Samuel thought Eli was calling him. Eli realized though that it was God. Eli told Samuel, "Go to sleep, and if you are called, reply, 'Speak, LORD, for your servant is listening'" (1 Samuel 3:9). When God called once more, Samuel answered him. Then God told Samuel about the things that he, the Lord, would do.

God was with Samuel, and did not permit "any word of his to be without effect. . . . The LORD continued to appear at Shiloh; he manifested himself to Samuel at Shiloh through his word, and Samuel spoke to all Israel" (1 Samuel 3:19, 21). Samuel became God's prophet. A **prophet** is someone who speaks on behalf of God, defends the truth, and works for justice.

Desperate Times   At this time many people continued to turn away from God. Israel's enemy, the Philistines, took advantage of Israel's disunity and threatened Israel's existence. The Philistines took so much land that some Israelites had to find a new home.

prophet

PROPHET

The Philistines even captured the ark of the covenant and kept it for a time.

Besides having enemies, the Israelites were themselves in a state of chaos and a civil war even broke out. Worse yet, God himself seemed to have abandoned his people.

During this time Samuel was called to gradually take over the leadership of Israel. He brought the ark back to a proper resting place. And Samuel offered sacrifice to God, praying for Israel's victory over the Philistines. Indeed, God would never abandon his people. His love for them would never end.

Like Samuel we are called to love and serve God. What do you think God is calling you to do? Write some ways you can answer God's call.

_____

_____

_____

_____

_____

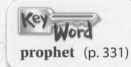

Key Word

prophet (p. 331)

prophet
PROPHET

Saul became Israel's first king.

As Samuel grew older, the Israelites cried out to him for a king. They wanted someone to lead and protect them.

Yet Israel's only king had always been the Lord. Now the people wanted to be like other nations. They wanted to be a monarchy. A **monarchy** is a kingdom or empire ruled by one person, either a king or a queen.

Samuel was displeased because he believed only God was Israel's king. Although God was also displeased, he told Samuel to let the people have an earthly king and become a monarchy.

The First King   Samuel was told by God to anoint Saul to be the first king of Israel. This anointing would be a symbol of Saul's consecration to God's service. Samuel poured oil on Saul's head and kissed him. As he anointed Saul, Samuel said, "The LORD anoints you commander over his heritage" (1 Samuel 10:1).

God spoke to Saul through Samuel. At first Saul followed Samuel's advice in leading the people. As commander of the Israelite army, Saul won battles against the Philistines. The Israelites were happy that they had a king.

Gradually, Saul stopped listening to Samuel. He was more concerned with his own interests than those of God's people. Saul began to act on his own. Once Saul even told his army to stop fighting and this error, which allowed the Philistines time to regroup, caused Israel to lose the battle.

As a result of Saul's actions, he no longer ruled with God's blessing. God said to Samuel, "I regret having made Saul king, for he has turned from me and has not kept my command" (1 Samuel 15:11). Therefore God would choose another king.

Key Word
monarchy (p. 331)

We learn from the Old Testament that being anointed with holy oil set a person apart to serve God as a king, a priest, or a prophet. Anointing is an important part of the life of the Church today. Each year just before the Easter Triduum, the bishop of the diocese blesses three holy oils at a special Mass called the Chrism Mass. These oils are then distributed for use in the celebration of some of the sacraments during the coming year. The oils are:

- the oil of catechumens, used during the Rite of Christian Initiation of Adults and before the celebration of Baptism
- the oil of the sick, used in the Anointing the Sick
- Sacred Chrism, used in Baptism, Confirmation, and Holy Orders.

Find out where the holy oils are kept in your parish church.

Imagine that you are living during Saul's reign. What advice would you give him about being king?

_____

_____

_____

_____

With a partner, role-play this scene.

God chose David to lead Israel.

Samuel followed God's instruction in choosing Israel's second king. God first sent Samuel to offer sacrifice in Bethlehem. Then God had Samuel invite Jesse and his family to the feast that followed the sacrifice.

Jesse and seven of his sons entered the feast. Samuel thought that surely one of these sons would be the new king. But none of these were acceptable to God. God said to Samuel, "Not as man sees does God see, because man sees the appearance but the LORD looks into the heart" (1 Samuel 16:7).

Then Samuel asked Jesse whether he had any more sons. Jesse told him that he had one more son, David. David, his youngest son, was in the fields tending the sheep. Samuel told Jesse to send for David.

David came before Samuel, "then Samuel, with the horn of oil in hand, anointed him in the midst of his brothers; and from that day on, the spirit of the LORD rushed upon David" (1 Samuel 16:13). God had chosen David to eventually replace Saul as Israel's king.

David and Goliath   The Philistines were again trying to overcome the Israelites. The Philistine army was gathered on a hill in Judah, and the Israelite army was on a neighboring hill. The Israelites, however, were afraid to attack because the Philistine army was led by a giant of a man named Goliath. Goliath was much taller than all the other men. His spear and shield were too heavy for most of them to lift. Every day Goliath challenged the Israelites to come and fight him. But no one accepted Goliath's challenge.

One day Jesse sent young David with supplies for his brothers who were in the Israelite army. As David entered the Israelite camp, Goliath began to shout his usual insults. The Israelites fled. David asked, "What will be done for the man who kills this Philistine and frees Israel of the disgrace?" (1 Samuel 17:26)

David's words were reported to Saul, who sent for David. David assured King Saul that he was prepared to fight Goliath. David told him that he had often killed a lion or bear when protecting his father's sheep. David said, "The LORD, who delivered me from the claws of the lion and the bear, will also keep me safe from the clutches of this Philistine" (1 Samuel 17:37). Saul then agreed to let David fight Goliath.

When David answered Goliath's challenge, Goliath cursed him. David, however, told Goliath that he came in the name of the God of Israel. David took a smooth stone, put it in his slingshot, and hurled the stone at Goliath. The stone hit Goliath in the forehead and knocked him down. Then David was able to kill Goliath. When the Philistines saw this they ran away.

David's courage came from trusting in God. Unlike Saul, David relied on the Lord completely. God had indeed saved David and the rest of Israel!

In groups dramatize a TV news segment in which David, Goliath, and Saul are interviewed about the upcoming battle between David and Goliath. Ask each of them the following questions:

• What happened here?

_____

_____

_____

• What is your role in this event?

_____

_____

_____

• What do you think will happen next?

_____

_____

_____

What can you learn from the events in the lives of Saul, David, and Goliath?

_____

_____

_____

_____

137

David was declared the king of Israel.

Around 1000 B.C. after the death of Saul, David was declared king of Israel by all the people.

David immediately set out to solve Israel's problems. As soon as he became king, he began to plan his attack against the Philistines, the Israelites' main enemy. David soon drove the Philistines from central Israel. In later battles David forced them out of the rest of the country. He even captured large parts of the Philistines' territory for Israel.

David dealt with another important task: taking over the areas in Israel that were still under Canaanite control. David captured most of these areas and the others simply surrendered to him. As a result, the Israelite takeover of Canaan was finally completed. Israel became a nation united.

One of the Canaanite cities that David conquered was Jerusalem. The city became the king's private property because he had captured it with his own soldiers. Thus, in biblical writings Jerusalem became known as the City of David.

Michaelangelo (1475–1564), *David*

The City of David   David decided to make Jerusalem the religious and political capital of all Israel. All the tribes agreed with David's choice. David brought the ark of the covenant to Jerusalem and ". . . came dancing before the LORD with abandon, as he and all the Israelites were bringing up the ark of the LORD with shouts of joy and to the sound of the horn" (2 Samuel 6:14–15).

David also set up a government in Jerusalem. As a leader, David proved to be brilliant. God was with David and under David's guidance Israel was transformed from a group of weak and disunited tribes into a strong kingdom. Through everything God was present in the lives of the people and in the life of the nation.

Throughout his years, David had been a shepherd, a storyteller, a poet, a musician, a warrior, and a great king. Yet he also had weaknesses. One was his love for a beautiful woman named Bathsheba. David wanted to marry Bathsheba, but she was already married.

David arranged to have Bathsheba's husband, Uriah, killed in battle. The prophet Nathan told David that Uriah's murder displeased God. David asked God's forgiveness saying, "I have sinned against the LORD" (2 Samuel 12:13). Then David prayed for God's forgiveness.

He did penance before the Lord, and God forgave David.

Once again in learning about the events in the life of God's people, we learn of God's great mercy. God always forgives those who are sorry for their sins.

Complete this profile to describe why you think David is chosen for person of the year in 999 B.C. Then pretend you are person of the year. Design your own profile.

David Person of the Year 999 B.C.	_____ (name) Person of the Year A.D. _____
Major Accomplishments _____ _____	Major Accomplishments _____ _____
Ways he showed love for God _____ _____	Ways you showed love for God _____ _____
Other interesting facts _____ _____	Other interesting facts _____ _____

WE RESPOND

In groups discuss the gifts and talents of Samuel, Saul, and David that made them good leaders of God's people.

What gifts and talents can you share with your parish?

Show What you Know

Classified ads found in newspapers or on Web sites are designed to attract offers of, or requests for, jobs, homes, apartments, cars, etc.

Write a classified ad for the **Key Words**.

What Would you do?

There is a new service club at school that does not have many members. Your teacher has praised your leadership skills and has nominated you to lead this club. You

_____

_____

_____

Pray Today

As Catholics, we are called to pray for the needs of the Church and the world. Pray the following prayer for civic leaders.

God our Father,
you guide everything in wisdom and love.
Accept the prayers we offer for our nation.
in your goodness,
watch over those in authority,
so that people everywhere may enjoy
freedom, security, and peace.
We ask this through our Lord Jesus Christ.
Amen.

DISCIPLE

Pray
Learn
Celebrate
Share
Choose
Live

Saint Stories

Ignatius Loyola was a courageous and adventurous Spanish soldier who lived during the sixteenth century. During a recovery from an injury, he read a book on the lives of the saints. Ignatius realized that, like the saints, he could be courageous and adventurous for Christ. He eventually became a priest. He founded the Society of Jesus, known as the Jesuits. These men were to serve Christ and the Church.

Ignatius wrote a book called *The Spiritual Exercises* to help people to become more like Christ. His book includes these important questions: "What have I done for Christ? What am I doing for Christ? What am I going to do for Christ?" The Church honors Saint Ignatius Loyola on July 31.

↳ **DISCIPLE CHALLENGE**
- Circle the phrase that explains why Ignatius founded the Society of Jesus.
- Underline the questions from *The Spiritual Exercises*. Choose one to answer on the lines below.

_____

_____

Reality Check

Samuel replied to God's call by saying,

"Speak, for your servant is listening" (1 Samuel 3:10).

What are some ways God "speaks" to you?

❏ In prayer

❏ In everyday occurrences

❏ _____

↳ **DISCIPLE CHALLENGE** How do you show that you listen?

Take Home

David asked God to bless his house. (See 2 Samuel 7:29.) As a family, write a prayer to God asking his blessing on your home.

_____

_____

_____

_____

CHAPTER TEST

Write the letter that best identifies the biblical character.

1. _D_ Saul   a. prayed for a child whom she promised to dedicate to God

2. _B_ Samuel   b. a leader and prophet of God who felt that only God should be considered Israel's king

3. _A_ Hannah   c. the father of David

         d. the first anointed king of Israel

4. _E_ David   e. the king of Israel who united and transformed the nation of Israel

Short Answers

5. How did Israel's enemy, the Philistines, take advantage of Israel's disunity?

They attacked, and stole the Ten Commandments

6. What was used to symbolize the consecration of Saul to God's service?

Holy Oil

7. What is the importance of the story of David and Goliath?

If to trust, and rely in God

8. What happened to the nation of Israel during King David's rule?

Israel became a united nation

Write a paragraph to answer this question.

9–10. What meaning do these words have in the story of David?
"Not as man sees does God see, because man sees the appearance but the LORD looks into the heart." (1 Samuel 16:7)

_____

_____

_____

_____

A Prosperous People

12

WE GATHER

✝ **Leader:** Jesus called the Apostle James a "son of thunder" because of his quick temper! But James became a wise man and taught the meaning of wisdom. Let us listen to his words.

Reader: A reading from the Letter of James

"Who among you is wise and understanding? Let him show his works by a good life in the humility that comes from wisdom. . . . But the wisdom from above is first of all pure, then peaceable, gentle, compliant, full of mercy and good fruits, without inconstancy or insincerity. And the fruit of righteousness is sown in peace for those who cultivate peace." (James 3:13, 17–18)

The word of the Lord.

All: Thanks be to God.

Leader: Let us pray for wisdom in our lives and in the lives of all people. We will respond, "Lord, hear our prayer."

Reader: For the wisdom to be gentle and peaceful with others,

For the wisdom to care for the earth and its creatures,

For the wisdom to be merciful toward those in need,

For the wisdom to be faithful and sincere with our friends,

For the wisdom to include and not exclude others,

All: We ask this in your name, Lord Jesus. Amen.

☀ Describe what the world would be like if everyone worked for peace.

WE BELIEVE
Solomon's reign was a time of peace and prosperity.

After forty years as king, David died. David's son Solomon succeeded him as king. Under Solomon's rule Israel achieved its greatest peace and prosperity. The story of Solomon's reign as king, which lasted for about forty years, is told in the First Book of Kings and the Second Book of Chronicles.

While his father, David, was remembered chiefly as a mighty warrior, Solomon was a diplomat. Solomon's reign was a time of peace. Solomon did not wage any wars. Rather, he made treaties, or agreements, with other kings and queens. These alliances kept Israel safe from attack and gave the country new business opportunities.

Solomon helped Israel to prosper by his success in overseas trade. During Solomon's time as king, Israel was richer than it had ever been before. For the first time in Israel's history, some of the common people—not just the powerful—began to enjoy a life of plenty.

To showcase Israel's power and success, Solomon began a great building program. This program was designed to strengthen the country's defenses and to beautify its cities, especially Jerusalem.

The most important of these building projects involved the construction of the Temple in Jerusalem. There were other projects including a palace for the king.

16th century depiction of the prosperity of Solomon's time. *Solomon with the Treasure of the Temple*, Frans Francken II, Flemish, (1581–1642)

Many forms of art also began to flourish in Israel. Among the most important were ivory carving, carpentry, stonework, and jewelry making.

Literature was also very important during Solomon's reign. The historical books of the Bible began to be written and compiled. Psalms, proverbs, and other kinds of poetry were also written. The first steps toward assembling the Bible were taken when Solomon was king.

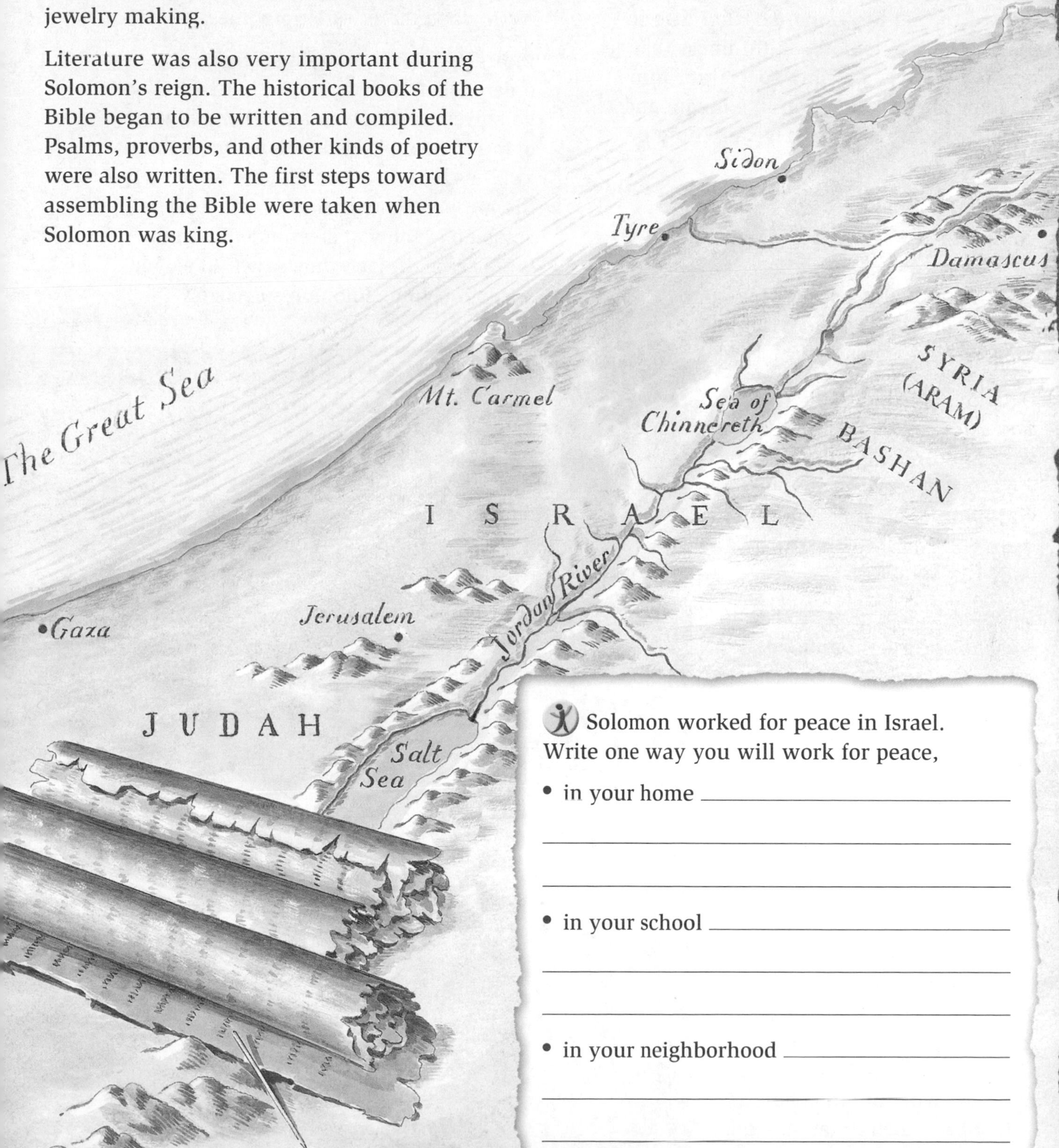

The Great Sea

Sidon

Tyre

Damascus

Mt. Carmel

Sea of Chinnereth

SYRIA (ARAM)

BASHAN

I S R A E L

Jordan River

Gaza

Jerusalem

J U D A H

Salt Sea

Solomon worked for peace in Israel. Write one way you will work for peace,

• in your home _____

_____

_____

• in your school _____

_____

_____

• in your neighborhood _____

_____

_____

Solomon gained fame for his wisdom.

When he was a young king, Solomon prayed to God for guidance. God was so pleased with Solomon's faithfulness that he decided to do something special for him. God appeared to Solomon in a dream and promised that he could have anything he desired.

Solomon replied to God, "I am a mere youth, not knowing at all how to act. . . . Give your servant, therefore, an understanding heart to judge your people and to distinguish right from wrong" (1 Kings 3:7, 9).

Delighted by Solomon's reply, God said: "I give you a heart so wise and understanding that there has never been anyone like you up to now, and after you there will come no one to equal you" (1 Kings 3:12).

Solomon was so grateful that he went to Jerusalem and stood before the ark of the covenant of the Lord. There he offered sacrifice and peace offerings. Then he gave a banquet for all his servants.

Solomon's Wisdom   Soon after God granted Solomon wisdom, it was tested. Two women, each recently having had a child, came to Solomon. One of the babies had died, and both women claimed to be the mother of the baby that was alive. One woman accused the other of switching the babies, and both women began to argue. How would Solomon possibly

determine which woman was telling the truth when there were no witnesses?

In order to test the women, Solomon ordered that the baby be cut in two and one half given to each woman. When only one of the women pleaded with Solomon not to kill the child, he saw that she was clearly the mother. All Israel was amazed by Solomon's ability to determine the truth in this case. In fact, they saw God's own wisdom behind Solomon's decision.

Solomon's story helps us understand the importance of wisdom. Wisdom is a gift from God. **Wisdom** is the knowledge and ability to recognize and follow God's will in our lives. It enables us to see as God sees and to act as God wants us to act. We need God's gift of wisdom to live a good life and to be faithful to our covenant with God.

wisdom (p. 331)

wisdom (p. 331)

As Catholics...

The Holy Spirit strengthens us to live as Christ's disciples and shares seven spiritual gifts with us. The gifts of the Holy Spirit are wisdom, understanding, counsel, fortitude, knowledge, piety, and fear of the Lord. In the Sacrament of Confirmation we receive the gifts of the Holy Spirit in a special way. These gifts help us to follow Christ's teachings and to give witness to our faith.

What is one gift of the Holy Spirit that you would ask for right now?

Wisdom is one of the gifts of the Holy Spirit. It helps us to see and follow God's plan for us. Identify some situations in which people call upon God for wisdom.

_____

_____

_____

_____

_____

_____

_____

This week ask God for wisdom in everything you do.

The Temple was built in Jerusalem.

To show his love for God and his desire to be faithful to the covenant, Solomon decided to build a great stone Temple in Jerusalem. This Temple was meant to be the center of worship of the one true God. It was meant to bind all the people to God and to Israel.

The Temple itself consisted of two main rooms: the sanctuary, or holy of holies, and the nave. The sanctuary, which was the innermost part of the Temple, was a small raised room reserved exclusively for God. Only the High Priest could enter the holy of holies. The sanctuary contained the ark of the covenant where God was believed to reside invisibly. Two huge statues of angels called *cherubim* served as symbols of God's presence in the sanctuary.

The nave of the Temple was a larger room in front of the sanctuary. It contained a small altar for burning incense. A flight of steps and a doorway with a curtain across it led from the nave to the sanctuary.

Temple Mount, Jerusalem
Many scholars believe this to be the site of ancient temples.

On three sides of the sanctuary and nave were smaller rooms used for storage or reserved for the priests. In front of the Temple stood the Court of the Priests. It contained a great altar designed for the offering of sacrifices of various kinds.

Beyond the Court of the Priests, was a series of larger walled courts that surrounded the entire Temple. One of the courts was reserved for male Israelites, one was designed for female Israelites, and one was for visitors who were not Israelites. A high retaining wall with elaborate gates and entranceways surrounded the whole structure of the Temple and its courts.

The completion of the Temple was considered so important that the writer of the First Book of Kings compared it to the founding of the Israelite nation on Mount Sinai. The successful completion of the Temple also symbolized God's permanent presence among his Chosen People in the promised land. Thus, the building of the Temple in Jerusalem was Solomon's greatest achievement.

An artist's representation
of the Temple of Jerusalem.

NAVE

SANCTUARY

Use the blueprint above to plan a sacred, or holy, space.
Design this space in a way that people will feel God's presence there.

The psalms teach us how to pray.

Many scholars believe that several sections of the Bible were completed, or at least begun, during the reigns of David and Solomon. The most important of these writings are the Book of Psalms and the Song of Songs.

The Book of Psalms, also known as the Psalter, is the great collection of Hebrew religious songs. A **psalm** is a poetic prayer designed to be sung or chanted. David is thought to have written many of the psalms. That would make sense because we know that David was a poet and a musician. Other psalms may have been composed by Solomon. And still others were written many centuries later.

As a Jew, Jesus prayed the psalms often. Today the psalms are still prayed by the Jewish People, and the psalms are also an important part of the liturgical life of all Christians. They help us to pray and to deepen our relationship with God.

The psalms are found in the Liturgy of the Hours, part of the official prayer of the Church, and in other prayer books. Psalms are found in the missals or song books that we use in church, and are prayed and sung during the celebration of Mass.

There are many kinds of psalms. They can be grouped most easily by content or mood.

- *Royal Psalms* These psalms were composed to celebrate various occasions in the reign of a king. In Christian tradition the royal psalms are also called *messianic psalms* because they apply to Jesus who was the Messiah, or Anointed One.

"LORD, the king finds joy in your power;
in your victory how greatly he rejoices!"
(Psalm 21:2)

- *Hymns praising God and Zion* These psalms focus on God's power or on the glory of Zion. Zion is another name for the hill on which Jerusalem is built.

"God is king over all the earth;
sing hymns of praise." (Psalm 47:8)

What are some psalms that you know?

_____   _____

_____   _____

_____   _____

_____   _____

Key Word

psalm (p. 331)

- *Laments* A lament is a poem or song expressing sorrow, mourning, or regret. Laments can come from individuals or whole communities.

"LORD, hear my prayer;
in your faithfulness listen to my pleading;
answer me in your justice." (Psalm 143:1)

- *Wisdom Poems* These psalms are designed to teach rather than to encourage prayer.

"How good God is to the upright,
the Lord, to those who are clean of heart!"
(Psalm 73:1)

The Song of Songs is another important Old Testament book. It is a collection of love poems. In the Song of Songs, the Lord is the one who loves, the Israelites are his beloved, and the covenant between them is described as their marriage. The Song of Songs contains some of the most beautiful love poems ever written.

WE RESPOND

Psalm 122: Qué Alegría/ I Rejoiced

Refrain:
I rejoiced when I heard them say,
"Let us go to the house of the Lord.
Let us go to the house of the Lord."

I rejoiced when they said to me,
"We will go to the house of the Lord."
And now inside your gates we
    stand, Jerusalem,
we stand, Jerusalem. (Refrain)

Refrain:
Qué alegría cuando me dijeron:
"Vamos a la casa del Señor.
Vamos a la casa del Señor".

Qué alegría cuando me dijeron:
"Vamos a la casa del Señor".
Y ahora en tus portales
entramos ya, Jerusalén,
entramos ya, Jerusalén. (Refrain)

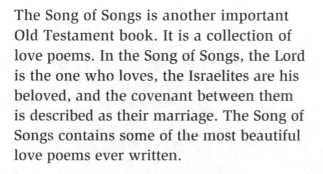

151

Pray Learn Celebrate Share Choose Live

Grade 6 Chapter 12 PROJECT

Show What you Know

Write the letters found by using the ordered pairs shown.

You will find the Key Words. Write a sentence for each.

✺	P	A	L
♥	D	S	M
❉	W	O	I
	★	◎	✿

1. ______ ______ ______ ______ ______ ______
(★,❉) (✿,❉) (◎,♥) (★,♥) (◎,❉) (✿,♥)

____

2. ______ ______ ______ ______ ______
(★,✺) (◎,♥) (◎,✺) (✿,✺) (✿,♥)

____

What's the Word?

David gave the following instructions to his son Solomon:

"I am going the way of all mankind. Take courage and be a man. Keep the mandate of the Lord, your God, following his ways and observing his statutes, commands, ordinances, and decrees as they are written in the law of Moses, that you may succeed in whatever you do, wherever you turn" (1 Kings 2:2–3).

- What does David mean when he tells Solomon, "I am going the way of all mankind"?

____

- Underline the phrase that describes what will happen to Solomon if he follows God and his ways.

Fast Facts

Seventy-three of the one hundred fifty psalms in the Book of Psalms are attributed to David. As a talented musician, he included musical instructions with the psalms he wrote, such as, "with stringed instruments," "with wind instruments," "for flute accompaniment," or "upon an eight-string lyre." David's psalms have many themes, including praise, thanksgiving, and sorrow.

King David as psalmist; illuminated manuscript, France, 13th century

DISCIPLE

**Pray
Learn
Celebrate
Share
Choose
Live**

Pray Today

Every church building is a house of prayer and a holy place. We show our reverence for this sacred space in many ways. We appreciate the work of the architect who planned this church building. We admire the work of the artists and craftspeople who contributed to its beauty. We thank God for all the people who sacrificed in the past to build this house of prayer. We are grateful for those who take care of the interior of the church, the vestments, and altar vessels.

DISCIPLE CHALLENGE Write a prayer to thank God for all of these people.

_____

_____

_____

_____

_____

Celebrate!

This week at Mass, or the celebration of other sacraments, pay particular attention when psalms are sung. Sing along, and let the presence of God truly enter your heart.

Take Home

Talk about the word *wisdom* with your family. Wisdom is a gift from God, and it enables us to live a good life and to be faithful to God.

Invite your family to share stories or experiences in which people, including your family members, asked God for wisdom.

CHAPTER TEST

Underline the correct answer.

1. Under the rule of (**David**/**Solomon**) Israel achieved its greatest prosperity and peace in ancient times.

2. In a dream, Solomon asked God for (**glory**/**wisdom**) to help him rule the Israelites.

3. Solomon built (**a temple**/**a palace**) to show his love of God and desire to be faithful to the covenant.

4. The (**sanctuary**/**nave**) of the Temple contained the ark of the covenant.

Choose a word(s) from the box to complete each sentence.

5. _Royal Psalms_ are psalms composed to celebrate various occasions in the reign of a king.

6. _Wisdom poems_ are psalms designed to teach rather than to encourage prayer.

7. _Laments_ are psalms that express sorrow, mourning, or regret.

8. _Hyms of God and Zion_ are psalms that focus on God's power or on the glory of Zion.

> Hymns of God and Zion
>
> Wisdom poems
>
> Laments
>
> Royal Psalms

Write a paragraph to answer this question.

9–10. How does the story of Solomon help us to understand the importance of wisdom?

~~Wisdom is important because~~

_____

_____

_____

"Then the wolf shall be the guest of the lamb,
and the leopard shall lie down with the kid;
The calf and the young lion shall browse together,
with a little child to guide them."

Isaiah 11:6

SEASONAL
CHAPTER 13

This chapter prepares us to celebrate the season of Advent.

During Advent, the Church prepares for the celebration of Christmas.

WE GATHER

✝ *Jesus, bring us peace as we prepare to celebrate your birth.*

What does the word *peace* mean to you? How would you describe peace in the world? in your neighborhood? in your school?

WE BELIEVE

The season of Advent is a time of waiting and expectation. We are preparing, celebrating, and anticipating the coming of Christ into the world.

The word *Advent* means "coming," and the four weeks of Advent are a special time of joyous anticipation and preparation.

- We hope for Christ's coming in the future, and we prepare by being faithful to him and living in peace with one another.

- We celebrate Christ's presence in the world today. Jesus comes to us every day in the celebration of the Eucharist, in all the sacraments, and in the love we have for one another. His presence gives us hope and strengthens us to make the world a more just, peaceful place.

- We wait with joyful expectation to celebrate that the only Son of God first came into the world over two thousand years ago in the town of Bethlehem in Judea.

The color violet is a symbol of this waiting and joyful expectation. It also reminds us of the need for penance. During Advent the celebration of the Sacrament of Penance and Reconciliation is an important way to prepare for the coming of Christ.

The prophet Isaiah   The powerful voice of Isaiah the prophet rings out in many of our readings during the season of Advent. Isaiah expresses the longings of God's people as they wait for the Savior God has promised to send. Isaiah assures them that the Messiah will come from among God's own people and that he will call the people to choose peace, not war. The Israelites believe that the Messiah will be a just king who will bring them freedom and peace.

During Advent and Christmas we hear the title Emmanuel. This, too, comes from the prophet Isaiah. In the Book of Isaiah we read of *Immanuel*, which is a Hebrew word meaning, "With us is God." Isaiah used this word as a name for the Savior, and he described Immanuel this way:

"For a child is born to us, a son is given us;
    upon his shoulder dominion rests.
They name him Wonder-Counselor, God-Hero,
    Father-Forever, Prince of Peace" (Isaiah 9:5).

The Messiah Isaiah speaks of will have authority. He will be wise and prudent. He will act as a warrior and defender of the people, like God himself. And his Kingdom will be one of peace.

Christians believe that the Savior, promised by God through his prophet Isaiah, has already come. We believe that Jesus Christ is the Messiah. He is our Emmanuel. He is the child and son born to us. Jesus Christ is God the Son who became one of us. He fulfills God's promises. He brings a message of love and respect for all of us, and he shows us how to do the same.

Isaiah used images to tell the people that the Savior would come and call them to turn violence into peace. Some of those images are of a wolf as a guest of a lamb, a cow and a bear as neighbors, a lion eating hay like an ox, and a baby playing in safety by a cobra's den. In groups work to list some images that Isaiah might use today to get across this same message. Then illustrate one image.

John the Baptist In the early weeks of Advent we hear the words of John the Baptist, often called a New Testament prophet. The writers of all four Gospels describe John with words from the prophet Isaiah.

"A voice of one crying out in the desert: 'Prepare the way of the Lord, make straight his paths.'" (Mark 1:3)

John fulfills the words of Isaiah. He prepares the people for the coming of the Messiah. He preaches a message of repentance and conversion. He points out Jesus as the Messiah. John's greatest joy is proclaiming that Jesus is the Messiah, the hoped-for Savior, "Behold, the Lamb of God, who takes away the sin of the world" (John 1:29).

We pray these words of John the Baptist at every Eucharist, before we receive the Body and Blood of Christ in Holy Communion. Jesus, the Savior of the world, is no longer a hope. He is truly "Emmanuel," truly God with us.

Isaiah the Prophet   Jesse Tree   John the Baptist

The Jesse Tree The Jesse Tree is a symbolic way of presenting the story of God's love and action in the lives of his people throughout the centuries. The name comes from Scripture:

> "But a shoot shall sprout from the
> stump of Jesse,
> and from his roots a bud shall
> blossom" (Isaiah 11:1).

The Jesse Tree is a way to connect the season of Advent to God's faithfulness to his people for over four thousand years. God promises Israel that the glory they had during King David's rule will be theirs again. There will be another king from David's family. Jesus was "of the house and family of David." The Jesse Tree is like a family tree that shows Jesus' ancestry.

Traditionally a different symbolic ornament is placed on the Jesse Tree for each of the days of Advent. There is also one for Christmas Day. The chart below lists some people and events that are part of the history of our salvation.

THE JESSE TREE

	People	Theme / Event	Symbolic Ornament
Week 1 of Advent	Abraham	The promise	Field of stars
Week 2 of Advent	Moses	God's leadership	Burning bush
	Israelites	Passover and Exodus	Lamb
	Samuel	The beginning of the kingdom	Crown
Week 3 of Advent	David	A shepherd for the people	Shepherd's crook or harp
	Isaiah	The call to holiness	Fire tongs with hot coal
Week 4 of Advent	John the Baptist	Repentance	Scallop shell
	Mary	The hope of the future	White lily
	Elizabeth (mother of John the Baptist)	Joy	Mother and child
	Joseph	Trust	Carpenter's square or hammer
	Magi	Worship	Star
Christmas Eve	Jesus	Birth of the Messiah	Manger
Christmas	Christ	The Son of God	Chi-Rho symbol

WE RESPOND

How does our preparation during Advent help us to remember the themes and events on the Jesse tree?

Research to find more people and events represented on the Jesse Tree.

✝ We Respond in Prayer

Leader: Our help is in the name of the Lord.

All: Who made heaven and earth.

Leader: In the short days and long nights of Advent, we realize how we are always waiting for deliverance from our God.

Reader: A reading from the Book of the Prophet Jeremiah

"The days are coming, says the LORD, when I will fulfill the promise I made to the house of Israel and Judah. In those days, in that time, I will raise up for David a just shoot; he shall do what is right and just in the land." (Jeremiah 33:14–15)

The word of the Lord.

All: Thanks be to God.

Leader: Lord our God,
we praise you for your Son, Jesus Christ:
he is Emmanuel, the hope of the peoples,
he is the wisdom that teaches and guides us,
he is the Savior of every nation.
Come, Lord Jesus.

All: Come quickly and do not delay.

🎵 Prepare the Way

Echo each line

Prepare the way for the coming of God!
Make a straight path for the coming of God!
Ev'ry valley will be filled in,
all hills and mountains will be made low;
crooked roads will be straightened out,
all the rough land will be made smooth.
And all the people on the earth
shall see the saving pow'r of God.

Pray
Learn
Celebrate
Share
Choose
Live

PROJECT DISCIPLE

Celebrate! Complete the sentences about the season.

1. The word *Advent* means "_____."

2. The color _____ is a symbol of waiting and joyful expectation. It also reminds us of the need for _____.

3. There are _____ weeks in the season of Advent.

4. During Advent and Christmas, we hear the title _____, which is a Hebrew word meaning, "With us is God."

5. The _____ is a symbolic way of presenting Jesus' ancestry and the people and events that are part of the history of our salvation.

Make it Happen

This week, invite _____ to
(name)
participate in the celebration of the Sacrament of Penance and Reconciliation with you.

Take Home

Encourage your family to prepare for Advent through good works and prayer. Participate in parish organizations that help to provide supplies, support, or prayer chains for our servicemen and women serving throughout the world. If there is no such program in your parish, you and your family might want to organize one!

Reality Check

Make a list of actions that you will do during Advent to promote peacemaking.

Week 1 _____

Week 2 _____

Week 3 _____

Week 4 _____

_____

"Come, you nations, and adore the Lord.
Today a great light has come upon the earth."

Introductory Rites, Monday after Second Sunday after Christmas

SEASONAL

CHAPTER 14

This chapter addresses the entire
Christmas season.

The season of Christmas is a time to celebrate the Incarnation.

WE GATHER

✝ *Lord, we thank you for your constant presence.*

How do you show others that you know they are present in your home? in your school? in your parish? in your life?

WE BELIEVE

What we celebrate on Christmas Day, and during the entire Christmas season, is the wonderful gift of Emmanuel, God-with-us. We celebrate that God is with us today and always.

The season of Christmas is a time to rejoice in the Incarnation, the truth that the Son of God became man. We celebrate Christ's presence among us now as well as his first coming into the world over two thousand years ago. We recall that God so loved the world that he sent his only Son to be our Savior.

The Christmas season begins on December 25 and ends with the Feast of the Baptism of the Lord. This feast is usually celebrated around the second week of January. During the Christmas season we have several feasts that help us to celebrate the Son of God's coming into the world and his presence with us today. Here are a few of them.

Saint Stephen   On December 26 we remember Saint Stephen, the first martyr for the faith. We read about Stephen's life in the New Testament in the Acts of the Apostles. He spread the Good News of Christ, the Son of God and Savior. Stephen preached in Jerusalem, and many people came to believe and were baptized. This angered the leaders in Jerusalem. They had Stephen taken out of the city and killed. He died praying for those who were about to take his life. Stephen's belief in Jesus, as well as his love for his enemies, is an example for all of us.

Saint John   On December 27 we remember Saint John, one of Christ's Apostles. John is credited with writing one of the four Gospels. His Gospel records the life and ministry of Jesus from his very personal view as Jesus' friend and disciple. John proclaimed that in the Son of God the Word became flesh for our salvation.

"And the Word became flesh
   and made his dwelling among us,
   and we saw his glory,
   the glory as of the Father's only Son,
   full of grace and truth." (John 1:14)

During the Christmas season we rejoice that the Word is among us, today and always. "The Word among us" and "the Word made flesh" are titles for Christ, but more importantly they are explanations for the Incarnation. In fact, the word *Incarnation* means "becoming flesh."

Holy Innocents   On December 28 we remember the children, called the Holy Innocents, who lost their lives near the time of Jesus' birth.

The wise men, or magi, from the East told King Herod about a newborn king of the Jews. Then they traveled on to find this child. They found the child Jesus, praised him, and offered him their gifts.

Herod, afraid that he would lose his power, wanted this newborn king killed. To be sure that this would happen Herod ordered his soldiers to kill all the baby boys in Bethlehem and the surrounding areas who were under two years of age. But the angel of the Lord had appeared to Joseph and told him to flee to Egypt with the newborn Jesus and Mary. So Jesus was saved.

Feast of the Holy Family   On the Sunday after Christmas, we honor Jesus, Mary, and Joseph, the Holy Family. We do not know much about Jesus' family life, but what we do know shows us that he grew up in a loving, faith-filled home. Mary, Joseph, and Jesus' relatives followed Jewish traditions, prayed, and celebrated the religious feasts of their time. Jesus was obedient to his parents, and as he grew older he continued to live by the covenant.

On Holy Family Sunday we pray for our own families, and hear readings at Mass that challenge us to be loving and obedient in our own family life. The Church teaches that our families should learn to be like the Holy Family and love and respect one another. All the members contribute to the holiness of the family by the way they live.

Mary, Mother of God   On January 1 we celebrate one of Mary's feasts. We say "Hail, holy Mother! The child to whom you gave birth is the King of heaven and earth for ever." We celebrate Mary's role in God's saving action in history. Jesus was truly human and truly divine. He is God the Son, the Second Person of the Blessed Trinity who became man. So Mary is the Mother of God. Mary's love for her son extends to his Church. We honor Mary as the Mother of the Church, too.

Epiphany On the Sunday between January 2 and January 8 we celebrate the Feast of the Epiphany. We celebrate that God the Father revealed his Son to all nations. On this day we celebrate Jesus' Epiphany, or the showing of Jesus, to the whole world. We hear in the Gospel of Matthew that when Jesus was born in Bethlehem, magi, or wise men, from the east traveled to find him. They arrived in Jerusalem asking, "Where is the newborn king of the Jews? We saw his star at its rising and have come to do him homage" (Matthew 2:2).

During the time of Jesus, many people believed that a new star appeared in the sky at the birth of a new ruler. The magi saw this star from lands far away and came in search of the new king. The magi themselves were not Jewish, but they still wanted to honor Jesus with gifts of gold, frankincense, and myrrh. On Epiphany Sunday we celebrate that Jesus' coming into the world was important to the whole world. The Good News of Jesus Christ is meant for everyone.

Baptism of the Lord On the Sunday after Epiphany we celebrate Jesus' baptism by John the Baptist at the Jordan River. Even though Jesus is without sin, he asks John to baptize him. John knows that Jesus does not need this baptism with water. He knows that Jesus is the Messiah. Yet Jesus convinces John to baptize him. By his baptism Jesus identifies himself with all of those who struggle to follow God's law and live by the covenant. Jesus shows that he understands what it means to be human.

And it is after Jesus' baptism that his divinity is revealed. The Spirit of God descended on Jesus, "And a voice came from the heavens, saying, 'This is my beloved Son, with whom I am well pleased'" (Matthew 3:17).

The Christmas season begins with the birth of Jesus and ends with his baptism. During the Christmas season, birth and baptism are connected for us, too. We celebrate Jesus, our Savior, born to us on earth, and we celebrate his new life born in us through the Sacrament of Baptism.

WE RESPOND

In groups brainstorm some special ways that you can celebrate the feasts of the Christmas season. As a class share your ideas. Then make a database of the top five and find a way to share your ideas with other classes.

✝ We Respond in Prayer

Leader: Glory to the Father, and to the Son, and to the
Holy Spirit:

All: as it was in the beginning, is now, and will
be for ever. Amen.

Reader: A reading from the Acts of the Apostles

"In truth, I see that God shows no partiality. Rather, in every
nation whoever fears him and acts uprightly is acceptable to
him. You know the word [that] he sent to the Israelites as he
proclaimed peace through Jesus Christ, who is Lord of all,
what has happened all over Judea, beginning in Galilee
after the baptism that John preached, how God anointed
Jesus of Nazareth with the holy Spirit and power. He went
about doing good and healing all those oppressed . . .
for God was with him." (Acts of the Apostles 10:34–38)

The word of the Lord.

All: Thanks be to God.

Side 1: "Here is my servant whom I uphold,
my chosen one with whom I am pleased,

Side 2: Upon whom I have put my spirit;
he shall bring forth justice to the nations."
(Isaiah 42:1)

🎵 Psalm 98: All the Ends of the Earth

Refrain

All the ends of the earth have seen
the saving pow'r of God.
All the ends of the earth have seen
the saving power of God.

The LORD has made his salvation known:
in the sight of the nations
he has revealed his justice.
He has remembered his kindness
and his faithfulness
toward the house of Israel. (Refrain)

PROJECT DISCIPLE

Celebrate!

Across

5. On December 26 we remember this first martyr for the faith.

6. On January 1 we celebrate her role in God's saving action in history.

7. On this feast we celebrate the showing of Jesus to the whole world.

8. On the Sunday after Christmas, we honor Jesus, Mary, and Joseph, the Holy _____.

Down

1. The _____ of the Lord ends the season of Christmas.

2. On December 28 we remember the children, called the Holy _____, who lost their lives near the time of Jesus' birth.

3. On December 27 we remember this Apostle and writer of one of the four Gospels.

4. The season of Christmas is a time to celebrate the _____, the truth that the Son of God became man.

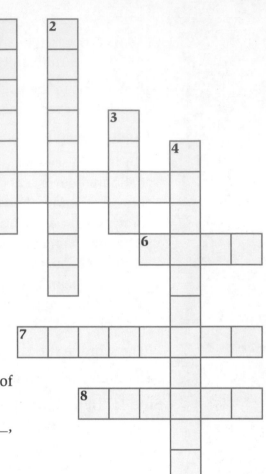

What's the Word?

Read about the birth of Jesus and the visit of the Magi. These accounts are found in the first two chapters of the Gospel of Matthew.

Take Home

The season of Christmas is a time of celebration. What are some Christmas traditions and celebrations that are unique to your family?

_____

_____

_____

Choose a word from the box to complete each sentence.

1. The word *exodus* comes from the Greek word for _____.

2. As Christians, when we read about God saving his people by helping them pass safely through the waters of the Red Sea, we are reminded of our _____.

3. In the Book of _____ we learn about the Israelites' years in Egypt and about God's carrying out his plan to bring his people to Canaan.

4. As the Israelites journeyed through the wilderness, God fed them with a sweet-tasting, bread-like food called _____.

5. To Christians, the twelve pillars of the altar that Moses set up in the wilderness are symbols not only of the twelve tribes of Israel but also of the _____.

6. To thank God for the gift of a son, Hannah dedicated her son _____ to God's service.

7. The great collection of Hebrew religious songs that Jesus prayed and that both Jews and Christians pray today is the Book of _____.

8. To show his love of God and his desire to be faithful to the covenant, _____ built the Temple in Jerusalem.

manna

Psalms

Solomon

Samuel

Apostles

Baptism

Exodus

departure

continued on next page

Write the letter of the phrase that best describes the person.

9. _____ Deborah

10. _____ Joshua

11. _____ Samson

12. _____ David

13. _____ Saul

14. _____ Ruth

15. _____ Solomon

16. _____ Moses

a. the first king of Israel

b. the shepherd-king who conquered the Philistines

c. the person God chose to lead his people out of slavery in Egypt

d. the judge who, with God's help, guided Barak to victory over the Canaanites

e. the person who said, "your people shall be my people and your God my God"

f. the leader who brought God's people into the land God had promised them

g. the king of Israel who prayed for an understanding heart and to whom God granted wisdom

h. the judge who was blessed by God with great strength

Write a paragraph to answer each set of questions.

17–18. How was King Solomon's reign different from King David's? For what is each king remembered?

_____

_____

_____

_____

19–20. What is the importance of the special meal of remembrance that Jewish families eat at the Passover? Why is the Passover meal that Jesus ate with his followers on the night before he died so important to Christians?

_____

_____

_____

_____

Redefining the Covenant People

Seasonal Chapters

In Unit 3 your child will grow as a disciple of Jesus by:

- learning the divisions among God's people, and the prophets who proclaimed God's faithfulness

- understanding that the people of Judah struggled to remain faithful to God, and the prophets who brought them comfort and hope from God

- appreciating the role of the prophets who continued to bring God's message to his people

- recognizing that the Jewish People lived and worshipped together, and how the Maccabees defended the Jewish faith

- learning Mary's and Elizabeth's roles in God's plan, and Jesus' Incarnation as the fulfillment of God's promise.

Saint Stories

The angel who brought the news to Mary that she would be the Mother of Jesus is Saint Gabriel the Archangel. Saint Gabriel is the patron saint of communications workers. Saint Clare of Assisi is the patron saint of television, and Saint Isidore of Seville is the patron of computer users and the Internet. Pope John Paul II sent text messages in 2004; Pope Benedict XVI sent texts to the participants at a recent World Youth Day. There are so many ways to spread the Good News today! How can your family spread the Good News of Jesus this week?

Saint Isidore of Seville

Picture This

Use the timeline on pages 172–175 as a review and a preview. Invite each family member to choose one person or event to look up in the text and then tell about to your entire family. In what ways do these events and people remind us of God's faithfulness?

Reality Check

"The Christian family is a communion of persons, a sign and image of the communion of the Father and the Son in the Holy Spirit."

(Catechism of the Catholic Church, 2205)

Pray Today

Throughout the Old Testament, God reveals himself as a faithful God. And God calls us to be faithful to him in return. Thank God for his faithfulness to our ancestors in faith and to your family. Pray that your family will be faithful to God in your decisions, actions and witness—today and every day.

Make it Happen

The prophets reminded God's people of their covenant with God and called them to be faithful. Who are the people in your life who remind you of God's presence and help you to respond to God's love? Have each family member name one person who is a "prophet" for him or her. Then decide on a way to thank these people for helping your family to be disciples of Jesus Christ.

Take Home

Be ready for this unit's Take Home:

Chapter 15: Standing up against injustice

Chapter 16: Respecting God, especially in family life

Chapter 17: Reading/discussing the story of Job

Chapter 18: Setting aside quality time for family

Chapter 19: Answering Jesus' call to discipleship

WE GATHER

Leader: The Lord speaks to us in many different ways and through many people. Here is the way he spoke to the prophet Elijah.

Narrator: The prophet Elijah challenged the king and the people to turn away from evil and keep their covenant with God. The queen then ordered the prophet to be killed. Elijah fled. He walked for forty days into the wilderness and took shelter in a cave. Then he heard,

All: "Why are you here, Elijah?" (1 Kings 19:9)

Narrator: Elijah answered:

Elijah: The Israelites have disobeyed your covenant, "torn down your altars, and put your prophets to the sword. I alone am left, and they seek to take my life" (1 Kings 19:10).

Narrator: "Then the LORD said,

All: 'Go outside and stand on the mountain before the LORD; the LORD will be passing by.'" (1 Kings 19:11)

Narrator: A strong and heavy wind was beating at the mountains—

All: "but the LORD was not in the wind.

Narrator: After the wind there was an earthquake—

All: but the LORD was not in the earthquake.

Narrator: After the earthquake there was fire—

All: but the LORD was not in the fire.

Narrator: After the fire there was a tiny whispering sound. When he heard this, Elijah hid his face in his cloak" (1 Kings 19:11–13).

All: For it was the voice of God.

Leader: Often God speaks to us in stillness. When we are quiet, we can hear God speaking to us in our hearts. Let us pause now in stillness and quiet, and invite the Lord to enter our hearts and minds. (Silent pause)

God, help us to listen carefully to your voice in the "tiny whispering sound" within our hearts and minds.

All: Amen.

☀ When do you find it easy to listen to someone? When is it difficult?

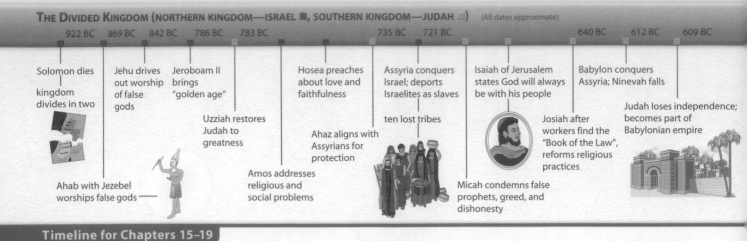

| 922 BC | 869 BC | 842 BC | 786 BC | 783 BC | 735 BC | 721 BC | 640 BC | 612 BC | 609 BC |

Solomon dies — kingdom divides in two

Jehu drives out worship of false gods

Jeroboam II brings "golden age"

Uzziah restores Judah to greatness

Ahab with Jezebel worships false gods

Amos addresses religious and social problems

Hosea preaches about love and faithfulness

Ahaz aligns with Assyrians for protection

Assyria conquers Israel; deports Israelites as slaves

ten lost tribes

Micah condemns false prophets, greed, and dishonesty

Isaiah of Jerusalem states God will always be with his people

Josiah after workers find the "Book of the Law", reforms religious practices

Babylon conquers Assyria; Ninevah falls

Judah loses independence; becomes part of Babylonian empire

Timeline for Chapters 15–19

WE BELIEVE
Solomon's kingdom was divided.

God loves us so much that he gives us the ability to love and care for one another. He also gives us the freedom to choose to love. God wants us to be happy and at peace. He wants what is best for us. However, our choices sometimes may lead us to live in ways that are not good for us.

It seems that this happened to King Solomon, the son of David. Some of Solomon's choices greatly hurt his friendship with God, and his heart was slowly turned away from God. Solomon gradually forgot the covenant and followed the ways of many false gods. Because of this God told Solomon that he would take the kingdom away from him and give it to someone else. But God also said, "I will not do this during your lifetime, however, for the sake of your father David; it is your son whom I will deprive. Nor will I take away the whole kingdom." (1 Kings 11:12–13).

King Solomon had ruled a united Israel and had completed many projects including the building of the Temple in Jerusalem. However, he had made the people pay heavy taxes and work long hours on these projects. Thus, by the time Solomon died in 922 B.C., the Israelites had grown discontent.

Solomon's son Rehoboam became the next king and announced that he would make the people's burdens even heavier. When the ten northern tribes heard this, they refused to accept Rehoboam as king. Instead they followed a man named Jeroboam. The words of the Lord to Solomon were fulfilled, and Solomon's empire was divided into two separate kingdoms. The kingdom made up of the ten northern tribes, with Jeroboam as king, was known as Israel. The kingdom made up of the two southern tribes, with Rehoboam as king, was known as Judah.

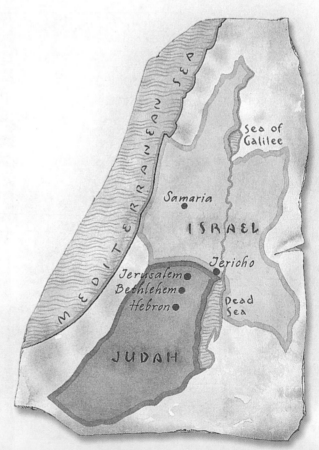

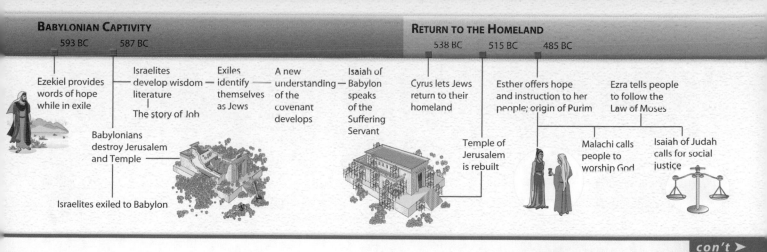

BABYLONIAN CAPTIVITY

593 BC   587 BC

Ezekiel provides words of hope while in exile

Israelites develop wisdom literature

The story of Job

Babylonians destroy Jerusalem and Temple

Israelites exiled to Babylon

Exiles identify themselves as Jews

A new understanding of the covenant develops

Isaiah of Babylon speaks of the Suffering Servant

RETURN TO THE HOMELAND

538 BC   515 BC   485 BC

Cyrus lets Jews return to their homeland

Temple of Jerusalem is rebuilt

Esther offers hope and instruction to her people; origin of Purim

Malachi calls people to worship God

Ezra tells people to follow the Law of Moses

Isaiah of Judah calls for social justice

con't ➤

Though God had given Jeroboam rule over Israel, Jeroboam did not keep God's commandments. He did not worship God with all his heart. He led Israel to forget their covenant with the one true God. By his actions, Jeroboam led the people into idolatry. **Idolatry** means giving worship to a creature or thing instead of to God. Idolatry is forbidden by the First Commandment.

The First Commandment calls us to love and honor God above all else. We honor God by our belief in him. We adore God through prayer and worship, by giving thanks and praise to him alone. The commandment also calls us to place our hope and trust in God. Even if we forget God's love and care for us, God's everlasting love for us remains.

Unfortunately neither king reminded the people of this. In Judah, Rehoboam, too, allowed the people to turn away from their covenant promise. So, both Jeroboam and Rehoboam led the people away from God. Their northern and southern kingdoms constantly battled with each other, and the divided kingdom continued to decline.

Key Word

idolatry (p. 330)

List some things that divide people today.

_____

_____

_____

_____

_____

_____

_____

_____

_____

In groups discuss how people can work to prevent or heal these divisions.

173

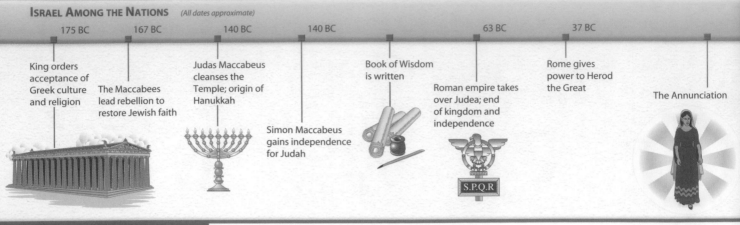

175 BC — King orders acceptance of Greek culture and religion

167 BC — The Maccabees lead rebellion to restore Jewish faith

140 BC — Judas Maccabeus cleanses the Temple; origin of Hanukkah

140 BC — Simon Maccabeus gains independence for Judah

Book of Wisdom is written

63 BC — Roman empire takes over Judea; end of kingdom and independence

S.P.Q.R

37 BC — Rome gives power to Herod the Great

The Annunciation

Timeline for Chapters 15–19

Elijah and Elisha proclaimed God's faithfulness.

After Jeroboam died, the northern kingdom continued to practice idolatry. Many of the kings that followed Jeroboam were not interested in leading the people back to God. One of the worst northern kings was Ahab. He "did evil in the sight of the LORD more than any of his predecessors" (1 Kings 16:30). Early in his reign Ahab married a foreign princess named Jezebel. She worshiped a false god named Baal, and King Ahab began to worship Baal, too. Ahab built a temple to Baal in Samaria the capital city of the northern kingdom. Ahab also used false priests and prophets as advisors.

Jezebel tried to plant her beliefs in the heart of the people of the northern kingdom. She set up statues of her gods everywhere. Eventually Ahab even allowed Jezebel to kill hundreds of people who believed in the one true God.

God tried to help the people of the kingdom of Israel to stay close to him. He sent prophets to guide the people in his ways. They experienced God's love and presence in their own lives. Because of this, the prophets clearly saw the wrongs that were taking place in their communities. The prophets told the people to stop and think about the way they were living. They called the people to be faithful to God just as God was faithful to them.

The Kings of Israel
The Northern Kingdom

Jeroboam I (jĕr′ ə bō′ əm)	922–901 B.C.
Nadab (nā′ dab)	901–900 B.C.
Baasha (bē′ ā shə)	900–877 B.C.
Elah (ī′ lā)	877–876 B.C.
Zimri (zim′ rī)	876 B.C.
Omri (ŏm′ rī)	876–869 B.C.
Ahab (ê′ hab)	869–850 B.C.
Ahaziah (ê ha zī′ ə)	850–849 B.C.
Jehoram (jē hō′ rəm)	849–842 B.C.
Jehu (jē′ hyōō)	842–815 B.C.
Jehoahaz (jē hō′ ə hǎz)	815–801 B.C.
Jehoash (jē hō′ ǎsh)	801–786 B.C.
Jeroboam II (jĕr′ ə bō′ əm)	786–746 B.C.
Zechariah (zek ə rī′ ə)	746–745 B.C.
Shallum (shal′ lum)	745 B.C.
Menahem (mĕn′ ə hĕm)	745–738 B.C.
Pekahiah (pē kə hī′ ə)	738–737 B.C.
Pekah (pē′ kə)	737–732 B.C.
Hoshea (hō shē′ ə)	732–721 B.C.

Broken idol of the false god, Baal.

174

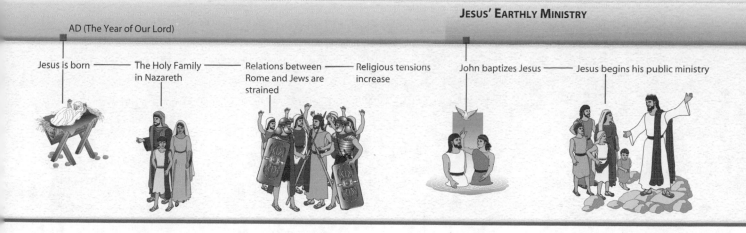

AD (The Year of Our Lord)

Jesus is born — The Holy Family in Nazareth — Relations between Rome and Jews are strained — Religious tensions increase — John baptizes Jesus — Jesus begins his public ministry

During the reign of King Ahab, the first prophet whom God sent to the northern kingdom was Elijah. The name Elijah means "Yahweh is my God." Elijah's message called the people to faith in the one true God.

Elijah eventually anointed Elisha to do God's work, too. Elijah threw his cloak over Elisha as a sign that he was called to the mission of a prophet. So Elisha had the spirit of God upon him, just as Elijah did. These two prophets spoke God's words to many and urged the people to live in justice and faithfulness.

The deeds of Elijah and Elisha are recorded in the First and Second Book of Kings. All of their works show that the power of a prophet comes from the one true God. Their words and actions show that God is loving and faithful to his people, even when they are not faithful to him.

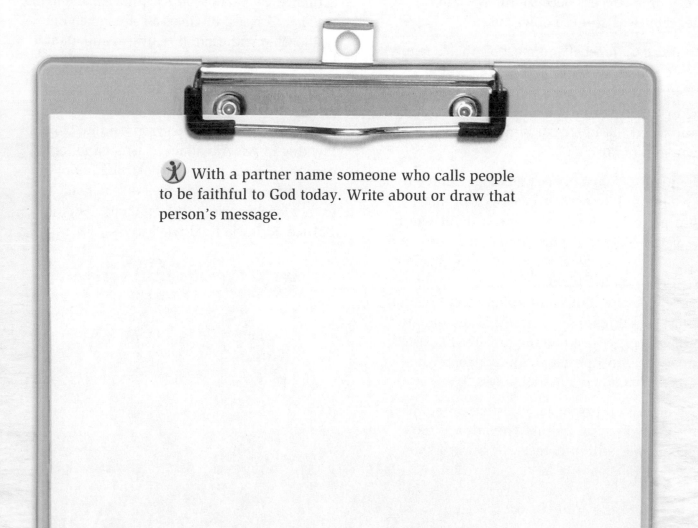

With a partner name someone who calls people to be faithful to God today. Write about or draw that person's message.

175

The Assyrians destroyed the northern kingdom.

In 850 B.C. King Ahab died in battle. He had led God's people away from their covenant with God. Ahab was first succeeded by one of his sons and then by another. They both tried to get Israel, the northern kingdom, to worship the one true God. However, they had very little success because their mother, Jezebel, was still too powerful.

In 842 B.C., Jezebel and most of Ahab's family were killed by Jehu, a general. Jehu also destroyed the places where false gods were worshiped. Jehu established himself as king and freed the northern kingdom from the worship of false gods.

In 801 B.C. Jehoash became king. His reign seemed to begin a period of power and prosperity. Under Jehoash's son, Jeroboam II, Israel even regained lost land in the north and established peace with the southern kingdom of Judah. Some people in Israel became very wealthy, but many others were poor. Most Israelites lived a hard life. Economic differences, which had not previously existed, now became a problem. Many people grew greedier and acted in evil ways.

Along with these social injustices, there were also religious problems. The faith of the people was still influenced by the worship of false gods. The real meaning of the covenant was forgotten. Many people no longer fulfilled their promises to God.

Faith is a gift from God. And even today we can lose faith if we do not turn to God to strengthen our faith. When we follow the example of Christ, and ask the Holy Spirit for help, our faith can grow. Spending time in prayer, studying Scripture, celebrating the sacraments, and living together as Jesus' disciples all strengthen our relationship with God. It is always important to keep our faith in God strong.

After Jeroboam II's death in 746 B.C., Israel's power and prosperity vanished due to a new power—the nation of Assyria. And in 724 B.C. the king of Assyria attacked Israel and took over the countryside. He took the king of Israel prisoner and occupied all the land except for Samaria, the capital city. Then in 721 B.C. Samaria finally fell to Assyria.

Great numbers of Israelites were sent away, or deported as slaves. The Assyrians filled the northern kingdom with people from other lands. Over twenty-seven thousand Israelites who were deported were never heard from again. They became known as the ten lost tribes of Israel. Thus, the northern kingdom of Israel became just another part of the Assyrian empire.

The experience of God's people shows us that sinfulness does not lead to life. Faithfulness to God and to one another is necessary for living as God calls us to live.

List some ways that your parish community can show faithfulness to God and one another.

_____

_____

_____

_____

177

Other prophets brought God's message to Israel.

A number of northern prophets left written records of their messages. The prophet Amos' message can be found in the Book of Amos, one of the prophetic books of the Old Testament.

Amos was from the Southern Kingdom of Judah, but God called him to go to the Northern Kingdom of Israel. Amos was a shepherd who lived during the middle of the reign of Jeroboam II, which seemed like a time of prosperity. In reality many social and religious problems existed in the northern kingdom. Amos addressed these problems fearlessly.

The message Amos delivered to Israel was difficult yet necessary for the people to hear. Amos told them that they were heartless, greedy, and dishonest. He accused them of turning their backs on God. He pointed out that they had forgotten those who were poor and orphaned, had unjustly taxed widows and farmers, and had committed crimes and other social injustices.

Amos told the people that God was not impressed by their religious practices when he saw that they were not living justly. He insisted that Israel's only hope of salvation was to act justly. He called the people of Israel to remember that their actions must show what was in their hearts. Amos proclaimed,

"Seek good and not evil,
 that you may live;
Then truly will the LORD, the God of hosts,
 be with you as you claim!" (Amos 5:14).

Unfortunately many people ignored Amos' message. Amos saw no clear sign that the people of Israel would change their ways. He predicted the kingdom's final destruction. His words later came true when Assyria took over Israel.

We, too, are called to act justly and stand up for what is fair and right. We all share in the work of social justice. The Church calls each of us to follow Christ's example of faith in God the Father and outreach to those who are oppressed, neglected, or in need. We cannot separate love for God and love for neighbor.

How can we follow Amos' message today?

Hosea, another northern prophet, lived around the time of Amos. We can read his story in the Book of Hosea. Hosea was married to a woman named Gomer. Gomer was not faithful to him. Though Hosea was horrified by her unfaithfulness, Hosea loved Gomer so much that he could not give her up. Hosea told the people that God felt the same way about Israel: God refused to abandon Israel even though its people had been unfaithful to him.

For Hosea, Israel's idolatry and injustices against the poor showed their lack of faith. Hosea told them that their promise of faithfulness to God was empty unless they could show their love by the way they lived.

How can we follow Hosea's message today?

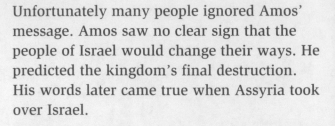

Faithful

WE RESPOND

Be a prophet! Plan a short commercial that encourages people to stay faithful to God.

_____

_____

_____

_____

_____

_____

_____

_____

_____

_____

As Catholics...

Through their words and actions, prophets remind us that justice, peace, and love of neighbor—especially those who are poor and oppressed—must be part of our Christian way of life. Such people in our modern times include Blessed Teresa of Calcutta, Blessed Pope John Paul II, Dorothy Day, César Chavez, Dr. Martin Luther King, Jr., and Sister Thea Bowman.

Choose one of these people to research. Discover why we call that person a prophet for today.

P R O J E C T

Show What *you* Know

Complete the flow chart to show the effects of the practice of idolatry during the following reigns.

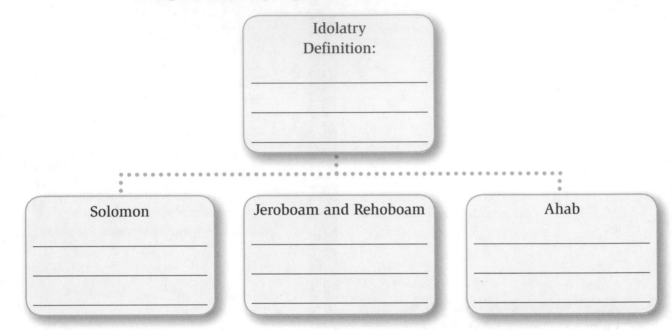

Idolatry Definition:

_____

_____

Solomon

_____

_____

Jeroboam and Rehoboam

_____

_____

Ahab

_____

_____

Fast Facts

Dr. Martin Luther King Jr. was inspired by the prophet Amos' call for social justice. King quoted Amos in his famous "I Have a Dream" speech. (See Amos 5:24.) The quote is the centerpiece of the Civil Rights Memorial in Montgomery, Alabama. This memorial honors those who lost their lives from 1954 to 1968 while working against racism and for social justice.

Question Corner

Which prophet would you like to learn more about?

❑ Elijah   ❑ Amos

❑ Elisha   ❑ Hosea

Why?

_____

_____

DISCIPLE

Pray
Learn
Celebrate
Share
Choose
Live

More to Explore

In 1943, the bishops of the United States founded Catholic Relief Services (CRS) to assist people outside of the United States who are in need in any way. CRS follows the teaching and example of Jesus Christ by trying to stop human suffering and poverty, by working for the development of people, and by encouraging peace and justice. CRS aids those who are in need of food, health care, homes, and education. It helps people to make their communities safer and to find better places to live. CRS also educates Catholics in the United States about the responsibilities of caring for all members of the human family.

DISCIPLE CHALLENGE

- Whose example does CRS follow?

  _____

- What does CRS do for Catholics in the United States?

  _____

  Visit Catholic Relief Services Web site (www.crs.org) to answer these questions:
- In how many countries does CRS operate?

  _____

- What kind of work did CRS do in Europe when CRS was first founded?

  _____

What Would you do?

What if you were asked to encourage others to be faithful to God? What would you say?

_____

_____

Now, pass it on!

Take Home

Just like God's people thousands of years ago, we are called to act justly and stand up for what is fair and right. As a family, decide on one way you will stand up against injustices that you see around you.

_____

_____

_____

CHAPTER TEST

Write the name of the prophet described.

1. _____ preached a message about the people of Israel being unfaithful to God.

2. _____ preached a message to address the social and religious problems that existed in the northern kingdom.

3. _____ was the first prophet God sent to the northern kingdom to call the people to have faith in the one true God.

4. _____ was anointed and had a cloak thrown over him to show that he was called by God to the mission of a prophet.

Jezebel

Elisha

Hosea

Elijah

Amos

Write True or False for the following sentences.
Then change the false sentences to make them true.

5. _____ God sent Israel prophets to keep them close to him and to guide them.

_____

6. _____ Judah was the kingdom of the ten northern tribes where Jeroboam was king.

_____

7. _____ Assyria was the kingdom of the two southern tribes where Rehoboam was king.

_____

8. _____ God refused to abandon Israel even though its people were unfaithful to him.

_____

Write a paragraph to answer these questions.

9–10. What is idolatry? Why is it forbidden by the First Commandment?

_____

_____

_____

_____

WE GATHER

**Leader: :** As God's people, we are called to faith in the one true God who is ever faithful.

Side 1: "Praise the LORD, all you nations! Give glory, all you peoples!

Side 2: The LORD's love for us is strong; the LORD is faithful forever."

(Psalm 117:1–2)

Side 1: Glory to the Father, and to the Son, and to the Holy Spirit:

Side 2: as it was in the beginning, is now, and will be for ever. Amen.

♫ **Though the Mountains May Fall**

Though the mountains may fall
and the hills turn to dust,
yet the love of the Lord will stand
as a shelter for all who will call on his name.
Sing the praise and the glory of God.

☀ Name someone you know who has made a difference in your life.

WE BELIEVE
Judah struggled to remain faithful to God.

Each person who ruled God's people had the responsibility to help them stay close to God. However, Rehoboam, the king of Judah, and his successor permitted the worship of false gods. This greatly affected God's people in Judah.

Asa, the next king, worked to free Judah from practices against the one true God. And, Asa's son Jehoshaphat also brought the people back to faithfulness to God.

Unfortunately, through the wife of the next king, the worship of the false god Baal was introduced into Jerusalem. Yet despite all that took place during each king's reign, the people's faith in God never completely failed.

During the reign of King Ahaz, Judah gave up its independence in exchange for Assyria's protection from Syria and Israel. Assyrians forced the people of Judah to recognize Assyria's false gods and they even set up a huge altar in the Temple in Jerusalem. As a result, the people practiced idolatry once again. The Assyrians also made the people of Judah pay heavy taxes. Poverty, suffering, and injustice began to spread in Judah just as they had in the northern kingdom of Israel.

Mistreated by the Assyrians, the people of Judah questioned God's power and doubted him. So God sent a great prophet to reassure his people. We call this prophet Isaiah of Jerusalem. Like Amos before him, Isaiah spoke out against all forms of idolatry and injustice. His message is recorded in Chapters 1—39 of the Book of Isaiah.

The Kings of Judah
The Southern Kingdom

Rehoboam (rē ə bō′əm)	922–915 B.C.
Abijah (ə bī′jə)	915–913 B.C.
Asa (ā′sə)	913–873 B.C.
Jehoshaphat (jē hŏsh′ə phăt)	873–849 B.C.
Jehoram (jē hō′rəm)	849 B.C.
Ahaziah (ā həz ī′ə)	842 B.C.
Athaliah (ăth ə lī′ə)	842–837 B.C.
Joash (jō′ash)	837–800 B.C.
Amaziah (ăm ə zī′ə)	800–783 B.C.
Uzziah (ŭ zī′ə)	783–742 B.C.
Jotham (jō′thəm)	742–735 B.C.
Ahaz (ā′hăz)	735–715 B.C.
Hezekiah (hez ə kī′ə)	715–687 B.C.
Manasseh (mə năs′ə)	687–642 B.C.
Amon (ā′mən)	642–640 B.C.
Josiah (jō sī′ə)	640–609 B.C.
Jehoahaz (jē hō′ə hăz)	609 B.C.
Jehoiakim (jē hoi′ək′ĭm)	609–598 B.C.
Jehoiachin (jē hoi′ək′ĭn)	598–597 B.C.
Zedekiah (zĕd ə kī ə)	597–587 B.C.

Isaiah reminded the king and the people of God's love for them. He told them how to be faithful to God. Isaiah warned the king that the people would suffer because of the Assyrians. But Ahaz and the people still turned from God. Yet, Isaiah told them God would make Judah pure and faithful again. Isaiah's message was one of hope and comfort.

Talk about why it is important for world leaders to make just decisions for their people and to treat neighboring countries with respect. In the space below write a prayer for world leaders.

Prophets brought Judah hope and comfort.

Isaiah called kings to act justly on behalf of God's people. King Ahaz did not listen, but King Hezekiah, his successor, did. He stopped practices against the one true God and removed foreign idols from the Temple.

Hezekiah also tried to help the poor and those who were suffering because of the many injustices in Judah. He managed to keep the people of Judah faithful to the worship of the one true God. "This Hezekiah did in all Judah. He did what was good, upright and faithful before the LORD, his God. . . . He did this wholeheartedly, and he prospered." (2 Chronicles 31:20–21)

Isaiah told Hezekiah that God would not allow Judah to be destroyed by foreign nations. Isaiah pointed out that even if events went against his people, God would be with them. God would bring new life out of death and destruction.

For Isaiah, faith was complete trust in God's plan and wisdom. He told the people that in his mercy God would spare a remnant of the people. A *remnant* is a small piece left over from something larger. This remnant, or small group of God's people, would survive and live just and holy lives as God's faithful community.

Micah was another prophet who preached in Judah. Micah had a deep understanding of people and their covenant relationship with God. His messages are recorded in the Book of Micah. Micah spoke out against false prophets who tried to become popular

by telling their listeners only what they wanted to hear. Unfortunately, people often ignored or rejected Micah's message.

Micah was angered by the greed, dishonesty, and corruption of God's people. Micah preached that goodness lies in the practice of social justice and in faithfulness to the one true God. Micah told the people that God required them,

"Only to do the right and to love goodness, and to walk humbly with your God"
(Micah 6:8).

The prophet Micah saw the terrible effects of sin at work and warned of the eventual destruction of both the northern and southern kingdoms. But Micah assured the people that God would not abandon his chosen people. God would welcome his people back and forgive their sins. He would restore them through the work of a new David.

As Christians we believe that this promise of a new David has been fulfilled in Jesus Christ. Jesus did what was right, loved goodness, and was humble before God his Father. He spoke out against injustices and, in a way no one else could, brought the people back to God.

If Micah or Isaiah were living today, what issues and concerns would they be preaching about? As followers of Jesus Christ, how can we address their issues and concerns? Write your answers on the chart below.

The Prophet's Message Today	Our Response as Followers of Jesus Christ

The kingdom of Judah came to an end.

When Josiah became king in 640 B.C., he helped Judah to slowly regain its independence. More importantly, while Josiah's workers were repairing the Temple, they found a copy of "the book of the law." This was probably an early version of the Book of Deuteronomy.

Josiah was surprised to discover how different the worship of his day was from that of the time of Moses. Thus, Josiah began a reform of religious practices in Judah. He banned all false practices. He closed local places of worship and brought all the priests to the Temple.

The prophet Zephaniah, whose message is in the Book of Zephaniah, appeared early in Josiah's reign. Zephaniah condemned the worship of false gods and welcomed Josiah's reforms. The prophet urged the people to return to the faith of Moses. Zephaniah said that God, in his great love, would allow a faithful remnant to at last enjoy the peace, prosperity, and justice that the covenant promised.

In 609 B.C., Josiah died in battle against the king of Egypt. Judah now had to pledge loyalty to Egypt. This did not last for long, however.

We read in the Book of Nahum that Assyria was eventually conquered. The king of Babylon destroyed Nineveh, the capital of Assyria and also defeated Egypt. So Judah became a part of the Babylonian empire. The king of Judah did not remain faithful to God, and he encouraged idolatry. Violence and social injustice flourished and many people turned their backs on God.

When the king of Judah was disloyal to the king of Babylon, Babylon invaded Judah. The king of Babylon ruined the crop and pasture lands and captured Jerusalem. He forced the new king of Judah, the court officials, and many other people to leave Judah and go to Babylon. This was the first step of the exile, or forced removal, of God's people from their own land.

The king of Babylon also carried off much of Judah's wealth, and he left Zedekiah in charge of Judah. Zedekiah later rebelled, and the king of Babylon invaded Judah a second time. He deported more of the people to Babylon and carried off more of Judah's wealth. In 587 B.C. the king of Babylon invaded Judah a third time. He destroyed Jerusalem, including the Temple, and deported even more people to Babylon. The people of Judah were in exile.

This was the end of Judah, the southern kingdom, and its proud line of kings descended from David.

Think about the messages of Isaiah, Micah, and Zephaniah. Then pretend you are a prophet calling the people of Judah to turn back to God. What is your message to them? Write some notes here.

_____

_____

_____

_____

_____

_____

_____

_____

_____

_____

_____

In small groups deliver your speeches to one another.

Prophets called the people to faithfulness.

Prophets served God by constantly calling the people to change their ways. One of these prophets was Habakkuk, who appeared between 605 and 597 B.C. His message can still be read in the Book of Habakkuk. The prophet questioned God's ways saying,

"Why do you let me see ruin;
    why must I look at misery?"
(Habakkuk 1:3).

God told him that Babylon was an instrument for purifying Judah of its sins. Those who were faithful to him and just to their neighbors would continue to remain in his love.

God calls each of us to be cleansed of our sins. It is in the Sacrament of Baptism that we are first freed from sin. We sometimes fail to follow God's laws and then it is in the Sacrament of Penance that we are forgiven our sins. Our promise to perform a penance shows that we are sorry for turning away from God and not loving others. Part of reconciling with God is our firm purpose to rely on God and not to sin again.

Another prophet named Jeremiah lived from around 650 B.C. until just after 583 B.C. These troubled times affected Jeremiah deeply and caused him to struggle with his vocation. A **vocation** is God's call to serve him. In Jeremiah's case, it was a call to be God's prophet.

God is with each of us too, as we work to serve God and others.

At first Jeremiah resisted God's call, saying,

"I know not how to speak; I am too young."
But God replied,
"Have no fear . . .
because I am with you . . ."
Then God touched Jeremiah's mouth and said,
"See, I place my words in your mouth!"
(Jeremiah 1:6, 8, 9).

Thereafter, Jeremiah was dedicated to God's service. When Jeremiah saw that people were performing religious ceremonies without understanding the covenant and how it called them to live justly, he wept at this unfaithfulness.

Jeremiah warned the people of Judah that God said that nothing would remain, not even a remnant, *unless* they started to live according to the covenant.

The people did not accept Jeremiah's message and accused him of blasphemy. **Blasphemy** is a thought, word, or act that refers to God without respect or reverence. Jeremiah was rejected, attacked, and imprisoned. He begged God to let him abandon his vocation. But God told Jeremiah to remain faithful, for God would be with him. So, Jeremiah continued to speak out against the sins of the nation.

The prophetic writing in the Book of Baruch was similar to that of Jeremiah. It was written to bring comfort to people who had lost their homeland. It stressed belief in the one true God, faithfulness to the Law of Moses, repentance, and hope.

Key Words

vocation (p. 331)
blasphemy (p. 330)

As Catholics...

As baptized Christians we all share a common vocation. We are called to grow in holiness, become more like Jesus Christ, and bring the Good News of Jesus to others.

God also calls each person to serve him in the single life, married life, religious life, or as a priest or deacon. The Holy Spirit guides us—and our family, friends, and teachers also help us—to discover how God is calling us to serve him.

In groups identify the vocations of different people in your lives.

WE RESPOND

The prophets, especially Jeremiah, called people to treat their "neighbors" justly. Who are our neighbors? With a partner list some ways that we can work for justice for all people.

_____   _____

_____   _____

_____   _____

_____   _____

_____   _____

Act out some of your ideas for the class. Have the members of your class try to guess your works of justice.

Pray Learn Celebrate Share Choose Live

PROJECT

Show What *you* Know

Write an online profile for Jeremiah. Include the **Key Words** in your profile.

Fast Facts

The prophet Isaiah's words of peace (see Isaiah 2:4) are inscribed in a granite wall in a park across the street from the United Nations in New York City. Ralph J. Bunche Park, named for the African-American diplomat and winner of the 1950 Nobel Peace Prize, is the site of the Isaiah Wall.

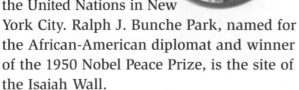

What's *the* Word?

"Then I [Isaiah] heard the voice of the Lord saying, 'Whom shall I send? Who will go for us?' 'Here I am;' I said; 'send me!' And he [God] replied: 'Go and say this to the people:
  Listen carefully, but you shall not understand!
  Look intently, but you shall know nothing!'"
(Isaiah 6:8–9)

↳ DISCIPLE CHALLENGE

• Underline the sentences that tell how Isaiah responds to God's call.

• What does the prophet Isaiah say to the people?

_____

_____

DISCIPLE

Pray
Learn
Celebrate
Share
Choose
Live

More to Explore

One way that the Church has carried on the mission of the prophets has been through encyclicals. Encyclicals are teachings that the popes have sent in letter form to the whole Church. Encyclicals help us to understand world events and how we can help society by living out the Gospel. In 1963, Pope John XXIII wrote an encyclical about the right of all people to live in peace and freedom. In 1995, Pope John Paul II wrote an encyclical on the value of human life. In 2007, Pope Benedict XVI wrote an encyclical on true Christian hope. Like the writings of the prophets, these letters from the popes give us words of wisdom for our times. They call us to live as faithful followers of Jesus Christ.

Pope John Paul II signing the encyclical *Veritas Splendor*, October 5, 1993

↳ DISCIPLE CHALLENGE

• What kind of writing is an encyclical?

_____

• Who writes encyclicals for the whole Church?

_____

Find out more about encyclicals.

Emblem of the papacy

Question Corner

Have you ever made a difference in someone's life?

❏ Yes   ❏ No

Has someone made a difference in your life?

❏ Yes   ❏ No

↳ **DISCIPLE CHALLENGE** Pray that as Jesus' disciple you can make a difference in the future.

Take Home

Plan a family discussion. Talk about the ways you use the name of God. Talk about the ways you can bring greater respect for God into your thoughts, words, and actions.

Now, pass it on!

CHAPTER TEST

Circle the letter of the correct answer.

1. _____ began a reform of religious practices in Judah, banning all false practices.

   a. Ahaz   **b.** Manasseh   **c.** Josiah

2. The life of the prophet _____ was tragic and his message was not often accepted, but he never lost hope. He knew that God was always with his people.

   a. Jeremiah   **b.** Jehoiakim   **c.** Josiah

3. _____ is a thought, word, or act that refers to God without respect or reverence.

   a. Blasphemy   **b.** Vocation   **c.** Remnant

4. God sent the prophet _____ to keep the people of Judah close to him. His message was one of hope and comfort to the people.

   a. Ahaz   **b.** Isaiah   **c.** Hezekiah

Short Answers

5. What was Jeremiah's vocation?

   _____

6. What was stressed in the prophetic writing in the Book of Baruch?

   _____

7. What happened to Judah after it became part of the Babylonian empire?

   _____

8. What did Micah say about goodness?

   _____

Write a paragraph to answer this question.

9–10. What did Isaiah say about a remnant of God's people?

_____

_____

_____

_____

The Exile and the Journey Home

17

WE GATHER

✝ **Leader:** There are many people in our world who live in exile, who have been sent away from their home or country. Let us pray for them.

Reader 1: For those who are homeless in our towns and cities, let us pray.

All: Lord, help us to help them.

Reader 2: For those in prison, especially for those who are unjustly accused, and for their families, let us pray.

All: Lord, help us to help them.

Reader 3: For refugees from war, famine, and oppression, let us pray.

All: Lord, help us to help them.

Reader 4: For all children without homes, let us pray.

All: Lord, help us to help them.

Reader 5: For all those in hospitals, let us pray.

All: Lord, help us to help them.

Reader 6: For those who are dying, that they may reach their heavenly home in peace, let us pray.

All: Lord, help us to help them.

Leader: Let us pray.
Lord, we remember all who are in exile today,
all who are kept from their homes by war, poverty, and illness.
May we find ways to help them in prayer and action.
We ask this in your name, Lord Jesus.

All: Amen.

ST PAUL'S HOSPITAL

HOSPITAL TOY DRIVE

☀ Have you ever been homesick? What was it like?

WE BELIEVE
Prophets continued to share God's message.

Following the destruction of Jerusalem, God's people mourned for their nation, their Temple, and the people who had been lost. The Book of Lamentations expresses the suffering and grief of the people. A **lamentation** is a sorrow that is expressed in the form of a poem. The Book of Lamentations contains five such poems describing the destruction of Judah and the suffering of the people. The biblical writer most likely the prophet Jeremiah, knew that only firm faith in God's love could comfort the people.

The prophet Ezekiel had a similar message for God's people. Ezekiel, a priest, was called to be God's prophet in 593 B.C. Ezekiel carried out his twenty-year ministry among the Israelites exiled in far-off Babylon. Ezekiel's

message, found in the Book of Ezekiel, called the people back to God and condemned all forms of social injustice, idolatry, and superstition. **Superstition** is the false belief that living creatures or things possess powers that in fact they do not have. Superstitions take away from the honor we owe the all-knowing and all-powerful God.

Ezekiel had a vision in which the glory of God first left the holy of holies, then the Temple itself, and finally the city of Jerusalem. Ezekiel declared that according to this vision the people had rejected God, and now God was leaving Jerusalem and leaving the Temple, his dwelling place.

Ezekiel's vision became a reality after the final destruction of Jerusalem in 587 B.C.

Key Words

lamentation (p. 330)

superstition (p. 331)

Then, during the time of the exile, Ezekiel began to offer words of hope and comfort to the people. He told them that God had said, "I will give you a new heart and place a new spirit within you" (Ezekiel 36:26). Ezekiel said that God would purify those who remained true to him. He would shepherd them triumphantly back to their homes in the promised land. Prosperity and justice would prevail under the guidance of the one true God. God would again choose Jerusalem as his dwelling place. He would give the city a new name meaning "The LORD is here" (Ezekiel 48:35).

 Imagine that Ezekiel had not spoken his message, but had painted a picture or made a sculpture to symbolize the return to the promised land. What might this look like? Design your own work here.

Babylonian ruins in the Middle East.

God's people in exile were given hope.

The experience of exile in Babylon helped God's people to grow in their faith. For the first time the exiles identified themselves as Jews and called their religion *Judaism*. More importantly, they began to realize just how unfaithful they had been to God.

The Jewish People began to see that birth in the promised land or citizenship in an independent Judah did not make a person one of God's people. Rather, being one of God's people meant truly following his will, having absolute faith in him, and making a personal commitment to follow the covenant.

In Babylon the Jews were able to remain a community. The Babylonians gave them fertile land on which to live and allowed the exiles to go freely about their lives. As a result, many of the exiles became quite wealthy, and some were even appointed to important positions at the royal court. In these ways God continued to protect his people and to set his plan for their future in place.

Late in the exile another prophet, Isaiah of Babylon, offered a clear message of hope to the people of Israel. His message is the second prophetic message in the Book of Isaiah and is found in Chapters 40—55.

Isaiah called the people to be faithful to God and to have hope. Like faith, hope is a gift from God. **Hope** enables us to trust in God's promise to be with us always. Hope enables us to be confident in God's love and care for us.

Isaiah reminded the people that God remained as faithful and loving as he was when they were in Egypt. But Isaiah said that salvation would come only through the suffering of a servant of the Lord, a servant who would be without sin.

Key Word

hope (p. 330)

The writers of the New Testament understand Isaiah's words to be fulfilled in Jesus Christ. He is the sinless servant who "did not come to be served but to serve and to give his life as a ransom for many" (Matthew 20:28).

As Christians we believe that God showed us his great love by sending his only Son to us. In Jesus Christ God's love is made present to us, so our hope is in Christ. Hope helps us to rely not on our own strength, but on the strength of God the Holy Spirit—sent to us by the Father and the Son.

As Catholics...

At Jesus' baptism, the Father made it known that Jesus was his Son. The Holy Spirit came upon him, anointing him as priest, prophet, and king.

We call Jesus a priest because he offered the perfect sacrifice that no one else could. Jesus offered himself to save us. Jesus was a prophet because he delivered God's message of mercy and spoke out for truth and justice. Jesus showed himself to be a king by the care he gave to all his people.

As baptized members of the Church, we share in Jesus' role as priest, prophet, and king. How can we serve others by what we say and do?

Pretend that you are in Babylon listening to Isaiah preach. With a group role-play the situation. Have one person be Isaiah and deliver God's message. Have others ask Isaiah questions about this message and about the way God would save them. Plan your role-play here.

_____

_____

_____

_____

_____

_____

_____

_____

_____

God's people searched for wisdom.

During the years in Babylon, and throughout their long history, the Jews were particularly attracted to the tradition of writing about wisdom. Some of this writing is contained in the wisdom books of the Old Testament. These books give practical guidance on how to live, and some use proverbs to teach. A **proverb** is a brief saying that gives wise advice. It makes a clear point that can be easily remembered.

The Wisdom Literature of the Old Testament

Book of Job	This book reminds us that suffering is a part of life for all people. Those who are innocent and faithful to God suffer, too, and are brought to a deeper trust in God.
Book of Psalms	This book is a collection of poetic prayers and songs known as psalms. These psalms help us to give worship to God. They are an important part of the Church's liturgy.
Book of Proverbs	This book gives advice on how to live. It covers a wide range of topics, from the simplest everyday concerns to the most complicated thoughts about God and our faith.
Book of Ecclesiastes	This book teaches us that riches, pleasure, and even wisdom, only bring happiness for a while. God alone can provide lasting happiness.
Song of Songs	This book is a collection of love poems that use symbolic language to help us understand God's love for us and our covenant relationship with him.
Book of Wisdom	This book is designed to urge people to live a good and holy life. For that reason it argues *against* greed, selfishness, and idolatry, and *for* faith in the one true God.
Book of Sirach (or Ecclesiasticus)	This book deals with growing in faith and teaches that we can grow in faith by living a good and holy life.

One of the most famous examples of wisdom literature is the Book of Job. It is the story of Job, who had a wonderful wife, a large family, many relatives and servants, and a great number of possessions. Job was a good and just man of God. Yet suddenly, he lost his children, his possessions, and even his own health. However, throughout his unexplainable suffering, he remained faithful to God. And eventually the Lord rewarded Job's faithfulness and gave Job back in a double measure everything that Job had lost.

Key Word

proverb (p. 331)

As a class start a book of proverbs that is a how-to manual for living a good and just life. What will you call your book of wisdom? Write the title and a few proverbs here.

_____

_____

_____

_____

_____

_____

_____

_____

_____

The long return to Judah happened in three stages.

God loved his people, Israel. He planned the stages of their return to the land that he had promised them. In 539 B.C. the Persians took over the Babylonian empire. A year later Cyrus, the Persian king, decided to let the Jews in exile return to their homeland. Though Judah would still belong to Persia and have a Persian governor, the Jews would be allowed to govern themselves in local and religious matters. This news was greeted with joyous celebrations.

In 538 B.C. Cyrus appointed a prominent descendant of David to lead a group of Jews back to Judah. This group began the rebuilding of the Jewish nation. Then Cyrus unexpectedly died in battle and all work was stopped. Still, the Jews were again in their homeland.

Around 520 B.C. the voices of two new prophets, Haggai and Zechariah, were heard. They cried out to those who had returned to stop concentrating only on their own interest and to rebuild the Temple. Their stirring arguments are in the Book of Haggai and in the Book of Zechariah.

Then a strong new ruler of the Persian empire appointed two prominent Jews to lead a large Jewish expedition back to Judah. This group succeeded in rebuilding the Temple and resettling a large part of the land. The first stage of God's plan to reestablish the exiled Jews in their homeland was now completed: Jews occupied the land, and the Temple was restored.

About seventy years after the Temple was rebuilt, Jewish territory in the south and southeast was invaded. Nehemiah was sent to rebuild the walls of Jerusalem and protect the city from these attacks. Thus, as we can read in the Book of Nehemiah, God completed the second stage of the return: Judah was freed from foreign attack.

Another Jew, Ezra, led a group of Jewish exiles back to Judah. Ezra reformed the religious and social practices in Judah. His work is recorded in the Book of Ezra.

In a dramatic scene in the Temple Ezra wept publicly and recalled the people's sins against God. The people were so moved that they repented and agreed to follow God's law. This law was found in the **Torah**, the Hebrew name for the first five books of the Old Testament. In this way God accomplished the last stage of the return to Judah: The people submitted fully to God's law.

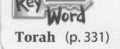

Key Word

Torah (p. 331)

WE RESPOND

We, too, are called to follow God's law. We do this when we live by the teachings of Jesus Christ.

With a partner brainstorm different ways that we, as members of the Church, can say and do the things that Jesus Christ taught us to do.

_____

_____

_____

_____

_____

_____

_____

Choose one thing that you will do this week to show that you follow Jesus' teaching.

Pray
Learn
Celebrate
Share
Choose
Live

PROJECT

Show What *you* Know

Write a summary of the Israelites' experiences during the exile in Babylon and the journey home. Be sure to use the **Key Words** in your summary.

Celebrate!

Psalms are an important part of the Church's liturgy. They help us to give worship to God. During Mass, when are psalms proclaimed?

❏ the Introductory Rites

❏ the Liturgy of the Word

❏ the Liturgy of the Eucharist

❏ the Concluding Rites

Picture This

The anchor was one of the most popular early Christian symbols of hope. The anchor as a symbol of hope is based on Scripture. (See Hebrews 6:18–19.) Think of your own symbol of hope and draw it in the space below.

Saint Stories

Saint Bonaventure was born in 1221 in Tuscany, Italy. At a young age he joined the Franciscans, a religious community founded by Saint Francis of Assisi. He moved to Paris, France, where he studied at the university. He wrote about God and became known for his great love of God. He kept a large crucifix on his desk. He said that he learned of all the beautiful things he wrote about God from Jesus, his only teacher. He also wrote a biography of Saint Francis of Assisi. Bonaventure's books made him famous, but he remained humble. In 1273, Bonaventure was made a cardinal. His knowledge and wisdom helped the pope and bishops. Saint Bonaventure University in Olean, New York, was named in honor of the saint. His feast day is July 15.

Devereux Hall on the campus of St. Bonaventure University, Olean, New York

↳ DISCIPLE CHALLENGE

- Underline the sentence that describes the source of Bonaventure's writing.
- Circle the name of the religious community that Bonaventure joined.

Visit *Lives of the Saints* on **www.webelieveweb.com** to find out more about other saints and holy people.

What's *the* Word?

The Book of Proverbs, one of the wisdom books of the Old Testament, gives advice on how to live. Read the following passage and explain its meaning.

"Rich and poor have a common bond:
the LORD is the maker of all." (Proverbs 22:2)

_____

_____

_____

_____

Take Home

As a family, read the story of Job found on page 201. Talk about Job's sufferings and his faithfulness. What situation in today's world reminds you of the story of Job?

_____

_____

_____

Write the letter that best defines each term.

1. ___C___ hope

2. ___D___ lamentation

3. ___E___ proverb

4. ___A___ superstition

a. false belief that living creatures or things possess powers that in fact they do not have

b. the Hebrew name for the first five books of the Old Testament

c. a gift from God that enables us to trust in God's promise to be with us always

d. a sorrow expressed in the form of a poem

e. a brief saying that gives wise advice

Short Answers

5. How are the messages of the prophets Ezekiel and Jeremiah similar?

Faith in God's love converts the people

6. Name one important change that took place while God's people were exiled in Babylon.

They realized that God should be first

7. What was the outcome of the third stage in God's plan for the return of the exiled people to Judah?

God is always with us

8. Name three wisdom books of the Old Testament that give practical guidance on how to live.

Job,

Write a paragraph to answer this question.

9–10. According to Isaiah of Babylon, how will God save his people?

Isiah's words will be in the name of Jesus

A Strong People

18

WE GATHER

✝ **Leader:** The wise walk in the ways of the Lord. They listen to the messages that God sends them.

Let us listen to these words of wisdom from Scripture.

Reader 1: "He who walks honestly walks securely, but he whose ways are crooked will fare badly."

(Proverbs 10:9)

All: Lord, give us wisdom to speak and act with honesty.

Reader 2: "Hatred stirs up disputes, but love covers all offenses."

(Proverbs 10:12)

All: Lord, give us wisdom to grow in love for all people.

Reader 3: "Better a little with virtue, than a large income with injustice."

(Proverbs 16:8)

All: Lord, give us wisdom to act justly and with compassion.

Reader 4: "He sins who despises the hungry; but happy is he who is kind to the poor!"

(Proverbs 14:21)

All: Lord, give us wisdom to find and serve you in all our brothers and sisters.

Reader 5: "A faithful friend is a sturdy shelter; he who finds one finds a treasure."

(Sirach 6:14)

All: Lord, give us wisdom to be faithful and true friends to others.

Reader 6: "A cheerful glance brings joy to the heart; good news invigorates the bones."

(Proverbs 15:30)

All: Lord, give us wisdom to understand the Good News that you send to us. Let it fill us with joy!

All: Lord, teach us your ways. Help us grow in grace and truth. Amen.

☀ Think of a book, television show, or movie that contains an important message for people. What is the message? How is it communicated?

207

WE BELIEVE
The Jews lived and worshiped together.

As we have seen, each of the prophets had a message for God's people. One of these prophets was known as Isaiah of Judah. His message, the third prophetic message in the Book of Isaiah, can still be read in Chapters 56—66 of that book. Isaiah not only focused on true worship, but also made a connection between worship and the fair and just treatment of others. He linked praising God and social justice. Worship, he said, must lead people to act with justice, especially toward those who suffer.

In the Book of Malachi we find another call to worship God and to be just. Malachi foresaw a day when God would come to judge his people. Malachi, meaning "my messenger," tells of a messenger who would prepare the way for repentance and true worship. We read about such a messenger in the Gospel of Matthew when John the Baptist appears in Judea:

"A voice of one crying out in the
    desert,
'Prepare the way of the Lord,
    make straight his paths.'"
    (Matthew 3:3)

The Book of Obadiah was written at a time when the Jewish People were having problems with the people in Edom. During the Jewish return from Babylon, the Edomites started to settle in southern Judah. The Book of Obadiah reminds us that God is just.

It presents the hope for the survival of the Jewish People and the return of the kingdom begun by David.

The Book of Joel uses images to show the people the need for true repentance.
"Rend your hearts, not your
    garments,
    and return to the LORD, your God"
(Joel 2:13), the prophet insists. He tells the people that only in this way will Israel be restored to God's favor.

The Book of Daniel gives insight into the long years of Babylonian exile and Persian domination. Stories about Daniel and his companions express hope and tell of the importance of behavior that is acceptable to the Lord. They show that God's people are able to be faithful to their religious traditions even in a foreign land.

The Book of Esther, like the Book of Daniel, is a kind of historical romance. It is a mixture of fact and fiction designed to offer hope and instruction to a defeated people. Esther was a virtuous Jewish girl married to the king of Persia. She stopped a terrible plot in which the king agreed that the Jews should be killed. The day of this terrible event would be decided by casting lots, or in Hebrew, *purim*. Jews everywhere still mark this day when through God's help Esther saved God's people. They celebrate it as the feast of Purim.

Esther appeals to the king of Persia. A page from the Megillat—
The Book of Esther, 18th century.

Throughout history God has worked through his people. What are some ways that God works through people

in your family?

My mother teaching CCD ~~and giving me wisdom above~~

in your parish?

My mother teaching CCD

in your city or town?

Places of worship

in your state or country?

celebrating holidays

in the world?

The Pope shares the good news of God.

God continued to work through his people.

Storytelling is an important way that the biblical writers help people to understand their relationship with God. The stories in the Bible are sometimes a part of historical or prophetic books. Other times the story is recorded in a specific book of the Bible—often bearing the name of a character in the story. Either way the stories contain symbolic, interesting characters who deal with the issue of God's providence. Providence is God's constant care for and protection of his people.

The Story of Tobit   The Book of Tobit is about a wealthy Jew living in Nineveh, Assyria. When he became blind, Tobit sent his son Tobiah to Persia where he met a woman named Sarah. There God sent the angel Raphael in disguise to help Tobit, Tobiah, and Sarah solve all their problems.

Tobit then sang a beautiful hymn praising God for his providence. It began,
"Blessed be God who lives forever,
    because his kingdom lasts for all ages"
(Tobit 13:1).

The Story of Judith   Providence is also the principal theme of the Book of Judith. As her story opens, the Jews had refused to help Assyria fight against its enemies. Thus, Assyria was about to punish the Jewish People.

The story goes on to portray Judith as a great heroine whose brave actions rescued the Jews. Through her courage, God saved his people from their enemies.

The Story of Jonah   One of the most interesting writings of the time is the short story that makes up the Book of Jonah. It is also known as a *parable*. A **parable** is a short story that has a message. A parable is usually about something familiar, but it is told to make a point about something else.

In the story, Jonah was called to be one of God's prophets. But he refused to carry God's message of doom to the sinful city of Nineveh. Instead Jonah sailed off on a ship, was thrown overboard, was swallowed by a huge fish, and after three days, was thrown safe and sound onto dry land. Then he was sent back to Nineveh by God to complete his mission.

Detail of *Judith*, by Giorgione (1476–1510)

As Christians, this symbolic story reminds us of the Resurrection. Just as God wanted Jonah to deliver a message, God sent Jesus Christ to bring his life and love to all people. And just as Jonah spent three days in the belly of the fish, Jesus Christ rose from the dead after three days in the tomb.

When Jonah went to Nineveh the people listened, repented, and were spared. Jonah complained to God that these wicked people should have been punished. God reminded Jonah that these people were also God's creation.

This story conveys a message: God extends his mercy to all who truly repent. It reminds us not to be narrow-minded but to have a tolerant attitude toward all people.

Make a mural that illustrates the meaning of one of the stories from the Books of Tobit, Judith, and Jonah. Write a caption to explain the importance of the story today.

As Catholics...

Jesus often used parables in his teaching. Jesus used examples from nature, farming, feasts, and everyday work to describe the Kingdom of God—the power of God's love coming into the world and into our lives. Jesus also told parables to help his disciples understand God's mercy and God's justice.

With your family read and discuss one parable from Chapter 13 of the Gospel of Matthew.

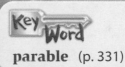

parable (p. 331)

The Maccabees defended the Jewish faith.

In 323 B.C. Judah, which was part of Palestine, came under Syrian-Mesopotamian rule. However, none of Judah's traditional political and religious arrangements changed.

In 175 B.C. the king of Syria-Mesopotamia was warned about the Roman empire trying to take over his land. He decided that his kingdom should be more united. So he required everyone to accept the Greek culture and religion.

This policy split the Jewish community in Palestine. Some Jews favored the introduction of Greek culture; they were called Hellenists, or the Greek party. Others disagreed; they were the Hasidim, or the Pious party. When the king saw that his policy was being resisted, he began to persecute the Hasidim. He also captured Jerusalem, removed the high priest, and damaged the Temple.

This caused a rebellion in 167 B.C. The events of this rebellion were recorded in the First and Second Books of Maccabees. In 166 B.C. Judas Maccabeus took charge of the revolt. The Hasidim joined Judas in rebellion and won many battles. Judas and his followers recaptured Jerusalem.

In 164 B.C. Judas cleansed the Temple and rededicated it to the worship of God. The Temple menorah, or lamp stand, was lit once again. Judas asked the people to remember this event with a festival. The festival was called the "the feast of lights" because a one-day's supply of oil in the menorah lasted for eight days. This was the origin of the festival of Hanukkah, which Jews still celebrate today. They celebrate the deeds of the people of God who refused to give up their faith.

When Judas died in battle in 160 B.C., his brother Jonathan led the people. For seventeen years they were successful in their struggle against Syria. Then Jonathan died, and his brother Simon took his place.

Simon took advantage of Syrian weakness and negotiated independence for Judah. Simon became the country's first Jewish king since 587 B.C. Simon was also the high priest. Judah was strengthened because Simon had both civil and religious authority.

The writers of the Books of Maccabees have shown us that God's providence and the heroism and diplomacy of many men and women helped save God's people and allowed them to again follow their faith.

During the time of the Maccabees how did God provide for his people? Illustrate ways God provides for people today.

Judea lost its independence to Roman rule.

In 134 B.C. Simon Maccabeus was killed and his son, John Hyrcanus, became king. John acquired a great deal of land in the south. Because he was also the high priest, he insisted that the people living there worship the one true God and give up their false religious practices.

During John's reign there was disunity and fighting among the Pious party, the Hasidim.

They questioned whether John had the right to the office of high priest. So different groups within the Hasidim formed. These groups were the Essenes, the Pharisees, and the Sadducees. Only the Sadducees recognized John's title and worked closely with him. Yet the Pharisees and the Sadducees joined with the community of Jews and continued to worship in the Temple in Jerusalem.

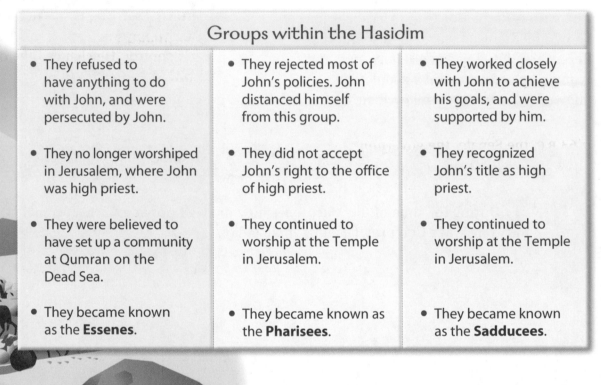

Groups within the Hasidim

• They refused to have anything to do with John, and were persecuted by John.	• They rejected most of John's policies. John distanced himself from this group.	• They worked closely with John to achieve his goals, and were supported by him.
• They no longer worshiped in Jerusalem, where John was high priest.	• They did not accept John's right to the office of high priest.	• They recognized John's title as high priest.
• They were believed to have set up a community at Qumran on the Dead Sea.	• They continued to worship at the Temple in Jerusalem.	• They continued to worship at the Temple in Jerusalem.
• They became known as the **Essenes**.	• They became known as the **Pharisees**.	• They became known as the **Sadducees**.

When John died, his younger son, Alexander Jannaeus, became king. He expanded his kingdom acquiring Galilee and Samaria. Alexander began to persecute the Pharisees because they opposed his policies. Still, when he died, he left behind him a much stronger Judea. Judea was a translation for Judah, the land where the Jews had resettled.

After Alexander Jannaeus died, a civil war broke out because of problems between his two sons. Rome sensed the trouble in Judea and decided to get involved.

In 63 B.C. the Senate, the governing body in Rome, sent Pompey the Great to settle matters in the East. Pompey made what remained of Syria-Mesopotamia a Roman province. He filled it with Roman troops. Pompey invaded Judea, captured Jerusalem, and brought the kingdom of Judea under Roman rule. This marked the end of the kingdom, as well as the end of Jewish independence for over two thousand years. The next thirty-three years or so saw a confused struggle for power, not only in Judea but also in Rome. During these conflicts, many Jews and many Romans, including Pompey himself, were killed.

When peace returned in 30 B.C., Judea found itself under Roman rule. Power in Judea was given to a complete outsider, Herod the Great. Herod was a descendant of one of the families from the southern lands that had been forced by John Hyrcanus to accept the one true God. For that reason many Jews doubted whether Herod was a Jew at all.

Herod's main concern was to survive in a dangerous world. So Herod tried to please the all-powerful Rome, now governed by the emperor Caesar Augustus. To do this Herod stopped all local attempts to free Judea from Rome's control. He changed the office of the high priesthood from one of inheritance to one of appointment. Herod also put to death all who challenged his authority. Thus he was hated by many Jews and admired by most Romans. In fact, the Romans were so happy with the way Herod was ruling that they made him king of Judea.

WE RESPOND

What can leaders do to show respect for the religious beliefs of their citizens? Write ways you can show respect for the religious beliefs of others.

_____

_____

_____

_____

_____

_____

_____

_____

_____

215

Pray Learn Celebrate Share Choose Live

PROJECT

Show What *you* Know Use the clues to complete the chart.

Clue	Your Answer
Jewish feast recalling that through God's help Esther saved God's people	
the country defeated by the actions of Judith	
the angel that helped Tobit, Tobiah, and Sarah	
he became king of Judah (Judea) when his father, John Hyrcanus, died	
the place of exile that is the setting of the Book of Daniel	
Hanukkah is "the feast of _____"	
Hasidim group that was persecuted by John Hyrcanus, and believed to have set up a community at Qumran on the Dead Sea	

↳ **DISCIPLE CHALLENGE** Look over your answers.

- Then, circle the first letter of each answer.
- Use the circled letters to write the Key Word:

____ ____ ____ ____ ____ ____ ____

The story of Jonah is a parable. What is its message?

_____

_____

Question Corner

You may have heard the saying, "When the going gets tough, the tough get going!" What helps you get "going" when the "going is tough"? Check all that apply.

❑ determination

❑ family and friends

❑ faith in God

❑ _____

Fast Facts

The phrase, "the whole megillah," comes from the Jewish feast of Purim. *Megillah* is the Hebrew word for "scroll." The scroll containing the Book of Esther is read in its entirety in the synagogue on Purim. So the phrase "the whole megillah" has come to mean a long, complicated story.

DISCIPLE

Pray
Learn
Celebrate
Share
Choose
Live

Saint Stories

Saint Genevieve was born in the fifth century in a small village near Paris. When she was fifteen she dedicated her life to God. After the death of her parents, she lived with her godmother in Paris. There she prayed every day and worked hard to care for those in need. Genevieve grew closer to Jesus and wanted to share his goodness with others. She became well known for her courage, faith, and just ways. Once she convinced the people of Paris to trust in God and remain in the city when an enemy attack was feared. She had them fast and pray to show their faith. Paris was spared! She is the patron saint of Paris. Her feast day is January 3.

↳ DISCIPLE CHALLENGE

- Underline the phrase that describes the characteristics for which Genevieve became well known.

- Circle the name of the city for which Genevieve is patron saint.

Visit *Lives of the Saints* on **www.webelieveweb.com** to find out more about other saints and holy people.

What Would *you* do?

Daniel, Esther, and Tobit remained faithful to God in lands where people did not know God. What if you lived among people that did not share your faith? How would you continue to live your faith and remember your relationship with God?

_____

_____

_____

Take Home

Within a home, everyone's schedule may be so full that it can be difficult to find enough time to eat a meal together, let alone sit down to talk.

This week, plan some "family time" to do something together. Attend Mass together and share a meal afterward. Make time to really "connect" with one another.

Underline the correct answer.

1. The prophet (**Isaiah**/**Malachi**) foresaw a day when God would come to judge his people, and mentioned a messenger who would prepare the way for repentance and true worship.

2. The Book of (**Obadiah**/**Daniel**) contains stories that express hope and tell of the importance of behavior that is acceptable to the Lord.

3. The Book of (**Tobit**/**Judith**) describes how on one occasion God rescued the Jews from their enemies through one person's courage.

4. The writers of the Books of the (**Maccabees**/**Romans**) show us that God's providence saved his people, and allowed them to again follow their faith.

Short Answers

5. What does the Jewish feast of Purim celebrate?

   _____

6. What is God's providence?

   _____

7. How did Judea lose its independence to Roman rule?

   _____

8. What does the Jewish feast of Hanukkah celebrate?

   _____

Write a paragraph to answer this question.

9–10. Why is the story of Jonah considered to be a parable? How is it symbolic of the Resurrection of Christ?

_____

_____

_____

_____

God Fulfills His Promise

19

WE GATHER

♫ **Christ, Be Our Light**

Refrain:
Christ, be our light!
Shine in our hearts.
Shine through the darkness.
Christ, be our light!
Shine in your church gathered today.

Longing for light, we wait in darkness.
Longing for truth, we turn to you.
Make us your own, your holy people,
light for the world to see. (Refrain)

Reader: The words of Isaiah the prophet are repeated as Saint Mark writes about the mission of John the Baptist.

A reading from the holy Gospel according to Mark

All: Glory to you, O Lord.

Reader: "Behold, I am sending my messenger
    ahead of you;
    he will prepare your way.
A voice of one crying out in the desert:
    'Prepare the way of the Lord,
        make straight his paths.'"

(Mark 1:2–3)

The Gospel of the Lord.

All: Praise to you, Lord Jesus Christ.

Refrain:
Christ, be our light!
Shine in our hearts.
Shine through the darkness.
Christ, be our light!
Shine in your church gathered today.

Longing for peace, our world is troubled.
Longing for hope, many despair.
Your word alone has pow'r to save us.
Make us your living voice. (Refrain)

☀ What is one important thing that has happened to you? Why is it important?

A painting from the *Annunciation Series*, by Maria Pia Marrella, 1995.

WE BELIEVE

Mary is blessed by God.

During the last year or two of King Herod's reign over Judea, the most important event in the history of salvation took place. In the town of Nazareth in Galilee, an angel of God gave a message to a young girl named Mary. Mary was engaged to Joseph, a descendant of King David.

The angel said to Mary, "Hail, favored one! The Lord is with you" (Luke 1:28). The angel continued, "Do not be afraid, Mary, for you have found favor with God. Behold, you will conceive in your womb and bear a son, and you shall name him Jesus. He will be great and will be called Son of the Most High, and the Lord God will give him the throne of David his father, and he will rule over the house of Jacob forever, and of his kingdom there will be no end" (Luke 1:30-33).

Mary did not understand how all of this would happen to her. She was not even married yet. But the angel explained, "The holy Spirit will come upon you, and the power of the Most High will overshadow you. Therefore the child to be born will be called holy, the Son of God" (Luke 1:35).

Take a moment to imagine how Mary must have felt.

The angel also told Mary that her relative Elizabeth, who was very old, would conceive a child. The angel said that nothing was impossible with God.

Mary spoke to the angel saying, "Behold, I am the handmaid of the Lord. May it be done to me according to your word" (Luke 1:38). Mary's words showed her complete faith in God and her choice to accept and follow God's plan.

The fulfillment of all that God had promised through the prophets had now begun. The long-awaited Messiah, the Savior of all people, would soon come into the world. The child that Mary had conceived was the Son of God. Through Mary, God the Son, the Second Person of the Blessed Trinity, would become one of us.

Joseph was unaware that this was all part of God's plan. So Joseph was going to leave Mary quietly. Then an angel of the Lord came to Joseph in a dream. The angel said, "Joseph, son of David, do not be afraid to take Mary your wife into your home. For it is through the holy Spirit that this child has been conceived in her. She will bear a son and you are to name him Jesus, because he will save his people from their sins" (Matthew 1:20-21).

Like Mary, Joseph did what the Lord asked of him.

Take a moment to imagine how Joseph must have felt.

Imagine that you have been asked to announce the coming of God's Son. Design a television news alert, a press release, or an Internet banner advertisement to share the Good News. Share your design with a partner; then discuss how you think people would react to the news.

Mary and Elizabeth had special roles in God's plan.

Throughout the history of the Jewish People, God had called many women to help his people to grow strong and faithful. God called Mary and Elizabeth to take roles in his plan of salvation.

After the angel's visit to her, Mary traveled to see her relatives Elizabeth and Zechariah. Zechariah had been visited by an angel, too. The angel told Zechariah that his wife, Elizabeth, would have a child and the child should be named John. Because Zechariah did not believe that this could happen, he lost his ability to speak. The angel told him that he would not speak again until his son was born.

When Mary arrived and greeted Elizabeth, the child that Elizabeth was carrying moved within her. Filled with the Holy Spirit, Elizabeth said, "Most blessed are you among women, and blessed is the fruit of your womb. And how does this happen to me, that the mother of my Lord should come to me? For at the moment the sound of your greeting reached my ears, the infant in my womb leaped for joy. Blessed are you who believed that what was spoken to you by the Lord would be fulfilled" (Luke 1:42–45).

The Visitation, Franco-Flemish school, 15th century

In response to Elizabeth's joyful words, Mary praised God in a song. Mary's song, or canticle, is also known as the *Magnificat* and can be found on page 326. Here is part of it:

"My soul proclaims the greatness of the Lord;
    my spirit rejoices in God my savior.
For he has looked upon his handmaid's
        lowliness;
    behold, from now on will all ages call me
        blessed.
The Mighty One has done great things for
    me, and holy is his name." (Luke 1:46–49)

Mary stayed with Elizabeth and Zechariah for about three months. Then she traveled home again. Elizabeth later gave birth to a son. Everyone thought that he would be called Zechariah. But his father wrote on a tablet "John is his name" (Luke 1:63). It was then that Zechariah was able to speak again. All his relatives and neighbors wondered "'What, then, will this child be?' For surely the hand of the Lord was with him" (Luke 1:66).

Then Zechariah, filled with the Holy Spirit, spoke. Zechariah's prophesy is called *The Canticle of Zechariah* and can be found on page 328. Here is part of it:

"Blessed be the Lord, the God of Israel,
    for he has visited and brought redemption
        to his people . . .
And you, child, will be called prophet of the
        Most High,
    for you will go before the Lord to prepare
        his ways,
to give his people knowledge of salvation
    through the forgiveness of their sins . . .
    to guide our feet into the path of peace."
(Luke 1:68, 76–77, 79)

John would have an important part in the fulfillment of God's promise to his people. Like the prophets before him, John would prepare the way for the coming of the Messiah.

What are some ways we can praise God for the things he has done for us?

_____
_____
_____
_____
_____
_____
_____
_____
_____
_____
_____
_____
_____

God the Son became man.

Mary and Joseph began their life together in Nazareth, a town in Galilee. They prepared for the birth of the child and for the life that they would share with him. God had spoken to each of them. However, the event that was about to take place was beyond Mary and Joseph's understanding. The child who was about to be born of Mary was the Son of God. This child, conceived by the power of the Holy Spirit, would save all people.

At this time in Judea, a census, or count of the people, was being taken. Joseph and Mary went to Bethlehem of Judea, the city of King David's birth. All men had to enroll their families in the city of their ancestors, and Joseph was a descendant of David. Mary, too, was of the house of David. It was in Bethlehem that Mary gave birth to her son. Thus, the words of the prophet Micah were fulfilled. Bethlehem is the birthplace of the "one who is to be ruler in Israel" (Micah 5:1).

Following the instructions of the angel in Joseph's dream, Mary and Joseph named the child Jesus. This name means "God saves." God the Son became one of us.
"And the Word became flesh
    and made his dwelling among us."
(John 1:14)

This mystery is called the Incarnation. The **Incarnation** is the truth that the Son of God, the Second Person of the Blessed Trinity, became man.

Mary and Joseph followed the laws of their Jewish faith, and so they traveled to Jerusalem to present Jesus in the Temple. There they met a holy man named Simeon to whom the Holy Spirit revealed that he would not die before he saw the Messiah. Mary and Joseph also met a prophetess named Ana. They both recognized the child Jesus as the fulfillment of God's promise to save his people.

In Nazareth, Jesus grew up with Mary and Joseph and many relatives and friends. Jesus heard about his Jewish ancestors and celebrated the Jewish feasts. On certain feasts his family traveled to the Temple in Jerusalem.

📖 Luke 2:41–52

Each year Mary and Joseph went to Jerusalem to celebrate the feast of Passover. When Jesus was twelve years old, he went with them. When the time came to return to Nazareth, Jesus remained in Jerusalem. But Mary and Joseph did not know this. They thought he was traveling with their relatives. When they could not find him, they went back to Jerusalem.

They found him three days later, listening and questioning the teachers. Mary and Joseph were astounded. Jesus told them that they should have known that he was in his Father's house. "But they did not understand what he said to them. He went down with them and came to Nazareth, and was obedient to them; and his mother kept all these things in her heart. And Jesus advanced [in] wisdom and age and favor before God and man" (Luke 2:50-52).

This is one of the few accounts of Jesus' early years. We learn from it that Jesus was a faithful, obedient Jewish child. We also see that he had deep understanding and knowledge of God.

Key Word

Incarnation (p. 330)

Role-play the story of Mary, Joseph, and Jesus during their visit to Jerusalem to celebrate Passover as found in Luke 2:41–52. Characters will include: a narrator, Mary, Joseph, Jesus (12 years old), friends and relatives, and teachers in the Temple. Write your own script and present your play.

John prepared the way for Jesus.

From the Gospels we do not learn much about Jesus' life until he was about thirty years old. During these "hidden" years, as they are called, things changed in Judea.

When Herod the Great, king of Judea, died, his relatives could not agree on his successor. So Caesar Augustus in Rome used this opportunity to weaken Judea by dividing Herod's territories among his sons Archelaus, Philip, and Herod Antipas.

Archelaus was a terrible leader, so Augustus removed him. To rule this part of Herod's old kingdom, Caesar Augustus set up a procurator, a kind of deputy governor. Rome was slowly taking over complete control of Judea, which the Romans called Palestine.

Judea was a divided country. Some regions were ruled directly by Rome, and others were governed by Jewish princes who were reporting to the Romans. Therefore, relations between Rome and the Jews were very strained.

Religious tensions were also a problem. The Jews feared that the Romans would interfere with their worship and observance of the covenant with God. Religious divisions and social injustices were widespread. It was in these troubled times that ". . . the word of God came to John the son of Zechariah in the desert" (Luke 3:2).

John began to prophesy and to urge people to repent and to ask God for forgiveness. He encouraged them to get ready for the coming of the Messiah, the Anointed One, the one foretold by the prophets.

Since people came to be baptized by him in the Jordan River, he was known as John the Baptist. This baptism by John showed people's willingness to change their lives.

John told the people, "I am baptizing you with water, but one mightier than I is coming. . . . He will baptize you with the holy Spirit and fire" (Luke 3:16).

It was about this time that Jesus left Nazareth and went to the Jordan River to hear John preach and to be baptized by him. "After all the people had been baptized and Jesus also had been baptized and was praying, heaven was opened and the holy Spirit descended upon him in bodily form like a dove. And a voice came from heaven, 'You are my beloved Son; with you I am well pleased.'" (Luke 3:21–22)

Like John, we can prepare the way for people to welcome Jesus, too. By Baptism, each of us is called to live as one of Jesus' disciples. When we do what is right and treat others fairly and with justice, we are showing what it is to be a follower of Jesus.

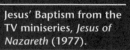

Jesus' Baptism from the TV miniseries, *Jesus of Nazareth* (1977).

WE RESPOND

Can you prepare the way for Jesus today? What will you say?
What will you do? Write some ways here. Role-play one of them.

_____

_____

_____

_____

_____

PROJECT

Show What *you* Know

Who am I? Write the letter that best describes the biblical character.

a. Anna

b. Elizabeth

c. John

d. Simeon

e. Zechariah

1. _____ I preached and encouraged the people to repent and to ask God for forgiveness.

2. _____ I lost my ability to speak when I did not believe the angel's announcement that I would have a son.

3. _____ I am a holy man. The Holy Spirit revealed to me that I would not see death until I had seen the Messiah of the Lord.

4. _____ I saw the presentation of Jesus in the Temple, and I spoke of him as the fulfillment of God's promise of salvation.

5. _____ I expressed joy when I recognized the presence of the God in an unborn child.

What's *the* Word?

"The angel said to them, 'Do not be afraid; for behold, I proclaim to you good news of great joy that will be for all the people. For today in the city of David a savior has been born for you who is Messiah and Lord. And this will be a sign for you: you will find an infant in swaddling clothes and lying in a manger.'" (Luke 2:10–12)

- Circle another name for Bethlehem in the passage.
- Why do you think the birth of Jesus involves so many visits from angels (to Mary, Joseph, Zechariah), and, in this passage, the shepherds?

_____

Fast Facts The accounts of Jesus' birth and childhood are called the *infancy narratives*. The infancy narratives are found in the first two chapters of the Gospels of Matthew and Luke.

DISCIPLE

More to Explore

The Liturgy of the Hours, part of the public prayer of the Church, helps us to praise God throughout the entire day. It is made up of psalms, readings from Scripture and Church teachings, hymns, and prayers. It is celebrated at various times during the day and night. At Morning Prayer, the Canticle of Zechariah is always prayed. In this canticle, Jesus is referred to as "the daybreak from on high." At Evening Prayer, the Canticle of Mary is always prayed. In this prayer we, along with Mary, praise God for all he has done for us. The Liturgy of the Hours reminds us that God is always active and present in our lives.

DISCIPLE CHALLENGE

- Underline the phrase that tells the purpose of the Liturgy of the Hours.
- Circle the phrase that describes Jesus in the Canticle of Zechariah.
- Find out more about the Liturgy of the Hours.

Pray Today

In 2005, Pope Benedict XVI presented the *Compendium of the Catechism of the Catholic Church.* He urged Catholics to learn the common prayers of the Church in Latin. Visit the *Latin Hall* on **www.weliveourfaith.com** to learn and listen to prayers of the Church in Latin.

Celebrate!

Every Sunday at Mass during the Profession of Faith, we profess our belief in the Incarnation— the truth that the Son of God, the Second Person of the Blessed Trinity became man. This week at Mass, listen closely as the words of the Creed are professed.

Take Home

When we do what is right and treat others fairly, we are showing what it is to be a follower of Jesus. Talk about our call to live as disciples, and ask your family members to share ideas for living out this call.

CHAPTER TEST

Circle the letter of the correct answer.

1. _____ told Mary that her relative Elizabeth was with child.

   a. Anna   **b.** An angel   **c.** Zechariah

2. _____ prepared the people for the Messiah.

   a. Elijah   **b.** Zechariah   **c.** John

3. Zechariah lost his ability to speak because he was _____ .

   a. old   **b.** sick   **c.** unbelieving

4. _____ was a descendant of King David.

   a. Joseph   **b.** Simeon   **c.** Zechariah

Short Answers

5. What role did angels play in the coming of the Messiah?

   _____

6. Why was Jesus born in Bethlehem?

   _____

7. What is the Incarnation?

   _____

8. Why is the story of the finding of Jesus in the Temple important?

   _____

Write a paragraph to answer this question.

9–10. How was Mary blessed by God?

_____

_____

_____

_____

Our hope is the God
of mercy and forgiveness.

SEASONAL

CHAPTER 20

**This chapter offers preparation for
the season of Lent.**

The season of Lent is a period of preparation for Easter.

WE GATHER

✝ *Jesus, help us to follow in your way.*

Have you ever been on a trip away from home? Where did you go? Was this a vacation trip or was it taken for another reason? What did you learn from your travels?

WE BELIEVE

The entire season of Lent is like a pilgrimage. A pilgrimage is a trip taken to a shrine or sacred place. As Christians, a pilgrimage is a prayer journey that helps us follow Christ more closely. During Lent we focus on following Christ and thinking about the relationship that we began with him at Baptism. In Baptism we are united to Christ and to all others who are baptized. Through the waters of Baptism we die with Christ only to rise to new life with him.

Lent is a journey during which we prepare to celebrate at Easter Christ's dying and rising to new life. The entire Church takes part in this preparation through our worship and by the way we live. This season is the final time of preparation for those who will celebrate the Sacraments of Christian Initiation at Easter. These three sacraments—Baptism, Confirmation, and the Eucharist—are called the Easter Sacraments. Those who receive them will share in Jesus' Death and Resurrection and have new life in Christ. We pray for them, support them, and welcome them into our parish.

On Ash Wednesday Catholics and other Christians can receive ashes, a sign of both sorrow and hope.

The season of Lent begins on Ash Wednesday and ends many weeks later on Holy Thursday evening. Absence and simplicity describe the season of Lent. There are signs of this absence in our churches and in our liturgy. During the liturgy, alleluia is not said or sung nor are bells rung. Dark purple is the color used in worship, and green plants and flowers may be removed from the churches. All of these changes remind us of our need to recommit ourselves to Christ and to the Church. They help us to prepare to renew our baptismal promises at Easter and to celebrate the new life Christ has won for us by his Cross and Resurrection.

The way we live during this season is also a sign of absence and simplicity. We are called to follow the Lenten practices of prayer, fasting, and almsgiving, or practicing works of compassion. The word *alms* comes from a Greek word meaning "compassion." Almsgiving can be the giving of time, money, or goods to those in need. Prayer, fasting, and almsgiving are always part of Christian living. However, during Lent they take on special meaning as we prepare to renew our Baptism.

Prayer

During Lent we focus on God's mercy and forgiveness. We call out to God to remember us and strengthen us to live by his laws. Lent is a good time to spend extra time in conversation with God. We may devote more time to personal prayer and to prayer with our parish community.

The Church prays especially for those who are preparing to receive the Sacraments of Christian Initiation. Many parishes gather for the Stations of the Cross and have special celebrations of the Sacrament of Penance.

Fasting

Fasting is a way to cleanse our bodies of harmful things and our hearts and minds of things that keep us from loving God and others. Fasting is also a form of penance. Doing penance helps us to turn to God and to focus on the things that are important in our lives as Christians. Doing penance is a way to show that we are sorry for our sins.

One way to fast is to give up things we enjoy, like a favorite food or activity. Catholics of a certain age are called to fast from food on Ash Wednesday and Good Friday. They are also called to give up meat on these days and on all the Fridays during Lent.

Almsgiving

During Lent we also show special concern for those in need. We follow Jesus' example of providing for the hungry and caring for the sick. We try to help other people to get the things they need and make sure that people have what is rightfully theirs.

Many parishes have food and clothing drives during this time of year. Families may participate in these drives and also volunteer at soup kitchens, visit those who are sick, and practice other works of mercy.

Stations of the Cross In Lent, as always, we are traveling toward the happiness of living forever with God. We have many opportunities to follow in the footsteps of Jesus. One of the most famous places to follow Jesus is the land where he once walked, or the Holy Land. Through the centuries, Christians have made pilgrimages to the Holy Land. They have walked in the footsteps of Jesus along the way of the cross. Since most people could not travel to the Holy Land, Stations of the Cross began to be placed in parish churches. In this way, everyone could follow Jesus on his path from Death to Resurrection. Everyone could be a pilgrim.

Following the Stations of the Cross became a devotion that takes place often during the season of Lent. The word *station* comes from a Latin word meaning "stopping point." In a parish the stations are usually fourteen statues, pictures, or crosses placed along the walls of the church. At each station we stop, we remember, and we pray.

At each station we usually pray this way:

We adore you, O Christ,
   and we bless you.
Because by your holy cross,
   you have redeemed the world.

WE RESPOND

Break into pairs or small groups and choose one station. Using various art materials design your station and write a meditation or prayer about that station. Use this space to brainstorm your ideas.

Stations of the Cross

1. Jesus is condemned to die.
2. Jesus takes up his cross.
3. Jesus falls the first time.
4. Jesus meets his mother.
5. Simon helps Jesus carry his cross.
6. Veronica wipes the face of Jesus.
7. Jesus falls the second time.
8. Jesus meets the women of Jerusalem.
9. Jesus falls the third time.
10. Jesus is stripped of his garments.
11. Jesus is nailed to the cross.
12. Jesus dies on the cross.
13. Jesus is taken down from the cross.
14. Jesus is laid in the tomb.

✝ We Respond in Prayer

Leader: Blessed are you, Lord, God of all creation:
All: you make us hunger and thirst for holiness.

Leader: Blessed are you, Lord, God of all creation:
All: you call us to true fasting:

Leader: to set free the oppressed,
to share our bread with the hungry,
to shelter the homeless and to clothe the naked.

All: Blessed be God for ever.

Reader: A reading from the Letter of Saint Paul to the Philippians

"Whatever is true, whatever is honorable, whatever is just,
whatever is pure, whatever is lovely, whatever is gracious,
if there is any excellence and if there is anything worthy
of praise, think about these things." (Philippians 4:8)

The word of the Lord.

All: Thanks be to God.

Leader: Let us now ask forgiveness of one another and of God.

All: I confess to almighty God,
and to you, my brothers and sisters,
that I have greatly sinned,
in my thoughts and in my words,
in what I have done
and in what I have failed to do,
through my fault, through my fault,
through my most grievous fault;
therefore I ask blessed Mary ever-Virgin,
all the Angels and Saints,
and you, my brothers and sisters,
to pray for me to the Lord our God.

235

Celebrate!

You have been asked to mentor a student who is younger than you. How would you explain the season of Lent to this student?

Pray Today

One traditional Lenten practice is prayer. Choose one of the seven Penitential Psalms (Psalms 6, 32, 38, 51, 102, 130, and 143) to pray during the season of Lent. Or pray one on each Friday of Lent. The message of these psalms is repentance. As you pray each psalm ask God for his help and forgiveness.

Now, pass it on!

Fast Facts

The Fourth Sunday of Lent is called Laetare Sunday. *Laetare* means "rejoice" in Latin. On Laetare Sunday, the opening prayer of the Mass and the prayer over the gifts during the Liturgy of the Eucharist speak of joy in anticipation of Easter. Rose-colored vestments may be worn by the priest to celebrate this Mass, and flowers may adorn the altar.

Rejoice

Laetare

Take Home

As a family, make time to develop good spiritual habits during the Lenten season. For example: encourage daily family prayer, daily examination of conscience, weekly Bible readings, participating in the Sacrament of Penance, and the Sacrament of the Eucharist. List other ideas here:

_____

_____

"Rejoice, O earth, in shining splendor,
radiant in the brightness of your King!
Christ has conquered! Glory fills you!
Darkness vanishes for ever!"

The Exsultet, the Easter Vigil

SEASONAL

CHAPTER 21

This chapter includes the three days from Holy Thursday evening until Easter Sunday.

WE GATHER

✝ *Jesus, take us with you into new life.*

Think about times when people count on a map to guide them in getting someplace. What would their experience be like without a map?

WE BELIEVE

The Easter Triduum guides us on a journey. We journey with Jesus Christ from Death to new life. When we celebrate the Easter Triduum, we are celebrating the most important three days of the year for Christians. These three days extend from the evening of Holy Thursday to the evening of Easter Sunday. They are counted as our Jewish ancestors in faith count their days—from sundown to sundown.

The liturgical celebrations of these three days are seen as one connected liturgy in which we celebrate Christ's passing from Death to new life. These days focus on the whole Paschal Mystery of Christ—his suffering, Death, Resurrection, and Ascension. Paschal comes from the word *pasch* which means "Passover." So the Paschal Mystery is the mystery of Christ's sacrifice of himself and of his passing over from Death to life.

Holy Thursday The Evening Mass of the Lord's Supper is not simply a reenactment of the events of the Last Supper when Jesus gathered to celebrate Passover with his disciples. It is a celebration of the new Passover, Christ's Body and Blood that he shared then and still shares with us today in the Eucharist. It is a celebration of the love and service Christ calls us to everyday.

During this Mass a ceremony of the washing of the feet takes place. This action commits us to follow the example of Jesus' love and service. He washed his disciples' feet as a sign of his love for them.

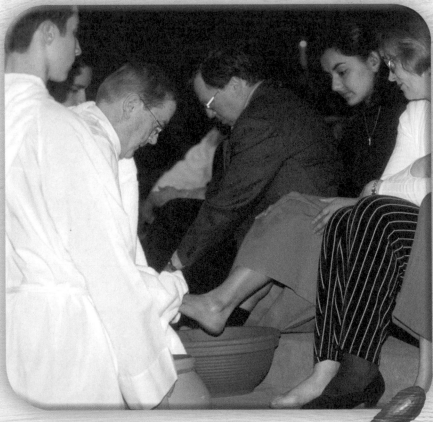

On Holy Thursday one way that we show our love and service for others is by contributing to a special collection for those who are in need.

Good Friday On this day we recall Jesus' suffering and Death. The celebration often takes place in the afternoon around three o'clock P.M.

We hear the Passion of Christ read from the Gospel of John, and we offer ten general intercessions that include prayers for the whole world. We also show reverence to the cross, for upon it hung the Savior of the world. The cross is the sign of Christ's Death and of the victory he wins for us by his Death. The cross is a symbol of the salvation Jesus Christ offers to the world.

Because the Liturgy of the Eucharist is not celebrated on Good Friday, a short communion service takes place and then all depart in silence.

Holy Saturday During the day we spend time thinking and praying. We remember that Jesus died to save all people and we thank God for this gift. We pray especially for those who will celebrate the Easter Sacraments. On Sundays and very important feast days, the Church begins the liturgical celebration on the night before with a vigil.

On Holy Saturday evening we gather with our parish for the celebration of the Easter Vigil.

The Easter Vigil is the most important vigil of the year and it is the highpoint of the Triduum. It begins after sundown on the Saturday before Easter Sunday. It is a time of watchful waiting. Two beautiful symbols of our faith are a central part of this night: light and water.

Throughout the history of salvation, fire has been a symbol of the presence of God. On the night of the Easter Vigil, a fire is made outdoors or in the back of the Church. The priest prepares the Paschal candle by marking the year on it. Then the Paschal candle is lit from this new fire and the priest says, "May the light of Christ, rising in glory, dispel the darkness of our hearts and minds." The fire represents the fire of the burning bush, and the Paschal candle reminds us of the pillar of fire that accompanied the Israelites on their journey out of Egypt. The Paschal candle is more, though. It is a symbol of the risen Christ among us. It is a reminder of our own passing with Christ from Death to life, from darkness to light.

239

The Paschal candle is carried into the dark church with great reverence. The deacon or priest sings "Christ our light" three times. The assembly responds "Thanks be to God" each time. Often those assembled light small candles from the Paschal candle, and the light of Christ spreads throughout the whole assembly.

Then the deacon or a parish member chants the Exsultet, or Easter Proclamation. To *exult* means to "rejoice with great joy and triumph." The Exsultet is a proclamation of our Easter faith. It is like a map of the celebration of Easter. The Exsultet proclaims God's plan, and notes that we are part of that plan.

"This is our passover feast," we hear. We also hear,
"This is the night when first you
         saved our fathers:
you freed the people of Israel
         from their slavery."

The waters of the Red Sea remind us of the waters of Baptism. Most importantly, we hear,

"This is the night when
    Jesus Christ
    broke the chains of death
    and rose triumphant
        from the grave."

This is the most beautiful and exciting night of the year! It is fitting that on this night new members of the Church are baptized, confirmed, and receive the Eucharist for the first time.

Water is another symbol that is very important to the Easter Vigil. It is important to the newly baptized and to all of us who renew our baptismal promises and are sprinkled with water. It is a symbol of our new Easter life. We, too, are risen with Christ.

Easter Sunday   Our joy continues at the Easter Sunday Eucharist as we pray:

"May the risen Lord
breathe on our minds
    and open our eyes
that we may know him in the
    breaking of bread,
and follow him in his risen life."

WE RESPOND

What can you do to help others to believe and experience the new life that comes from Christ?

How can you spread the light of Christ in your home? your school? your parish? the world?

✝ We Respond in Prayer

Leader: Let us rejoice in the Resurrection of Jesus.

🎵 **Resucitó/He Is Risen**

Refrain:

Resucitó, resucitó, resucitó, aleluya.
Aleluya, aleluya, aleluya, resucitó.
(He is risen, alleluia.)

Leader: Let us pray the great Easter Proclamation.

Group 1: "Rejoice, heavenly powers! Sing, choirs of angels!
Exult, all creation around God's throne!
Jesus Christ, our King, is risen!
Sound the trumpet of salvation!"

All: (*Sing Refrain.*)

Group 2: "Rejoice, O earth, in shining splendor,
radiant in the brightness of your King!
Christ has conquered! Glory fills you!
Darkness vanishes for ever!"

All: (*Sing Refrain.*)

Group 3: "Rejoice, O Mother Church! Exult in glory!
The risen Savior shines upon you!
Let this place resound with joy,
echoing the mighty song of all God's people!"

All: (*Sing Refrain.*)

Group 4: "Most blessed of all nights, chosen by
God to see Christ rising from the dead!

Of this night scripture says:
'The night will be as clear as day:
it will become my light, my joy.'"

All: (*Sing Refrain.*)

PROJECT DISCIPLE

Celebrate!

Write the day of the Triduum (HT = Holy Thursday, GF = Good Friday, HSE = Holy Saturday Evening) that corresponds to each statement.

1. _____ The priest prepares the Paschal Candle by marking the year on it, and the candle is lit and carried into the dark church with great reverence.

2. _____ Around 3P.M. a celebration often takes place at which we recall Jesus' suffering and Death.

3. _____ At an evening Mass we celebrate the events of the Last Supper—when Jesus gathered to celebrate Passover with his disciples.

4. _____ During Mass a ceremony of the washing of feet takes place.

5. _____ A short communion service takes place because the Liturgy of the Eucharist is not celebrated.

6. _____ New members of the Church are baptized, confirmed, and receive the Eucharist for the first time.

7. _____ The Easter Vigil is celebrated after sundown.

8. _____ We hear the Passion of Christ read from the Gospel of John, offer ten general intercessions for the whole world, and show reverence to the cross.

What's the Word?

"You call me 'teacher' and 'master,' and rightly so, for indeed I am. If I, therefore, the master and teacher, have washed your feet, you ought to wash one another's feet. I have given you a model to follow, so that as I have done for you, you should also do." (John 13:13–15)

DISCIPLE CHALLENGE

- Circle the names the disciples use for Jesus.
- Why does Jesus ask his disciples to wash one another's feet?

_____

Take Home

One of the most ancient traditions of the Catholic Church is the veneration of the cross on Good Friday. The cross is the sign not only of Christ's Death, but also of the victory Christ won for all humankind by his Death. Place a cross or crucifix in a prominent place in your home. Remember to always treat this symbol of our faith with reverence.

Choose a word from the box that best completes each sentence.

1. Jesus' birth in the town of Bethlehem in Judea fulfilled the words of the prophet _____ .

2. The great prophet _____ told King Hezekiah that God would not allow foreign nations to destroy Judah; he would always be with the people of Judah.

3. _____ , the son of Elizabeth and Zechariah, was sent by God like the prophets before him to prepare the way for the coming of the Messiah.

4. God called the prophet _____ from the southern kingdom of Judah to go to the northern kingdom of Israel and tell the people there to live justly or their kingdom would be destroyed.

5. King _____ began a reform of religious practices in Judah, banned pagan practices, and returned true worship to the Temple in Jerusalem.

6. The prophet-priest _____ told the people that God would purify those who remained true to him and would shepherd them back from exile to the promised land.

7. In the Book of _____ we are reminded that God alone can provide lasting happiness.

8. When Jews celebrate the festival of _____ , they recall that through God's help Esther saved God's people.

9. In the Book of _____ we read about God's rescue of his people through the brave actions of a remarkable woman.

Judith
Amos
Ecclesiastes
Ezekiel
Herod
Isaiah
John
Josiah
Malachi
Micah
Purim

continued on next page

Underline the correct answer.

10. God sent the prophet **(Jonah/Elijah)** to the northern kingdom of Israel to show the people that the gods worshiped by King Ahab were false gods.

11. The prophet **(Hezekiah/Jeremiah)** was accused of blasphemy, rejected, and imprisoned, but he never lost hope because he knew that God is always with his people.

12. The prophet Elijah anointed a man named **(Elisha/Isaiah)** to carry on his work among God's people.

13. When Judah was invaded a third time, the city of Jerusalem—including the Temple— was destroyed and even more people were deported to **(Babylon/Assyria)**.

14. The Book of **(Wisdom/Lamentations)** contains five poems describing the destruction of the kingdom of Judah and the sufferings of the people.

15. When Judas **(Maccabeus/Malachi)** rededicated the Temple, he asked the people to remember the event with a "feast of lights" that Jews celebrate today as the festival of Hanukkah.

16. During **(King Haman's/Herod's)** reign over Judea, an angel of God was sent to Mary to tell her she would be the Mother of the Son of God.

Write a paragraph to answer each question.

17–18. In the Book of Jonah we read of a prophet who is swallowed by a huge fish. What symbolic meaning does the story of Jonah have for us as Christians?

_____

_____

_____

_____

19–20. The prophet Isaiah, preaching to God's people in exile in Babylon, said that salvation would come only through the suffering of a servant of the Lord—a servant without sin. How are these words of Isaiah's important to Christians?

_____

_____

_____

_____

The Covenant Fulfilled in Jesus

UNIT 4

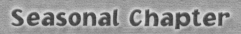

Seasonal Chapter

Pray
Learn
Celebrate
Share
Choose
Live

In Unit 4 your child will grow as a disciple of Jesus by:

- understanding Jesus as teacher and healer who worked signs and wonders among the people
- thanking Jesus for giving his life for us and rising so that we would have new life
- appreciating the coming of the Holy Spirit on Pentecost and the witness of early Christians who were persecuted for their faith
- recognizing that the Church continues Jesus' ministry by sharing the Word of God, the Bible, celebrating the sacraments, and working for social justice
- living as Catholics who are united, holy, welcoming and faithful.

Fast Facts The Church of the Beatitudes is built on the hill where many people believe Jesus first taught the Beatitudes. The Church overlooks the Sea of Galilee and is octagonal in shape, with each of eight sides representing one of the Beatitudes. The dome symbolizes the ninth saying, "for great is your reward in heaven."

What's the Word?

God continues to tell us who he is through his only Son, Jesus. What does Jesus teach us about God? Have each family member share one of the stories of Jesus' life and what it tells us about who God is. Give thanks to God for the Bible.

Reality Check

"Parents must regard their children as *children of God* and respect them as *human persons*."
(*Catechism of the Catholic Church, 2222*)

Show That You Care

As disciples of Jesus Christ, we are called to work for the unity of Christians and to respect people of all faiths. As a family, learn more about one of the Christian churches or one of the other faiths. You may have friends who belong to another church or faith whom you could invite to share with you. Pray together for all God's people.

Picture This

The Unit 4 timeline is on pages 248–251. Look over the timeline together, and invite your 6th grader share an event which was most memorable to him or her. The timeline ends with today's disciples. What family events would you add to the timeline as significant moments of faith?

Take Home

Be ready for this unit's Take Home:

Chapter 22: Remembering favorite teachers

Chapter 23: Praying the Stations of the Cross

Chapter 24: Praying to the Holy Spirit

Chapter 25: Learning more about the Bible

Chapter 26: Redesigning *Project Disciple's* logo

Jesus, Teacher and Healer

WE GATHER

✝ **Leader:** A reading from the holy Gospel according to Matthew

"As he was walking by the Sea of Galilee, he saw two brothers, Simon who is called Peter, and his brother Andrew, casting a net into the sea; they were fishermen. He said to them, 'Come after me, and I will make you fishers of men.' At once they left their nets and followed him. He walked along from there and saw two other brothers, James, the son of Zebedee, and his brother John. They were in a boat, with their father Zebedee, mending their nets. He called them, and immediately they left their boat and their father and followed him." (Matthew 4:18–22)

The Gospel of the Lord.

All: Praise to you, Lord Jesus Christ.

Leader: We want to follow Jesus—but what must we leave behind?

Reader 1: May we leave behind selfishness, and follow Jesus in the spirit of gratitude and generosity.

All: Jesus, we want to follow you.
(Response to three petitions)

Reader 2: May we leave behind injustice, and follow Jesus with hope and help for those who suffer.

Reader 3: May we leave behind fear and self-consciousness, and follow Jesus by using our talents and abilities to help others.

♫ **Pescador de Hombres/ Lord, You Have Come**

Tú has venido a la orilla, no has buscado ni a sabios ni a ricos; tan sólo quieres que yo te siga.

Lord, you have come to the seashore, neither searching for the rich nor the wise, desiring only that I should follow.

Refrain:
Señor, me has mirado a los ojos, sonriendo has dicho mi nombre, en la arena he dejado mi barca, junto a ti buscaré otro mar.

O Lord, with your eyes set upon me, gently smiling, you have spoken my name; all I longed for I have found by the water, at your side, I will seek other shores.

☀ Why do you prepare for an important event? What are some ways that you get ready for it?

247

The wedding at Cana — Jesus brings God's love to all people — Many become disciples — Sermon on the Mount, the Beatitudes — Jesus works many signs and miracles — At Last Supper, Jesus gives a new covenant — Jesus prays at Garden of Gethsemane — Judas betrays Jesus

Timeline for Chapters 22–26

WE BELIEVE

God makes himself known in his Son.

After Jesus' baptism at the Jordan River, the Holy Spirit led him into the desert. Jesus stayed there for forty days and forty nights. He prayed to his Father and fasted as a sign of his obedience. Jesus was preparing for his public life, his life among the people.

Jesus then returned to Galilee and began to preach this message: "This is the time of fulfillment. The kingdom of God is at hand. Repent, and believe in the gospel" (Mark 1:15). The Gospel is the Good News about God at work in Jesus Christ. Jesus showed that the **Kingdom of God** is the power of God's love coming into the world and into our lives. The Kingdom came into the world with the coming of God the Son.

The Jewish People had been waiting for this fulfillment of God's promises. They were waiting for God's Kingdom of justice and fair rule. Many hoped Israel would be restored to its place of power with God as king.

However, the Kingdom Jesus announced was not political. It was the power of God's love active in the lives of the people. When Jesus said that the Kingdom, or reign, of God was near, he was saying that:

• God's presence and rule can be found in him and in the things he said and did

• freedom from sin and the gift of God's life of grace are offered to everyone

• by living in God's presence and for the Kingdom, people can begin to live in God's life, the very life that we believe is life with God forever.

Jesus' mission was to share the life and love of God his Father with all people and to reconcile all people to God. Jesus brought God's love to all people and began to change the world. "The people were astonished at his teaching, for he taught them as one having authority." (Mark 1:22) During his ministry Jesus encouraged all people to turn to God. He accepted and welcomed all people into his life. He showed concern for people who were ignored or neglected by the rest of society. Jesus' life was a sign of God the Father's love and care. The Holy Spirit was truly active in Jesus.

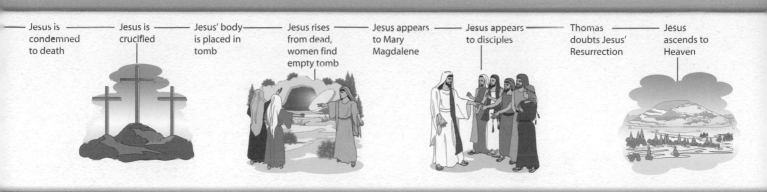

Jesus is condemned to death — Jesus is crucified — Jesus' body is placed in tomb — Jesus rises from dead, women find empty tomb — Jesus appears to Mary Magdalene — Jesus appears to disciples — Thomas doubts Jesus' Resurrection — Jesus ascends to Heaven

con't ➤

Jesus also forgave the sins of those who sought God's forgiveness and healed those who were suffering from many different kinds of illnesses. These actions of healing and forgiving were special signs that Jesus was not only human, but also divine.

The things that Jesus said and did are the greatest Revelation of who God is and of how God loves us. And the ways we speak and act and live our faith show our belief in God's own Son, Jesus Christ.

Think about the Kingdom of God. Work together to list some signs that God's love is active in our lives. Using these signs as captions, make a poster entitled "The kingdom of God is at hand" (Mark 1:15).

As Catholics...

God revealed his Kingdom to us in the words of Christ, in the works of Christ, and in the very presence of Christ among us. After Christ's Resurrection the Church was planted like a seed in the world. Our mission is to bring forth the fruits of the Kingdom of God. What are these fruits? They are many, "but the greatest of these is love" (1 Corinthians 13:13).

What are some of the other fruits, or signs, of the Kingdom of God?

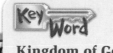

"The kingdom of God is at hand." (Mark 1:15)

Key Word

Kingdom of God (p. 330)

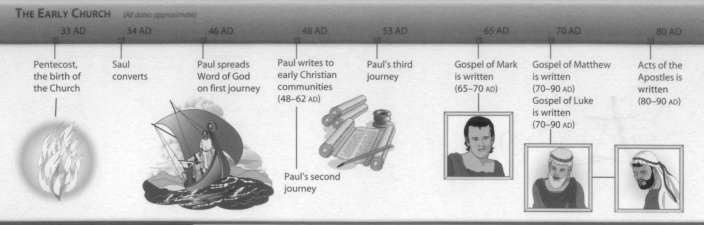

33 AD	34 AD	46 AD	48 AD	53 AD	65 AD	70 AD	80 AD
Pentecost, the birth of the Church	Saul converts	Paul spreads Word of God on first journey	Paul writes to early Christian communities (48–62 AD)	Paul's third journey	Gospel of Mark is written (65–70 AD)	Gospel of Matthew is written (70–90 AD) Gospel of Luke is written (70–90 AD)	Acts of the Apostles is written (80–90 AD)

Paul's second journey

Timeline for Chapters 22–26

Many people heard Jesus' message and became his disciples.

Jesus' message gave people hope. Many people wanted to know Jesus better and learn more about God's love. So they began to follow Jesus. He invited all different kinds of people to follow him and live by his teachings. These women and men became his disciples.

One day a large crowd followed Jesus to the mountains. The message that Jesus gave to the people that day has become known as the *Sermon on the Mount*. In the first part of this sermon Jesus taught that people would be happy only if they trusted in God and lived as he did.

We call these teachings that describe the way to live as Jesus' disciples the **Beatitudes**. In the Beatitudes *blessed* means "happy." As disciples of Jesus, we too are called to follow the Beatitudes.

Jesus' message of hope for all those who live the Beatitudes is: "Rejoice and be glad, for your reward will be great in heaven" (Matthew 5:12).

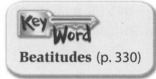

Beatitudes (p. 330)

Read about the Beatitudes on the chart on page 251.
Make a mural to show others a way to follow the Beatitudes.

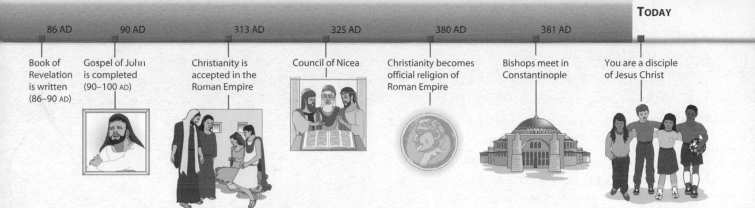

TODAY

86 AD — Book of Revelation is written (86–90 AD)

90 AD — Gospel of John is completed (90–100 AD)

313 AD — Christianity is accepted in the Roman Empire

325 AD — Council of Nicea

380 AD — Christianity becomes official religion of Roman Empire

381 AD — Bishops meet in Constantinople

You are a disciple of Jesus Christ

The Beatitudes	Living as Disciples
📖 Matthew 5:3–10	
"Blessed are the poor in spirit, for theirs is the kingdom of heaven."	We should not be overly attached to possessions. Our confidence should be in God.
"Blessed are they who mourn, for they will be comforted."	We are to be signs of hope and comfort to those who suffer injustice and loss.
"Blessed are the meek, for they will inherit the land."	We realize that our talents and abilities come from God, and we use them to show love for God and others.
"Blessed are they who hunger and thirst for righteousness, for they will be satisfied."	We put our trust in God and carry out Christ's work of justice.
"Blessed are the merciful for they will be shown mercy."	We show compassion to all people and will receive love and forgiveness ourselves in God's Kingdom.
"Blessed are the clean of heart, for they will see God."	We accept God and God's law. As faithful Christians, we find Christ in others.
"Blessed are the peacemakers, for they will be called children of God."	We are called to be reconcilers in our homes, communities, and world.
"Blessed are they who are persecuted for the sake of righteousness, for theirs is the kingdom of heaven."	We are to live out our Christian faith even when others do not understand our beliefs.

Jesus taught about living and growing closer to God.

In the Sermon on the Mount, Jesus said, "You are the salt of the earth. But if salt loses its taste, with what can it be seasoned? . . . You are the light of the world. . . . your light must shine before others, that they may see your good deeds and glorify your heavenly Father" (Matthew 5:13, 14, 16).

Jesus was telling his disciples that just as salt and light were important and necessary, so were they. They were to take an active part in their communities and to serve the Kingdom of God by sharing God's love and life with others.

List some benefits of salt and light in our lives.

_____

_____

_____

_____

_____

How can we be like salt and light in our communities? How can we help others to live and grow in God's love?

_____

_____

_____

_____

_____

_____

Catholic cathedral carved in salt mines near Kracow, Poland.

During his Sermon on the Mount, Jesus also taught his disciples about prayer. Jesus himself often prayed in silence and alone. And at times he also prayed with others. Through prayer, the disciples learned to speak to God and listen to God speaking to them.

Jesus told them that God the Father knows what we need before we ask, and Jesus instructed them to pray to God our Father. So Jesus taught the disciples a very special prayer—the Lord's Prayer, one of the most important prayers in the Gospels and of the Church. This prayer is also called the Our Father. As followers of Jesus Christ, we pray the Lord's Prayer during Mass and at many other times in our lives. It sums up Jesus' whole message of trust in and love for the Father.

We pray:	Our words mean:

Our Father,
who art in heaven
hallowed be thy name;
thy kingdom come;
thy will be done on earth as it is
   in heaven.
Give us this day our daily bread;
and forgive us our trespasses
   as we forgive those who trespass
   against us;
and lead us not into temptation,
but deliver us from evil.
Amen.
	God is present to all who love him. We have become God's people and he is our God. We look forward to being with him forever.
	
	We ask God to unite us with the work of Christ and pray for God to bring about his Kingdom. We pray to God for the ability to do his will.
	
	We ask God for everything we need for ourselves and for the world. We use his gifts to work toward his plan of salvation. We ask God to heal us and we ask for forgiveness from others when needed. We follow the example of Christ and forgive those who have hurt us.
	
	We pray that God will protect us from all that could draw us away from his love. We ask him to guide us to choose good in our lives, and we ask him for the strength to follow his law.

Pray the Lord's Prayer together.

Work in a group and list different ways that prayer can be part of our lives.

_____

_____

_____

_____

Jesus worked signs and wonders among the people.

A miracle is an extraordinary event that is beyond human power and brought about by God. It is an action beyond the ordinary laws of nature. Jesus worked many miracles. They were all signs that he was the Son of God and that the Kingdom of God had arrived in him.

According to the Gospel of John, Jesus performed his first sign or miracle at a wedding feast in Cana of Galilee.

 John 2:1–12

One day Jesus and his mother, Mary, and some of Jesus' other disciples went to a wedding in the village of Cana. Cana was a few miles from Nazareth. At the wedding, however, the wine ran out in the middle of the banquet. Mary went to Jesus and told him that there was no more wine. Then Mary told the servants, "Do whatever he tells you" (John 2:5).

Jesus listened to his mother Mary. She knew the wedding party needed his help. Jesus pointed to some jars and told the servants, "Fill the jars with water." After they filled them to the top, Jesus said, "Draw some out now and take it to the headwaiter" (John 2:7, 8).

The servants did as he said. But Jesus had changed the water into wine. When the headwaiter tasted it, he was amazed that the wine was so good. He called the bridegroom and said to him, "Everyone serves good wine first, and then when people have drunk freely, an inferior one; but you have kept the good wine until now" (John 2:10).

Through this miracle, Jesus revealed his divinity. His followers began to see who Jesus was and to believe in him and praise God.

Signs and Wonders Everywhere Jesus went, to villages, towns, or farms, he helped those who expressed faith in him.

Once two blind men followed Jesus asking him for help. When Jesus approached them, he asked if they believed he could help them. They said yes, and Jesus touched their eyes saying, "Let it be done for you according to your faith" (Matthew 9:29). Immediately their eyes were opened, and they could see.

Some of Jesus' miracles involved nature or everyday needs, such as calming a storm or feeding a multitude of people. We learn that as Jesus' disciples were crossing the sea in a boat, a great storm frightened them. Jesus "rebuked the winds and the sea, and there was great calm" (Matthew 8:26).

Another time Jesus was worried about a crowd of thousands of people who had been listening to him preach and had had nothing to eat. Among all the people there were only seven loaves of bread and a few fish. Jesus gave thanks and broke the loaves and gave them to his disciples to give to the people. "They all ate and were satisfied. They picked up the fragments left over—seven baskets full." (Matthew 15:37)

Jesus worked miracles because he loved people, especially those suffering and in need. He wanted them to have his Father's comfort and peace in their lives. He also wanted to strengthen their belief in the power of God's love and forgiveness. Through signs and his deep compassion and concern for others, the Kingdom of God continued to be made known.

WE RESPOND

How can you show that you are Jesus' disciple? Write one or two things you will do this week.

_____

_____

_____

_____

_____

_____

_____

_____

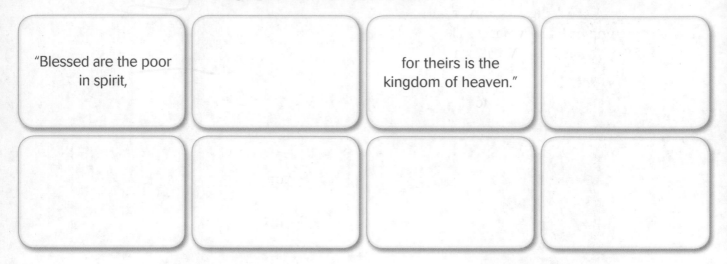

PROJECT

Show What *you* Know

Write the first part of each Beatitude in different squares. Then, write the remaining part of the Beatitudes in the other squares. Cover each square with paper. With a partner, play a Beatitude Memory Game by choosing squares to find each match.

"Blessed are the poor in spirit,		for theirs is the kingdom of heaven."	

 Reality Check

All kinds of media (TV shows, commercials, Web sites, music, email campaigns) tell us how to find happiness. List a few examples:

_____

As a disciple of Jesus Christ, what do you think of these messages?

_____

_____

 **Pray Today**

In his gift of the Lord's Prayer, Jesus encouraged us to turn to God for all our needs. Pray the Lord's Prayer each day.

DISCIPLE

Pray
Learn
Celebrate
Share
Choose
Live

Saint Stories

Saint Angela de Merici was concerned with the lack of education that was available for girls. She founded the Company of Saint Ursula, known as the Ursulines. The Ursulines were the first group of women religious to work outside the cloister and the first teaching order of women. The Church celebrates the feast day of Saint Angela de Merici on January 27.

↳ **DISCIPLE CHALLENGE**

- What is another name for the Ursulines?

_____

- Underline the phrases that tell what the Ursulines were "first" to do.
- Visit *Lives of the Saints* on **www.webelieveweb.com** to learn more about Saint Angela de Merici.

Fast Facts

The Sisters of the Good Shepherd provide support to women and families through counseling. They help those in prison and those trying to start their lives again. They staff social service offices, and work to change unjust laws.

What's the Word?

Jesus used parables to teach about the Kingdom of God. Read the parables found in Mark 4:30–32 and Matthew 13:47–50. What is the Kingdom of God compared to in each of these parables?

_____

↳ **DISCIPLE CHALLENGE** What image could you use today to explain the Kingdom of God?

_____

Take Home

Read the *Saint Stories* feature about Saint Angela de Merici with your family. Point out that like Jesus, Saint Angela de Merici was a teacher. Invite family members to recall favorite teachers and talk about ways these teachers made a difference in their lives. Discuss ways your family can help educate children throughout the world.

Underline the correct answer.

1. An extraordinary event that is beyond human power and brought about by God is a (**Beatitude/miracle**).

2. The (**Torah/Gospel**) is the Good News about God at work in Jesus Christ.

3. The (**Beatitudes/Apostles**) are the teachings of Jesus that describe the way to live as his disciples.

4. The (**Kingdom of God/Lord's Prayer**) is the power of God's love coming into the world and our lives.

Short Answers

5. What message did Jesus give to the people at the Sermon on the Mount?

   bea't, tude

6. What are two things we ask God when we pray the words of the Lord's Prayer?

   our further

7. What did Jesus tell his followers about the Kingdom of God?

   to help us to live our lives wa

8. Why did Jesus work miracles?

   turb water

Write a paragraph to answer this question.

9–10. What did Jesus do to show God's love to people?

_____

_____

_____

_____

Jesus, Redeemer and Savior

23

WE GATHER

✝ **Leader:** Lord Jesus, you are the Savior and Redeemer of the world. Blessed be your name.

All: Blessed be your name for ever.

Leader: Our passage from death to new life can only be made in our dying and rising with Christ. Listen as Saint Paul reminds his friends of the Paschal Mystery.

Reader 1: "You were buried with him in baptism, in which you were also raised with him through faith in the power of God, who raised him from the dead."(Colossians 2:12)

All: Lord Jesus, you are the Savior and Redeemer of the world.

Reader 2: "And whatever you do, in word or in deed, do everything in the name of the Lord Jesus, giving thanks to God the Father through him." (Colossians 3:17)

All: Lord Jesus, you are the Savior and Redeemer of the world.

Leader: It is Christ's perfect sacrifice of love and obedience that saved us from sin and grants us salvation. All praise and honor be yours, now and for ever.

All: Amen.

☀ Talk about events that you have heard of or experienced that do not seem to have a clear explanation.

259

WE BELIEVE
Jesus gave us a new covenant.

Many people said that Jesus was the Messiah. This worried some of the authorities in Jerusalem who feared that Jesus might lead a revolt against the Roman government.

Despite the political tension Jesus and the disciples went to Jerusalem as the feast of Passover approached. They were a family to one another. So like every other family, they prepared the Passover meal. At sundown they gathered for the meal.

Everything about the meal—the unleavened bread, the wine, the lamb, the bitter herbs—reminded Jewish families of the great events of the Exodus from Egypt. It also reminded them of their covenant with God. The Passover meal has the same meaning for Jews today.

Jesus, however, gave the Passover meal a new meaning. During the meal Jesus took some bread, prayed over it, broke it, and gave it to the disciples saying, "This is my body, which will be given for you" (Luke 22:19). Then he took a cup of wine, prayed over it, and gave it to them saying, "This cup is the new covenant in my blood, which will be shed for you" (Luke 22:20). Jesus was giving his followers a new covenant and a new covenant meal. The Passover celebration now had a new meaning. As the priest of the new covenant, Jesus was offering himself as the Paschal lamb. Jesus told his disciples to "do this in memory of me" (Luke 22:19). We call the Passover meal that Jesus shared with his disciples on the night before he died the **Last Supper**.

Jesus' disciples continued to share this meal as a memorial to Jesus. Jesus was with them as they broke the bread and drank from the cup. Christ's own Body and Blood were present under the appearances of bread and wine. Jesus' love and his sacrifice would forever be remembered in the celebration of the Eucharist. For Christians the Eucharist is the new Passover of God's people.

Jesus knew that the next day would be one of suffering and of death. So he went to the Mount of Olives with his disciples. In these final hours, Jesus prayed to his Father in the olive grove called Gethsemane. Jesus asked his disciples to pray also.

As he prayed, Jesus asked to be relieved of the pain that he would suffer, yet he wanted to do his Father's will. During his prayer Jesus chose to be obedient to and to trust his Father. Jesus freely chose to offer his life for us so that we might be freed from sin.

Jesus had given himself in the Eucharist and was now preparing to give his life for all of humanity.

Key **Word**

Last Supper (p. 330)

Leonardo da Vinci (1452–1519),
The Last Supper

Illustrate the Passover of the Jewish People and the new Passover that has been given to us by Jesus Christ. What can you do to remember Jesus' Last Supper this week?

Jesus gave his life for us.

While Jesus was praying in Gethsemane, Judas, one of his Apostles, entered with Temple guards. Judas had promised to hand over Jesus for thirty pieces of silver. Judas had told them that the one he kissed was the one they were looking for. So Judas greeted Jesus with a kiss. Jesus said, "Friend, do what you have come for" (Matthew 26:50). Then the guards arrested Jesus.

First they took Jesus before Caiaphas, the high priest. Caiaphas insisted that Jesus was guilty of blasphemy, of referring to God in a disrespectful or irreverent way. Then this group took him before Pontius Pilate, the Roman governor. When Judas learned what had happened to Jesus because of his betrayal, he regretted what he had done. He tried to return the thirty pieces of silver and said, "I have sinned in betraying innocent blood" (Matthew 27:4). But it was too late to stop what had begun!

Pilate found nothing for which to condemn Jesus. However, Pilate feared that there would be unrest or even a revolt unless he took action. Pilate ordered that Jesus be whipped and crucified.

Jesus was crucified between two criminals. The dying Jesus was insulted by the soldiers, chief priests, and scribes. They said that if he were the king of Israel he would be able to save himself.

When Jesus took his last breath, the veil of the sanctuary in the Temple was torn in two. The soldier who stood in front of Jesus and watched him die said, "Truly this man was the Son of God!" (Mark 15:39). We further read in the Gospel of Mark that there were women watching from a distance. Mary Magdalene, Mary the mother of the younger James, and Salome had followed Jesus when he was in Galilee. Other women followers who had come with Jesus to Jerusalem were there, too.

After Jesus died, his body was placed in the tomb of Joseph of Arimathea, a follower of Jesus. A heavy stone was rolled across the entrance of the tomb. It was Friday, the day before the Jewish Sabbath. Christians call the day that marks Jesus' Death Good Friday because it was on this day that Jesus died to save us. This is why we call Jesus our Redeemer. By his Death and Resurrection Jesus gained our salvation and brought us the hope of new life.

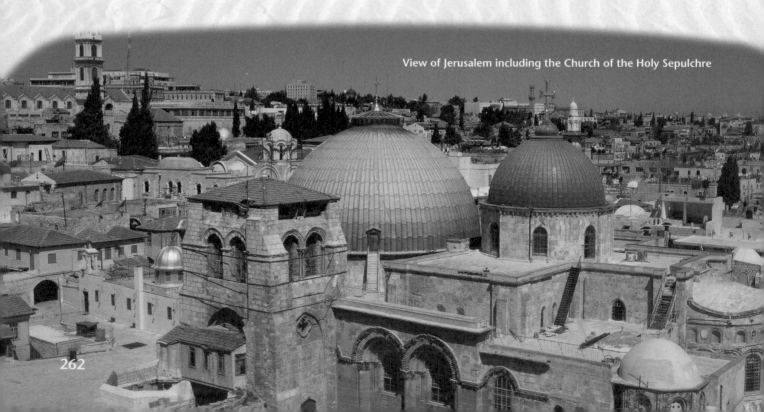

View of Jerusalem including the Church of the Holy Sepulchre

Let us make an imaginary pilgrimage now to the Holy Land. Let us walk where Jesus walked during the last days of his life.

Our first stop is the *Chapel of the Cenacle*. The word *cenacle* comes from a Latin word meaning "dining room." In the Upper Room on the second floor, Jesus celebrated the Last Supper with his Apostles. At this meal, Jesus gave us the gift of his Body and Blood, the Eucharist.

The Church of the Holy Sepulcher, Jerusalem

The Chapel of the Cenacle, Jerusalem

Our second stop is the *Garden of Gethsemane*. This garden was a special place for Jesus. This was where he went after the Last Supper to prepare for his eventual suffering on the cross. It was here that he endured the agony in the garden.

Our last stop is the *Church of the Holy Sepulcher*. This is an impressive stone building with a shining dome. It combines two churches. The upper chapel of the church is said to be the site of Jesus' Crucifixion. The site of Jesus' tomb is said to lie beneath the dome, but the actual tomb was destroyed.

If you were in these sacred places, what would you pray for?

_____

_____

_____

_____

_____

What would you say to Jesus, who died and rose here, and is with us now, today?

_____

_____

_____

_____

_____

The Garden of Gethsemane, Jerusalem

Jesus Christ rose from the dead.

As it had been foretold in the Scriptures, Jesus was raised from the dead on the third day after his Death. The mystery of Jesus' being raised from the dead is called the **Resurrection**.

Mark 16:1–11

"When the sabbath was over, Mary Magdalene, Mary, the mother of James, and Salome bought spices so that they might go and anoint him. Very early when the sun had risen, on the first day of the week, they came to the tomb. They were saying to one another, 'Who will roll back the stone for us from the entrance to the tomb?' When they looked up, they saw that the stone had been rolled back; it was very large. On entering the tomb they saw a young man sitting on the right side, clothed in a white robe, and they were utterly amazed. He said to them, 'Do not be amazed! You seek Jesus of Nazareth, the crucified. He has been raised; he is not here. Behold, the place where they laid him. But go and tell his disciples and Peter, "He is going before you to Galilee; there you will see him, as he told you. . . . When he [Jesus] had risen, . . . he appeared first to Mary Magdalene, . . . She went and told his companions who were mourning and weeping. When they heard that he was alive and had been seen by her, they did not believe."

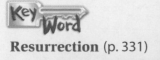

Key Word

Resurrection (p. 331)

The Holy Women at the Sepulchre by Laura James (Contemporary Artist)

We can read in the Gospel of Mark that the risen Christ appeared to other disciples, too. They also told the group what they had seen. But the group of disciples did not believe until Christ also appeared to them.

We believe in Jesus Christ and his Resurrection through the gift of faith. By faith we not only believe in Jesus risen among us, but also live as his disciples each day.

Pretend that you are a news reporter in Jerusalem. You are interviewing Mary Magdalene and the other women on the day of Jesus' Resurrection. Plan your interview here. With a group role-play the interview.

Christ appeared to his disciples.

Later on the day of Jesus' Resurrection, the risen Jesus appeared to his disciples to strengthen them and to increase their faith in his Resurrection. He wanted his disciples to believe in all that he had told them and in all that he had done.

Jesus came and stood among the disciples. He showed them his side and his hands and said, "Peace be with you. As the Father has sent me, so I send you" Then he breathed on them and said, "Receive the holy Spirit." (John 20:21, 22) This began the new life in which humanity now can share because of Jesus' Resurrection.

Thomas, one of Jesus' Apostles, was not with the others when Jesus appeared to them. He said to the other Apostles, "Unless I see the mark of the nails in his hands and put my finger into the nailmarks and put my hand into his side, I will not believe" (John 20:25).

When all of the disciples, including Thomas were together again, Jesus appeared. He told Thomas, "Put your finger here and see my hands, and bring your hand and put it into my side, and do not be unbelieving, but believe" (John 20:27). Thomas told Jesus he believed Jesus was the Lord, his God. But Jesus said, "Blessed are those who have not seen and have believed" (John 20:29).

🎵 **Jesus Is Risen**

Refrain:
> Alleluia! Alleluia! Alleluia!
> Jesus is risen, alleluia!

Now it no longer could be denied,
seeing his feet and his hands and his side.
"Indeed you are Lord! You are God!" they
  cried.
"Conquering death, you have risen!" (Refrain)

As disciples of Christ we are called to believe everything we have learned about Jesus from the Gospels and the other writings of the New Testament. We are called to believe that Jesus Christ died and rose to new life. We believe that Jesus is the Son of God, our Savior. We are called to believe what the Church teaches us about Christ.

The Holy Spirit that Jesus breathed on his Apostles is the same Holy Spirit who gives us life. The Holy Spirit guides us as we live each day. Jesus has not left us alone, but is with us always. We believe that through the risen Jesus we have new life and the hope of sharing this life with him forever.

WE RESPOND

Think about the appearances of Jesus after his Resurrection. Prepare a short advertisement using your favorite appearance to convince the public that Jesus is risen!

PROJECT

Show What *you* Know

You are a journalist living in the time of Jesus. Write a news article to explain the  **Key Words** Last Supper and Resurrection.

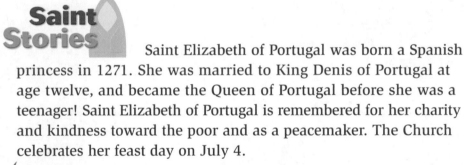

Saint Stories

Saint Elizabeth of Portugal was born a Spanish princess in 1271. She was married to King Denis of Portugal at age twelve, and became the Queen of Portugal before she was a teenager! Saint Elizabeth of Portugal is remembered for her charity and kindness toward the poor and as a peacemaker. The Church celebrates her feast day on July 4.

↳ **DISCIPLE CHALLENGE** Saint Elizabeth showed charity and kindness to others. How can you do the same?

Fast Facts

 **INRI**

The letters *INRI* that appear on the crucifix are an acronym of the Latin *Iesus Nazarenus, Rex Iudaeorum*, which translates to English as Jesus of Nazareth, King of the Jews. Pontius Pilate ordered this inscription to be placed on Jesus' Cross. (See John 19: 19.)

What's *the* Word?

In the Gospel of Luke there is a story of the risen Jesus' appearance to two of his disciples on the road to Emmaus. Read Luke 24:13–35 with a friend. Take turns reading the verses. Would you have recognized Jesus?

D1SC1PLE

More to Explore

The Congregation of the Most Holy Redeemer was founded by Saint Alphonsus Liguori, and serves all around the world to spread the Good News and deepen the faith of youth, young adults, and adults. Its members are priests, brothers, and lay missionaries who follow the example of Christ the Redeemer by preaching God's Word to the poor and abandoned. Known as the Redemptorists, they work in parishes, preach at parish programs, run retreats and conference centers, work with those suffering from AIDS and other terminal illnesses, serve as missionaries throughout the world, and manage Liguori Publications, a Catholic publishing company.

↳ DISCIPLE CHALLENGE

- Underline the phrase that describes how the Redemptorists follow the example of Christ the Redeemer.
- Circle the name of the Redemptorists' founder.
- Name three ways the Redemptorists serve.

_____

_____

Visit www.cssr.com to learn more about the Redemptorists.

Question Corner

Who Am I?

I betrayed Jesus for thirty pieces of silver.

_____

I ordered Jesus to be whipped and crucified.

_____

I was first to see the risen Jesus.

_____

I needed to see "proof" before I could believe that Jesus had appeared after his Resurrection.

_____

Take Home

As a family, read about the Stations of the Cross on page 328. Visit www.webelieveweb.com to find appropriate stations and meditations to use at your parish church, or at a nearby shrine or retreat center that has outdoor stations. Then, pray the Stations of the Cross. At each station after silent reflection, pray:

We adore you, O Christ,
   and we bless you:
Because by your holy cross,
   you have redeemed the world.

Afterwards, gather together as a family and talk about the experience.

Complete the following.

1. At the Last Supper when Jesus was celebrating the _____ meal with his

   disciples, he gave them the _____ .

2. The mystery that Jesus _____ on the third day after his Death is called the

   _____ .

3. The risen Jesus appeared to his _____ to strengthen them and to increase

   their _____ in his Resurrection.

4. Christians call the day that marks Jesus' Death _____ , because on this day

   Jesus died to _____ .

Write True or False for the following sentences.
Then change the false sentences to make them true.

5. _____ On the evening of the Resurrection, the risen Jesus appeared to all
   his Apostles.

   _____

6. _____ On the night before he suffered and died, Jesus prayed to his Father.

   _____

7. _____ Christians celebrate the Eucharist as the new Passover given to us by Christ.

   _____

8. _____ By his Death, Jesus gains our salvation and brings us the hope of new life.

   _____

Write a paragraph to answer this question.

9–10. What happened at the Last Supper?

_____

_____

_____

_____

The Church Begins

24

WE GATHER

Leader: Come, Holy Spirit, fill the hearts of your faithful.

All: And kindle in them the fire of your love.

Reader: A reading from the Letter of Saint Paul to the Ephesians

"You are fellow citizens with the holy ones and members of the household of God, built upon the foundation of the apostles and prophets, with Christ Jesus himself as the capstone. Through him the whole structure is held together and grows into a temple sacred in the Lord; in him you also are being built together into a dwelling place of God in the Spirit . . . it has now been revealed to his holy apostles and prophets by the Spirit, that the Gentiles are coheirs, members of the same body, and copartners in the promise in Christ Jesus through the gospel." (Ephesians 2:19–22; 3:5–6)

The word of the Lord.

All: Thanks be to God.

Leader: The Holy Spirit moves us to become one in Christ's body, his Church. From the apostles to the martyrs to all the holy ones in the faith, we have learned that the Spirit knows our needs even before we ask the Father. Jesus teaches us to pray. The Spirit leads us to pray in freedom as sons and daughters of God. And so we pray.

All: Amen! Amen! Amen!

Imagine you have been asked to start a new group to accomplish a task. What would you do to begin?

WE BELIEVE
With the coming of the Holy Spirit the Church began.

Jesus was about to leave his disciples and return to his Father in Heaven. But he left them with the mission that he had begun. He had brought the Good News of the Kingdom of God. He showed the people his Father's love and forgiveness. He spoke to them about the power of the Holy Spirit. He lived in the spirit of justice and peace. And Jesus passed his mission on to his disciples. He wanted them to continue to bring more people into the community of believers.

Jesus knew that his disciples needed strength and courage to carry on his mission. He knew that the Holy Spirit would help them to live out their faith and love in the one God. Jesus told his disciples to be his witnesses and to spread the Good News. Then he said, "And [behold] I am sending the promise of my Father upon you; but stay in the city until you are clothed with power from on high" (Luke 24:49).

Jesus then went with his disciples "as far as Bethany, raised his hands, and blessed them. As he blessed them he parted from them and was taken up to heaven" (Luke 24:50–51). We call this the Ascension.

The disciples went back to Jerusalem as Jesus had instructed them. They were filled with joy and praised God, remembering all that had just taken place. Mary, the mother of Jesus, and other women and men who were disciples of Jesus prayed and stayed close to one another. This included Matthias, the Apostle chosen to take Judas's place.

Acts of the Apostles 2:1–4, 7, 17, 41

While the Jewish feast of Weeks, or Pentecost, was taking place, the disciples were gathered together. "And suddenly there came from the sky a noise like a strong driving wind, and it filled the entire house in which they were. Then there appeared to them tongues as of fire, which parted and came to rest on each one of them. And they were all filled with the holy Spirit and began to speak in different tongues, as the Spirit enabled them to proclaim." (Acts of the Apostles 2:2–4) Everyone was astounded and Peter told them that the prophecy of Joel was now fulfilled.

"God says,
'that I will pour out a portion of my spirit
 upon all flesh.'" (Acts of the Apostles 2:17)

We call the day the Holy Spirit came upon the first disciples **Pentecost**.

It was on this day that Peter and the other Apostles baptized about three thousand people. This was the beginning of the Church. The fact that each person understood what was being said in his or her own language helps us to know that Christ's message of love and peace is for all people.

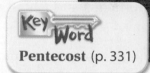

Pentecost (p. 331)

In groups discuss what we can do to share Christ's message of love and peace. How can his message be shared throughout the entire world? Draw or write some of your ideas here.

The Good News of Christ spread to many places.

The Church continued to grow and be strengthened through the power of the Holy Spirit. In carrying out Jesus' command to love God, themselves, and others, the Apostles and other disciples shared everything. They contributed to a common fund to help needy members and "they devoted themselves to the teaching of the apostles and to the communal life, to the breaking of the bread and to the prayers" (Acts of the Apostles 2:42).

Some disciples called themselves "followers of the Way," recalling that Jesus described himself as "the way and the truth and the life" (John 14:6). Others called themselves Nazarenes, indicating that they were followers of Jesus of Nazareth. About ten years after Jesus' Death, in a large city called Antioch, the followers of Jesus Christ were first called "Christians."

As the number of the disciples increased, the Temple authorities in Jerusalem became uneasy. As Peter and the others continued to preach, fear about their influence and acceptance grew. It was not long before a persecution of Christ's disciples broke out.

Acts of the Apostles 9:1–8, 17–18

One of the leaders of these persecutions was a young Pharisee and Roman citizen named Saul.

Saul asked the high priest for permission to arrest Christians there and bring them back to Jerusalem for trial. The high priest granted his request. As Saul approached Damascus, however, a blinding light flashed around him. He fell to the ground and heard a voice saying to him "Saul, Saul, why are you persecuting me?" He said, "Who are you, sir?" The voice replied, "I am Jesus, whom you are persecuting" (Acts of the Apostles 9:4–5). With these words Jesus was telling Saul that in persecuting Christians, he was persecuting Jesus because Jesus and his followers were one body, the Church.

When Saul got up from the ground, he could not see. The men he was traveling with brought him to Damascus. Three days later he recovered his sight in the presence of one of Jesus' disciples and Saul was baptized. This event is one of the most well-known examples of conversion in the Bible.

Within a short time Saul, better known by his Roman name, Paul, became one of the great leaders of the early Church. In three missionary journeys, Paul brought the Good News of Jesus Christ to the major cities of the eastern Roman empire.

- His first journey took him to the island of Cyprus and to Antioch and other cities of Syria and Asia Minor (modern Turkey).

- His second journey, which is the most extensive, included an eighteen-month stay in Corinth, Greece.

- Most of his third journey was spent establishing the Church community in Ephesus, a large and important city in Asia Minor.

During his travels Paul wrote letters to the new Christians in these places. Some of these letters can be found in the New Testament.

In caring for these members of the Church, Paul suffered insults, the hatred of his enemies, shipwreck, and even imprisonment. Yet he never wavered from his faith. He led many to believe in Jesus and to become members of the Church. From the moment of his conversion, Paul's life was guided by his devotion to Jesus, who was the center of his preaching and teaching.

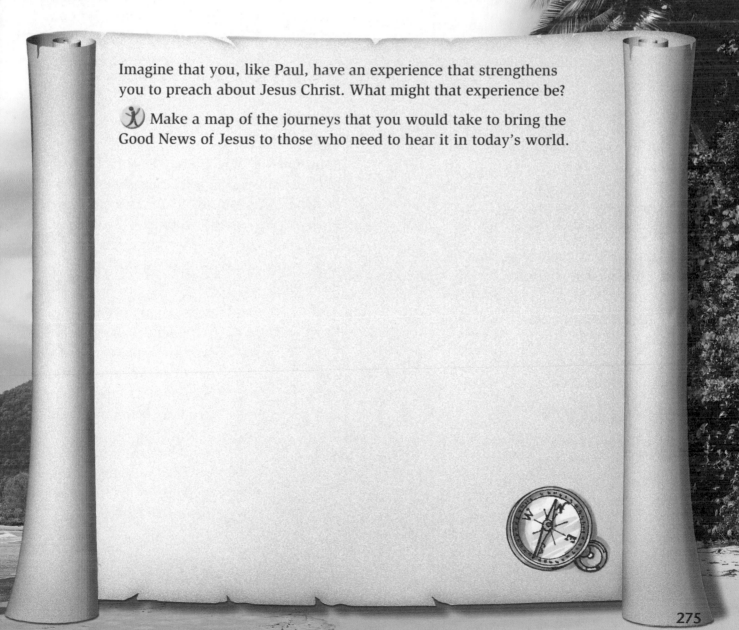

Imagine that you, like Paul, have an experience that strengthens you to preach about Jesus Christ. What might that experience be?

Make a map of the journeys that you would take to bring the Good News of Jesus to those who need to hear it in today's world.

Christians were persecuted for their faith.

Paul's missionary trips were very important to the development of the Church. Because of his work, Christianity spread beyond Judea and to people other than only those of the Jewish faith. It grew to include Greeks and Romans. Thus from its beginning, the Church has included people of different cultures who live throughout the world.

As the Church grew, Christians refused to honor and worship the false gods of the Romans. Roman officials began to believe that Christians threatened the authority and security of the empire. Christianity was not an accepted religion during the first three centuries, and this put the Christians at risk. Christians were persecuted, and some were imprisoned and forced to accept false gods. Others were treated as outcasts. However, this did not stop Christians from believing in Christ. Many even became martyrs for their faith. A **martyr** is a person who dies rather than give up his or her belief in Jesus Christ. The word *martyr* actually comes from the Greek word for "witness."

We do not have a record of all of the thousands of Christians who died for their faith. However, the stories of some martyrs have been passed down to us.

Key Word

martyr (p. 331)

Saint Lawrence

Lawrence lived in Rome during the third century. He was one of the deacons of the Roman Church. One legend about Saint Lawrence recounts that when Pope Sixtus was led away to be executed, he told Lawrence that he would also die. So Lawrence sold all the sacred vessels and gave the money to the poor, the widows, and the orphans of Rome. When ordered to bring all the Church's valuables to the chief Roman officer, Lawrence presented Christian people who were neglected and abused by society as "the Church's treasure." We celebrate Saint Lawrence's feast day on August 10.

Saint Cecilia
Cecilia is believed to have lived in Rome during the third century. She was a Christian who wanted to dedicate her life to Christ. But her father wanted her to marry. It is said that during the wedding ceremony Cecilia was silently singing to God and praying for his help.

Cecilia convinced her husband that an angel of God protected her, and soon her husband and his brother became Christians. These two men were martyred, and Cecilia, too, was then persecuted and martyred. We celebrate the feast day of Saint Cecilia, patroness of music, on November 22.

Saint Agnes Agnes lived during the third century in Rome. At age thirteen, she dedicated her life to Christ and vowed to remain pure of heart. She refused to worship the false gods of her time and was ridiculed for her chaste ways. This abuse did not weaken her faith. She withstood the mistreatment but eventually died as a martyr because she refused to give up her Christian ways. We celebrate Saint Agnes' feast day on January 21.

List some ways people give witness to their faith today.

_____

_____

_____

_____

_____

_____

_____

_____

Christianity became an accepted religion.

The fourth century was a dramatic one for the Church. In the year 380 Christianity became the official religion of the Roman Empire. The years of persecution were finally ending. However, not all Romans accepted Christianity, and sometimes even members of the same family did not practice the same faith. The family of Saint Martin of Tours is one example of this.

Martin is one of the first saints that we remember as a witness who was able to live out his Christian faith. He was born in a Roman province in the early years of the fourth century. He felt a strong calling to serve God. Since his parents continued to worship false gods, Martin had to study Christianity secretly.

At age fifteen he was required to join the Roman army because his father had served in the military. As a young soldier he showed great compassion for those in need. Once he gave half of his cloak to a beggar. That night Jesus appeared to Martin and soon after Martin was baptized.

A few years later he left the army and went to Tours, France. He devoted his time to stopping false beliefs in France. Eventually Martin became the Bishop of Tours. He prayed, taught, and preached everywhere. Through his work many came to believe in Christ.

We celebrate the feast of this bishop and saint on November 11.

Professing the Faith Eventually it became necessary to summarize the faith into professions of faith, or creeds, for those being baptized. One of the earliest creeds, the Apostles' Creed, is found on page 325. It is about the First Person of the Blessed Trinity and the great work of creation, the Second Person of the Blessed Trinity and the redemption all of us have because of him, and the Third Person of the Blessed Trinity from whom the Church's and our holiness come.

It later became necessary for the Church to come together to ensure that the teaching of Jesus and the Apostles was passed on to future generations. In the year 325 the bishops gathered together in Nicea for the first ecumenical council. An *Ecumenical Council* is a gathering of the pope and bishops to make decisions on issues of faith, Christian living, and the life of the Church. Another council took place in Constantinople in 381. The result of these two councils is stated in the Nicene Creed. We still say this creed at Mass. It can be found on page 327.

Both the Apostles' Creed and the Nicene Creed are part of Tradition. Tradition refers to the written and spoken beliefs and practices that have been passed down to us from the time of Christ and the Apostles. The Catholic Church teaches us that Tradition is one of the two means by which God's Revelation comes to us. The Bible is the other.

WE RESPOND

Profess your faith by praying the Apostles' Creed or Nicene Creed together.

Write a prayer to thank God for the gift of faith.

_____

_____

_____

_____

_____

_____

The Third Council of Constantinople (680–681) from a fresco in the Vatican circa 1868.

PROJECT

Show What *you* Know

Use the code to find each **Key Word** . Then, write a sentence using the word.

A	B	C	D	E	F	G	H	I	J	K	L	M	N	O	P	Q	R	S	T	U	V	W	X	Y	Z
1	2	3	4	5	6	7	8	9	10	11	12	13	14	15	16	17	18	19	20	21	22	23	24	25	26

1. ____ ____ ____ ____ ____ ____
   13   1   18   20   25   18

_____

2. ____ ____ ____ ____ ____ ____ ____ ____ ____
   16   5   14   20   5   3   15   19   20

_____

Fast Facts

Saint Paul was one of the great leaders of the early Church. June 2008–2009 was declared the "Year of Saint Paul" by Pope Benedict XVI. Special liturgies, publications, Web sites, events, videos, and symposiums were based on the 2,000th anniversary of the birth of Saint Paul.

Reality Check

Take this Evangelizer Survey.

I can be an evangelizer by:

❑ speaking and acting in ways that reflect God's love

❑ telling others about the wonderful things that Christ has done

❑ encouraging others who already believe in Christ to continue to grow in their faith.

❑ other _____

DISCIPLE

Pray
Learn
Celebrate
Share
Choose
Live

Saint Stories

As a religious in the Daughters of Charity, Saint Catherine Laboure experienced visions of the Virgin Mary. In one of the visions, Mary instructed Catherine to have a medal honoring the Immaculate Conception made. This medal is commonly known as the miraculous medal. The Church celebrates Saint Catherine Laboure's feast day on November 25.

Visit *Lives of the Saints* on **www.webelieveweb.com** to learn more about saints and holy people.

Make it Happen

We are called to give witness to our faith. We give witness when we speak and act based upon the Good News. We tell others about the wonderful things that Christ has done. We show them what it means to be a disciple. Giving witness to our faith is an important part of the Church's mission of evangelization. Evangelization takes part in our everyday lives. We evangelize those who have not yet heard the message of Jesus Christ. We also evangelize those who have heard the message but need encouragement to live out the gift of faith that is theirs.

↳ **DISCIPLE CHALLENGE** Be an evangelizer! Live out the Gospel, and the people around you will see your faith in action. How can you do this today?

_____

_____

_____

Now, pass it on!

Take Home

The Church was made strong through the power of the Holy Spirit. Call upon the Holy Spirit to strengthen your family. Pray together the following prayer:

Come Holy Spirit,
fill the hearts of your faithful.
And kindle in them the fire of your love.
Send forth your Spirit and they shall be created.
And you will renew the face of the earth.
Amen.

281

Underline the correct answer.

1. Christianity was (accepted/~~not accepted~~) as a religion during the first three centuries.

2. The Church began with the coming of (the Holy Spirit/Matthias).

3. (Romans/Nazarenes) were followers of Jesus Christ who were later called Christians.

4. The Apostles' Creed and the Nicene Creed are part of (Tradition/Scripture).

Short Answers

5. What are two ways the Holy Spirit helps Christ's disciples?

   ~~It tells us~~ . He tells us right from wrong

6. What do we call the day on which the Holy Spirit came upon the first disciples?

   Pentacos

7. Why was the fourth century important for the Church?

8. Why is Paul considered to be a great leader of the early Church?

Write a paragraph to answer this question.

9–10. What are some ways Christians have given witness to Christ?

The Bible and the Church Today

25

WE GATHER

Leader: The prophets such as Amos, Micah, Jeremiah, Isaiah, and John the Baptist announced God's special love for those who are poor and in need. They called the people to live justly.

Reader: Jesus, the Messiah, began his ministry by proclaiming these words of the prophet Isaiah in the synagogue in Nazareth,

"The Spirit of the Lord is upon me,
  because he has anointed me
    to bring glad tidings to the poor.

He has sent me to proclaim liberty to
  captives
  and recovery of sight to the blind,
    to let the oppressed go free,
and to proclaim a year acceptable to the
  Lord" (Luke 4:18–19).

How does your family record and share memories?

🎵 God Has Chosen Me

God has chosen me,
God has chosen me to bring good
  news to the poor.
God has chosen me,
God has chosen me to bring new
  sight to those searching for light:
God has chosen me, chosen me:

Refrain:
And to tell the world that God's
  kingdom is near,
To remove oppression and break
  down fear,
Yes, God's time is near,
God's time is near,
God's time is near, God's time is near.

God is calling me,
God is calling me in all whose cry is
  unheard.
God is calling me,
God is calling me to raise up the
  voice with no power or choice:
God is calling me, calling me: (Refrain)

WE BELIEVE

The New Testament is made up of different types of writings.

The Bible is a book of faith. It is a record of the ways that God has remained faithful to his people. Christians see the events and truths of faith in the Old Testament as leading us to Jesus and his teachings found in the New Testament.

The New Testament is a collection of twenty-seven books. The writers of these books were inspired by the Holy Spirit to use their own abilities to record the truths of faith that are so important for living as Christians. Like the Old Testament, the New Testament includes different types of writings.

Matthew
Mark
Luke
John

The Gospels The Gospels of Matthew, Mark, Luke, and John are in many ways historical writings. The writers of the Gospels describe Jesus' mission and ministry, his call to discipleship, and his love. They help us to understand that Jesus Christ is the Messiah and the Son of God. This is why Christians consider the Gospels the most sacred books of the Bible.

The Letters to the Christian Communities
The letters, or Epistles, include twenty-one writings from leaders such as Paul, James, Peter, John, and Jude to different Christian communities. These letters have a variety of purposes. Some are written to discuss specific problems in the community, to instruct the people on how to live and worship, and to explain the role of the leaders of the community.

Other Writings   The Acts of the Apostles and the Book of Revelation are the other books of the New Testament. The Acts of the Apostles records the coming of the Holy Spirit and the ministry of the Apostles. It describes the beginning and growth of the Church and the various missionary trips of the Apostles and disciples. The Acts of the Apostles is actually a continuation of the Gospel of Luke.

The Book of Revelation is the final book in the New Testament. In many ways it is like parts of the Old Testament Books of Ezekiel, Zechariah, and Daniel. The Book of Revelation is based on visions and dreams and the interpretation of them. As a Christian prophecy, the Book of Revelation deals with Christ's second coming at the end of time. The book uses symbols, poetry, and images. It is not written to foretell specific events, but to spread the message of God's Kingdom.

We treat both the Old and New Testaments as sacred, or holy. The Holy Spirit inspired the biblical writers, so God is the true author of Scripture.

The New Testament, like the Old Testament, helps us to know that God loves us and is with us today. God is calling us to respond to his love and to follow his Son.

 List some ways Scripture is a part of your life.

_____

_____

_____

_____

_____

The Bible is an important source for Christian living and worship.

The Bible is an important guide for Christian living. From the Bible we learn the Ten Commandments, the Beatitudes, the Great Commandment, and Christ's new commandment. These laws and teachings are the foundation of our moral life as Catholics. They help us to relate to God, ourselves, and one another.

Jesus obeyed God his Father and accepted the law as his guide. In fact, he told his disciples, "Do not think that I have come to abolish the law or the prophets. I have come not to abolish but to fulfill" (Matthew 5:17).

Jesus used the teachings of the Old Testament writers to teach his own disciples about following God's law. Jesus was asked which commandment of God's law was the greatest. He combined two Old Testament teachings into one which is known as the Great Commandment: "You shall love the Lord, your God, with all your heart, with all your soul, and with all your mind. This is the greatest and the first commandment. The second is like it: You shall love your neighbor as yourself." (Matthew 22:37–39)

Jesus fulfilled the law by living it completely and totally. He showed us the way to love God and one another and gave us the *new commandment*. "I give you a new commandment: love one another. As I have loved you, so you also should love one another. This is how all will know that you are my disciples, if you have love for one another." (John 13:34–35)

Prayer and Worship   Sacred Scripture is an essential part of the liturgy, the Church's official public worship. God's Word is proclaimed at every Mass. In fact, the first main part of the Mass is called the Liturgy of the Word. On Sundays and certain feast days of the Church, the Liturgy of the Word includes three readings and a Responsorial Psalm. The first reading is usually from the Old Testament. We hear of God's saving action in the lives of his people. We then sing or recite a Responsorial Psalm. The second reading is from one of the New Testament books other than the four Gospels. This reading encourages us to follow Christ's teachings and to be faithful disciples. The third reading is always from one of the four Gospels.

We show our reverence for the Good News of Jesus Christ by standing for the proclamation of the Gospel. The deacon or priest kisses the Book of Gospels, which was also honored in procession at the beginning of the Mass. And while the deacon or priest proclaims the Gospel, altar servers often stand on either side of him holding candles. These are just some of the ways we show how important the Gospels are to our lives as Christians.

The deacon or priest then gives a homily that helps us to reflect on the ways that God's Word calls us to live as faithful followers of Christ.

Hearing the Word of God is also a part of the other sacraments and liturgical celebrations of the Church. For example, the Liturgy of the Hours is a beautiful combination of praying, singing, and listening to God's Word.

We can use the Bible in study and personal prayer to get to know God and ourselves better. This reflection can help us to understand God's will for us.

Discuss some ways that you can learn more about Scripture. Write one way here.

_____

_____

_____

As Catholics...

Christ calls all of us to love one another as he has loved. When we read the Gospels we find many examples of the way Jesus lived. He cared for the needs of others, especially those who were neglected, poor, or oppressed. Jesus identified himself with those he served, and he once told his disciples, "whatever you did for one of these least brothers of mine, you did for me" (Matthew 25:40). The Corporal Works of Mercy come from this part of Matthew's Gospel. All the Works of Mercy are acts of love that help us to care for the needs of others. They can be found on page 329.

The Corporal Works of Mercy deal with the physical and material needs of others. The Spiritual Works of Mercy deal with the needs of people's hearts, minds, and souls.

Select one Work of Mercy and perform it this week.

The Church continues Jesus' ministry through the Seven Sacraments.

The Church continues Jesus' ministry of welcoming, healing, forgiving, and feeding others through the sacraments. A sacrament is an effective sign given to us by Jesus through which we share in God's life. We call the life of God within us grace. Grace is God's gift to us. Christ instituted the sacraments so that his followers would always experience his presence.

The sacraments are part of the liturgy of the Church, and they are our most important celebrations. The whole Body of Christ celebrates each sacrament. The priest and other members of the Church who participate in the sacraments represent the whole Church. The sacraments join Catholics all over the world with Jesus and with one another. They unite us as the Body of Christ.

Sacraments of Christian Initiation Our initiation into the Church takes place through three sacraments:

Baptism is the sacrament in which we are freed from sin, become children of God, and are welcomed into the Church.

Confirmation is the sacrament in which we are sealed with the Gift of the Holy Spirit.

The Eucharist is the Sacrament of the Body and Blood of Christ in which Jesus is truly present under the appearances of bread and wine.

Sacraments of Healing   Two sacraments are known as Sacraments of Healing:

Penance and Reconciliation is the sacrament by which our relationship with God and the Church is restored and our sins are forgiven.

The Anointing of the Sick is the sacrament by which God's grace and comfort are given to those who are suffering because of their old age or because of serious illnesses.

Sacraments at the Service of Communion
Church members who receive these sacraments are strengthened to serve God and the Church through one of two particular vocations:

Holy Orders is the sacrament in which baptized men are ordained to serve the Church as deacons, priests, and bishops.

Matrimony is the sacrament in which a man and woman become husband and wife and promise to be faithful to each other for the rest of their lives.

Write your answer to each of these questions.

What sacraments have you received?

_____

_____

_____

How have you participated in the celebration of these sacraments?

_____

_____

_____

How did your family and parish take part?

_____

_____

_____

What are some signs of these sacraments?

_____

_____

_____

Why are these sacraments important to your parish? to you?

_____

_____

The Church continues Jesus' ministry through her work for social justice.

Through the prophets God called his people to work for social justice, and told them that love of God could not be separated from love of neighbor.

Jesus Christ, the Son of God and Messiah, worked for justice. He tried to make sure that people had what they needed. He spoke out against leaders who did not take care of people.

Catholic social teaching calls us to work for justice and peace as Jesus did. Jesus' life and teaching are the foundation of Catholic social teaching. There are seven themes of Catholic social teaching.

Themes of Catholic Social Teaching

Life and Dignity of the Human Person
Human life is sacred because it is a gift from God. Because we are all God's children, we all share the same human dignity. Our dignity—our worth and value—does not come from the way we look or the things we accomplish. Our dignity comes from being made in the image and likeness of God. This dignity makes us equal. As Christians we respect all people, even those we do not know.

Call to Family, Community, and Participation
We are all social. We need to be with others to grow. The family is the basic community in society. In the family we grow and learn values. We learn what it means to be part of a group. Families are groups of people that contribute to society in many ways. As Christians we are involved in our family life and community.

Rights and Responsibilities of the Human Person
Every person has a fundamental right to life. This includes the things we need to have a decent life: faith and family, work and education, health care and housing. We also have a responsibility to others and to society. We work to make sure the rights of all people are being protected.

Option for the Poor and Vulnerable
We have a special obligation to help those who are poor and in need. This includes those who cannot protect themselves because of their age or their health. At different times in our lives we are all poor in some way and in need of assistance.

Dignity of Work and the Rights of Workers
Our work is a sign of our participation in God's work. People have the right to decent work, just wages, safe working conditions, and to participate in decisions about their work. There is value in all work. Our work in school and at home is a way to participate in God's work of creation. It is a way to use our talents and abilities to thank God for his gifts.

Solidarity of the Human Family
Solidarity is a feeling of unity. It binds members of a group together. Each of us is a member of the one human family, equal by our common human dignity. The human family includes people of all racial, cultural, and religious backgrounds. We all suffer when one part of the human family suffers whether they live near us or far away from us.

Care for God's Creation
God created us to be stewards, or caretakers, of his creation. We must care for and respect the environment. We have to protect it for future generations. When we care for creation, we show respect for God the Creator.

Questions

What are some ways the dignity of students or teachers is not respected during class? Why do you think this happens?

What are some conflicts in your school that have been resolved in a way that recognizes the dignity of those involved?

What are some virtues that individuals practice? that families practice? that neighbors practice?

How does the practice of these virtues influence society as a whole?

What is the difference between needing and wanting something?

What are some ways people might be poor?

What are some ways people are vulnerable?

How might different kinds of work make people feel?

How can we make people feel respected and valued for whatever work they do?

What are some problems or challenges that we face in our country?

How are they similar to those of other countries? How are they different?

What are some examples of society not protecting the environment?

How can these situations be changed?

The whole Church is called to live by this social teaching. Together we can work to change the things in society that allow unjust behaviors and conditions to exist.

WE RESPOND

In groups select one theme of Catholic social teaching. Dramatize some examples of people following the teaching and of people not following it. What are the effects of each of these examples on our society?

PROJECT

Show What *you* Know

How can you teach others about Catholic social teaching?
Be creative. Write your ideas here:

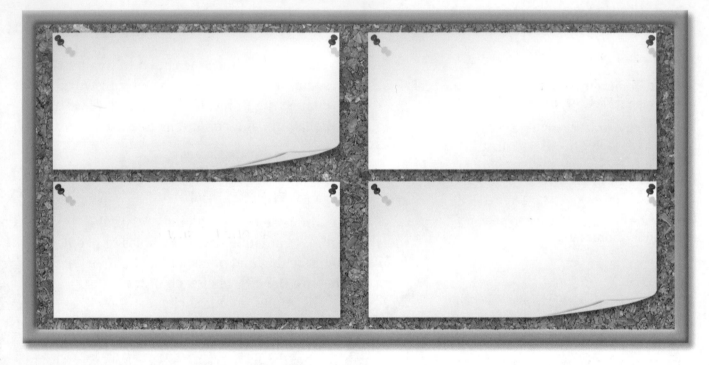

Celebrate!

The Seven Sacraments are part of the liturgy of the Church, and they are our most important celebrations.

↳ **DISCIPLE CHALLENGE** Invite your friends and family to take a "sacrament survey." Ask them which sacraments they have received. Record your results here:

Name	Sacraments Received

DISCIPLE

Pray
Learn
Celebrate
Share
Choose
Live

Saint Stories

Saint Thomas Aquinas is known as one of the greatest theologians in the history of the Church. He was a Dominican priest and a brilliant student. He is the patron saint of all universities and of students. The Church celebrates his feast day on January 28.

Visit *Lives of the Saints* on **www.webelieveweb.com** to learn more about saints and holy people.

What's *the* Word?

"They [the early Christians] devoted themselves to the teaching of the apostles and to the communal life, to the breaking of the bread and to the prayers... Every day they devoted themselves to meeting together in the temple area and to breaking bread in their homes. They ate their meals with exultation and sincerity of heart, praising God and enjoying favor with all the people. And every day the Lord added to their number." (Acts of the Apostles 2:42, 46–47)

• Which sacrament is described in the first verse?

_____

• Circle the sentence above that implies that more and more people were being baptized and following Jesus.

Question Corner

As you near the end of the Grade 6 *We Believe* program, what questions do you still have about the Bible?

_____

_____

_____

_____

Take Home

Read the *Question Corner* with your family. Talk about your response(s). Work together to find the answers. Invite family members to share favorite Bible stories or passages that were introduced to them through the Grade 6 *We Believe* program.

CHAPTER TEST

Write True or False for the following sentences.
Then change the false sentences to make them true.

1. __T__ Catholic social teaching calls us to work for justice and peace as Jesus did.

   _____

2. __F__ The writers of the New Testament were inspired and guided by Paul to record the truths of faith God wanted revealed to us.

   _____ guided by the holy spirit

3. __T__ The sacraments join Catholics all over the world with Jesus and one another, and unite the Church as the Body of Christ.

   _____

4. __F__ The dignity of work is an important source for Christian living and worship.

   _____ The bible _____

Short Answers

5. What kinds of books are in the New Testament?

   _____ letters /other writings _____

6. Name two ways we live out Jesus' new commandment.

   _____ put God and others first -JOY _____

7. What is a sacrament?

   _____ Tradition _____

8. There are seven themes of Catholic social teaching. List three.

   _____

Write a paragraph to answer this question.

9–10. How does the Church use Scripture?

_____
_____
_____
_____

WE GATHER

Leader: Blessed be God who made us to be his Church.

Blessed be the name of the Lord.

All: Now and for ever.

Reader: A reading from the holy Gospel according to Matthew

All: Glory to you, O Lord.

Reader: Jesus "said to them, 'But who do you say that I am?' Simon Peter said in reply, 'You are the Messiah, the Son of the living God.' Jesus said to him . . . 'you are Peter, and upon this rock I will build my church.'" (Matthew 16:15–18)

The Gospel of the Lord.

All: Praise to you, Lord Jesus Christ.

What do you believe in? How do you show others what you believe in?

🎵 **Who Am I?**

Who do people say I am?
Tell me who I am!
Are you Elijah? No, I'm not.
John the Baptist? No, I'm not.
Jeremiah? No, I'm not.

Who do you say I am?
Tell me who I am!
You are Jesus! Yes, I am.
Christ the Lord! Yes, I am.
Son of God! Yes, I am.

On your faith I'll build my Church.
We will build your Church!
Will you follow? Yes, we will!
Love each other? Yes, we will!
Share the Good News? Yes, we will!

Tell the people who I am.
Tell them who I am.
We will tell the people,
you are Christ the Lord, Son of God!

WE BELIEVE
We live as one people.

Each time we gather for Mass, we profess our faith by praying the Apostles' Creed or the Nicene Creed. We declare our belief in Jesus Christ, the Blessed Trinity, and the Church. In the Nicene Creed we state, "We believe in one holy catholic and apostolic church." One, holy, catholic, and apostolic are the four essential features, or identifying marks, of the Church. They are also called the **marks of the Church**.

The members of the Church believe in and follow the one Lord, Jesus Christ. The Church is one because its members are joined to Christ, who "is the head of the body, the church" (Colossians 1:18). Saint Paul wrote, "As a body is one though it has many parts, and all the parts of the body, though many, are one body, so also Christ. For in one Spirit we were all baptized into one body, whether Jews or Greeks, slaves or free persons" (1 Corinthians 12:12–13).

The Church is one because

- Jesus Christ unites us by his Death and Resurrection

- the one Holy Spirit draws us together and guides us as a community

- the pope and bishops are called to lead us and continue the work of the Apostles

- the Seven Sacraments unite us and enable us to share in God's grace.

All members share the same Baptism in the name of the Father, and the Son, and the Holy Spirit. Because of our common Baptism, we participate in the Sacrament of the Eucharist. In the Eucharist, we are nourished by the Word of God and receive the Body and Blood of Christ. We are joined more closely to Christ and one another to form the Body of Christ, the Church. We show that we are filled with the life of Christ by the way that we live.

The Catholic Church teaches that it is the Church founded by Christ himself. It is the one, holy, catholic, and apostolic Church. However, the Catholic Church respects all other Christians and recognizes the good in other Christian traditions. We have an especially close connection to the members of the Orthodox Churches. Other followers of Christ include: Episcopalians, Lutherans, Methodists, Presbyterians, Baptists, and Pentecostals.

Jesus wanted his followers to be united. The Catholic Church works with other Christian communities to bring about the unity of the Church. This work to promote the unity of all Christians is called **ecumenism**. The task of ecumenism involves all of us. We are called to know and share our faith and the teachings of the Church. We are called to grow as disciples of Christ and to pray that all Christians may be one.

Key Words

marks of the Church (p. 330)

ecumenism (p. 330)

How can you show that you believe in ecumenism? Make a poster illustrating some possible ways to bring about ecumenism.

Ecumenical Prayer Service, Toronto, Canada

We live as a holy people.

We learn from the Old Testament that the one true God is good and holy. He shared his goodness with all of his creation, most especially with humans.

Christ offered his goodness and holiness to us through his life, Death, Resurrection, and Ascension. Christ shares his holiness with us today through the Church. **Holiness** is sharing in God's goodness and responding to his love by the way we live. This holiness comes from the gift of God's life that he shares with us through the sacraments and from living as faithful Christians every day. The Holy Spirit helps us to respond to God's love and to follow Christ's example.

The Apostles taught the early Christians that by Baptism they shared in the very life and holiness of Christ. Saint Paul wrote to the new community at Corinth, "Do you not know that you are the temple of God, and that the Spirit of God dwells in you?. . . the temple of God, which you are, is holy." (1 Corinthians 3:16, 17)

To Paul, *holy* was another way of saying "belonging to God." He told the Corinthians, "you who have been sanctified in Christ Jesus, called to be holy, with all those everywhere who call upon the name of our Lord Jesus Christ" (1 Corinthians 1:2). Paul, Peter, and the other Apostles encouraged Christ's disciples to live lives of holiness. We, too, share this call to holiness.

From the beginning of the Church, some of God's holy ones have been honored as saints. Saints have stood up for their faith in many ways. Some saints preached the Good News of Christ in times when the Church was misunderstood by society. Others put Jesus' words into action in the midst of injustice. Many others dedicated their lives to prayer and penance. And others were martyrs.

The Church officially declares a disciple of Christ a saint by a process called *canonization*. These women and men are friends and servants of God. Their lives are models for us and teach us about true discipleship. Because the saints are closely united to Christ, they pray for us constantly. They help the Church to grow in holiness.

We are all God's holy ones, and his Church is holy. Yet at times we do not live as God calls us to live. However, through the grace of the Sacrament of Penance, we are again freed from sin and made holy. The Sacrament of the Eucharist also strengthens us to follow Christ's example of holiness. Praying, respecting all people, living fairly, and working for justice and peace help us to respond to God's grace in our lives and to help the Church to grow in holiness.

Key Word

holiness (p. 330)

👤 In groups identify some ways you and your families can show others that you "belong to God."

_____

_____

_____

_____

_____

_____

_____

_____

_____

_____

_____

Then as a class plan to present some of these ways to a class of younger students. Design the presentation to include role-plays that involve the younger students.

Venerable Pierre Toussaint

Saint Elizabeth of Portugal

Saint Cecilia

Saint Martin of Tours

Saint Paul

Saint Mary Magdalene

We live as a welcoming people.

The word *catholic* means "universal." The Church welcomes all people everywhere who seek God's love and mercy. Jesus commissioned the Apostles and sent them to make disciples of all nations. Some of them traveled to other parts of the world to preach the Gospel, baptize believers, and establish local Church communities. This was the beginning of the universal Church.

Catholics belong to a great variety of cultures. Our different customs and expressions of faith are a gift to the Church. We have many languages and customs, but we are united by our love for Christ and our common call to holiness. Together we make the Church catholic.

Because the Church is catholic, all people are invited to believe in Jesus and to be baptized in the faith of the Church. The mission of the Church is to share the Good News of Christ and to spread the Kingdom of God.

Each of us is called to take part in the mission of the Church. We are called to share the Good News of Christ and to live lives of holiness. We can do this by our prayers, good works, and everyday living.

Some members of the Church are missionaries who share their faith with those they serve. They also may build homes, schools, and hospitals with the people whom they serve. They may teach people to farm and to provide for their needs in other ways, too. These works of service put the Good News of Christ into action.

Illustrate ways your parish is one community made up of many different people.

There are many other religions beside Christianity. As Catholics we respect the rights of others to practice and live their faith. As you have learned, Christianity has its roots in Judaism. The Jewish People are our ancestors in faith, and many of our beliefs, prayer practices, and traditions are based in Judaism. Today Jewish People everywhere continue to live as God's people and follow the covenant.

Islam is another religion with which Christians and Jews share belief in the one true God. People who practice the religion of Islam are called Muslims. Muslims, Jews, and Christians have the important connection of worshiping God and consider Abraham a common ancestor. Muslims follow the teachings of the prophet Muhammad, who lived in the sixth and seventh centuries.

People of other religions and faiths include Buddhists, Hindus, and members of many native tribes. The Church respects the rights of all people to practice their faith, and we join with them and with people of no religious belief in trying to make the world a better place for all people.

 What might your class do to show respect for people whose beliefs are not the same as yours? List three ideas here and then decide on ways to make them a part of your daily life.

_____

_____

_____

_____

_____

We live as a faithful people.

The Church is apostolic because it is built on the faith of the Apostles. ". . . you are fellow citizens with the holy ones and members of the household of God, built upon the foundation of the apostles and prophets, with Christ Jesus himself as the capstone" (Ephesians 2:19-20).

Jesus chose the Apostles to care for and lead the community of believers. The faith we profess and practice is based on the faith that the Apostles shared and spread.

The life and leadership of the Church is based on that of the Apostles. When the Apostles established local communities of believers, they appointed local leaders to represent them in the community. The Apostles passed on to these leaders what Christ had given them: the Gift of the Holy Spirit and the authority to carry out the mission of Jesus Christ. These leaders who continued the Apostles' ministry were the successors of the Apostles and eventually became known as bishops. As the Church grew, the bishops commissioned others to continue the ministry of the Apostles. In this way, the leadership of the Church throughout history can be traced back to the Apostles.

As the Bishop of Rome, the pope is the successor of the Apostle Peter, who was the first leader of the Church of Rome. The pope continues Peter's ministry and has a special responsibility to care for the Church. The bishops, with the pope as their head, are called to lead and guide the whole Church.

The whole Church shares in the mission that Christ first gave to his Apostles. But as a body has different parts with different functions, so the members of the Church have different roles in sharing in this mission.

The laity are the baptized members of the Church who share in the Church's mission to bring the Good News of Christ to the world. The laity are also known as laypeople or the Christian faithful. Right now you are a layperson, and every day you are growing as Jesus' disciple. You do not have to wait to be an adult to be an active member of the Church. As a layperson you are called to share the Good News at home, in school, and in your neighborhood. You can take part in your parish celebrations and be an example of Christian living for others. Laypeople are called to participate in the celebration of the sacraments and to support their parishes.

Laypeople are called to bring the Good News of Christ to their work places and local communities. Women and men in the laity are called to be involved in city, state, and national governments. They have a responsibility to act and make decisions based on the teachings of Jesus and on their faith.

It is truly a blessing that all in the Church can work to bring about God's reign. We are one people who can show by our love of others that we are living as Christ's disciples in the world.

WE RESPOND

What are the different ways that the Church serves the world?

_____

_____

_____

_____

What are the different ways that people your age participate in the mission of the Church?

_____

_____

_____

_____

PROJECT

Show What *you* Know

Across

3. the successor of the Apostle Peter and leader of the Church

4. the work to promote unity among all Christians

Down

1. a word that means "universal"

2. sharing in God's goodness and responding to his love by the way we live

6. The _____ of the Church are the four essential features of the Church: one, holy, catholic, and apostolic.

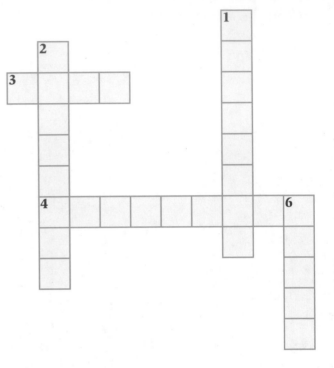

Question Corner

How do you share in the Church's mission as a sixth-grader? Check all that apply.

❏ I share the Good News at home, at school, and in my neighborhood.

❏ I take part in parish activities.

❏ I live as Jesus taught.

❏ I am an example of Christian living.

❏ I participate in the celebration of the sacraments.

❏ other _____

Now, pass it on!

DISCIPLE

Saint Stories

Saint Maximilian Kolbe was a Franciscan priest. During World War II, he was imprisoned in a Nazi concentration camp. There he offered his life in place of another man, a husband and father, who had been chosen to die. Saint Maximilian is an example of unselfish love for all people. The Church celebrates his feast day on August 14. How can you show that you are unselfish at home? in your community?

Visit *Lives of the Saints* on www.webelieveweb.com to learn about more saints and holy people.

Pray Today

We are called to pray that all Christians may be one. A special time to pray for this is during the Week of Prayer for Christian Unity. The Week of Prayer for Christian Unity is traditionally celebrated every year from January 18 to 25.

↳ **DISCIPLE CHALLENGE** Write a prayer for Christian unity.

_____

_____

_____

_____

Take Home

Redesign the logo for *Project Disciple* with your family. You might want to use the outline on the left for your ideas.

Be sure to live it out!

CHAPTER TEST

Complete the following.

1. The Church is one because _____
   _____

2. The Church is holy because _____
   _____

3. The Church is catholic because _____
   _____

4. The Church is apostolic because _____
   _____

Circle the letter of the correct answer.

5. _____ is sharing in God's goodness and responding to his love by the way we live.

   a. Ecumenism   **b.** Catholic   **c.** Holiness

6. The _____ are all the baptized members of the Church who share in the Church's mission to bring the Good News of Christ to the world.

   a. bishops   **b.** laity   **c.** Apostles

7. The Catholic Church is the Church founded by _____.

   a. Jesus Christ   **b.** Peter   **c.** Paul

8. The work to promote unity among all Christians is called _____.

   a. ecumenism   **b.** holiness   **c.** marks of the Church

Write a paragraph to answer this question.

9–10. What can young people do to help the Church to grow?

_____

_____

_____

_____

"The love of God has been poured into our hearts by his Spirit living in us, alleluia."

Introductory Rites, Pentecost Vigil Mass

SEASONAL

CHAPTER 27

This liturgical chapter celebrates the entire Easter season.

During the Easter season, we celebrate our new life in Christ and the coming of the Holy Spirit.

WE GATHER

✝ *Lord Jesus, may we rise with you to new life in the Holy Spirit!*

Think of a time when a person was welcomed into your family. How did you celebrate?

WE BELIEVE

The Easter season is a special time to rejoice in the new life we have in Christ. It is a time for bringing new members into the Church—for celebrating the Sacraments of Baptism and Confirmation, both of which lead to the table of the Eucharist. And during the Easter season the whole Church grows in their experience of the risen Christ, and through liturgical celebrations, reflects with joy on Christ's Paschal Mystery. We welcome the new members of the Church and pray with them each week.

The Easter season lasts for fifty days. During this time we celebrate the Resurrection and Ascension of Jesus Christ and the coming of the Holy Spirit on Pentecost. We hear stories of the risen Jesus' appearances to his disciples. We learn about the beginning of the Church from the Acts of the Apostles.

Easter Monday in Nigeria The day after Easter Sunday is an important day of worship in Nigeria. In many towns and villages, Catholics and other Christians gather in a common place which they name "Galilee" for the day. They believe that, like the Apostles and first disciples, they are to be in "Galilee" to meet the risen Lord. Christians of all faiths gather together to celebrate Christ's Resurrection with preaching, singing and dancing, sharing a meal, and participating in all types of sports and games. This "Galilee" gathering is possible because Easter Monday is traditionally a public holiday in Nigeria.

Ascension   During the season of Easter we recall the last event of Jesus' public life, his Ascension. Jesus ascended, or returned to his father in Heaven forty days after he rose from the dead. Thus the Church celebrates the Feast of the Ascension around forty days after Easter. In many dioceses of the United States this feast is a holy day of obligation. We read about Jesus' Ascension in the Acts of the Apostles.

Christ the Redeemer,
Rio de Janiero

Acts of the Apostles 1:3–12

Forty days after his Resurrection, the risen Jesus had gathered with his Apostles outside of Jerusalem. He told them, "'You will receive power when the holy Spirit comes upon you, and you will be my witnesses in Jerusalem, throughout Judea and Samaria, and to the ends of the earth.' When he had said this, as they were looking on, he was lifted up, and a cloud took him from their sight." (Acts of the Apostles 1:8–9).

The Apostles went back to the upper room and waited in prayer.

Pentecost Fifty days after Easter we celebrate the Feast of Pentecost. The word *Pentecost* comes from a Greek word meaning "fiftieth." Pentecost is celebrated on the last Sunday and final day of the Easter season. On Pentecost Sunday we celebrate the coming of the Holy Spirit to the first disciples. We also celebrate the beginning of the Church, and we rejoice because the Holy Spirit fills our hearts today.

The Jewish feast of Pentecost was celebrated fifty days after Passover, as a thanksgiving for the harvest. The "first fruits" of field and orchard were blessed and shared. So it is fitting that on this feast God the Father and God the Son, chose to share the "first fruits" of Jesus' Resurrection—the Holy Spirit, the power sent from on high. This Gift of the Holy Spirit was a great gift of God's love. The Apostles now shared in the fellowship of the Holy Spirit.

What a difference the Holy Spirit made in the lives of the Apostles! During Jesus' trial and Death, the Apostles were afraid. After his Resurrection, they remained hidden. When the Holy Spirit came, the Apostles began to remember the words of Jesus and to act on them. They began preaching and teaching. They were no longer alone. Neither are we alone because the Holy Spirit will be with us always.

The Apostles and Mary spent the time between the Ascension and Pentecost in prayer. The Church keeps the days between Ascension and Pentecost as days of waiting and prayer for the Holy Spirit. During this time the liturgy is full of prayerful longing for the coming of the Holy Spirit.

WE RESPOND

Pray this prayer together.

"Father,
let your Spirit come upon us with power
    to fill us with his gifts.
May he make our hearts pleasing to you,
    and ready to do your will."

Prepare for the feast of the coming of the Holy Spirit.
Write a prayer, a poem, a favorite quotation from Scripture,
or a "Spirit-filled" action you can do.

✞ We Respond in Prayer

Leader: Lord, send out your Spirit.

All: And renew the face of the earth.

Reader: A reading from the first Letter of Saint Paul to the Corinthians

"There are different kinds of spiritual gifts but the same Spirit; there are different forms of service but the same Lord. . . As a body is one though it has many parts, and all the parts of the body, though many, are one body, so also Christ. For in one Spirit we were all baptized into one body, whether Jews or Greeks, slaves or free persons, and we were all given to drink of one Spirit." (1 Corinthians 12:4–5, 12–13)

The word of the Lord.

All: Thanks be to God.

🎵 Envía Tu Espíritu

Refrain:
Envía tu Espíritu, envía tu Espíritu,
envía tu Espíritu,
sea renovada la faz de la tierra.
Sea renovada la faz de la tierra.

Spirit of the living God,
burn in our hearts,
and make us a people of hope
and compassion. (Refrain)

Wind of promise, wind of change,
friend of the poor,
empower your people to make
peace and justice. (Refrain)

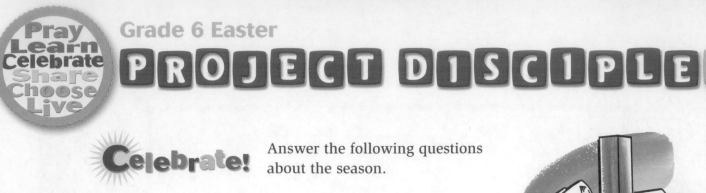

PROJECT DISCIPLE

Celebrate! Answer the following questions about the season.

1. How long is the season of Easter? _____

2. During the season of Easter, what do we recall as the last event of Jesus' public life? _____

3. What are we celebrating on Pentecost Sunday? _____

4. When do we celebrate Pentecost? _____

5. Which feast during the Easter season is also a holy day of obligation in many dioceses in the United States? _____

What's *the* Word?

"God raised this Jesus; of this we are all witnesses. Exalted at the right hand of God, he received the promise of the holy Spirit from the Father and poured it forth, as you see and hear." (Acts 2:32–33)

• What two liturgical events does Peter describe in this passage?

_____

• Underline the phrase that describes how the Apostles are part of the Easter story.

Picture This

Design an e-card to send during the Easter season. If possible, include symbols of Easter in your design, such as the Paschal Candle, a flowering plant, a white dove, etc.

Take Home

The Irish phrase *Cead Mile Failte* (kayd me-lay fall-chuh) means "a hundred thousand welcomes." The season of Easter is a time of welcoming new members into the Church.

How can your family welcome these new members? Make a list here:

_____

_____

UNIT TEST

Fill in the circle beside the correct answer.

1. The Church teaches us that _____ is one of the two means by which God's Revelation comes to us. The Bible is the other.

   ○ Tradition   ○ liturgy   ○ the Council of Nicea

2. In the first part of the Sermon on the Mount, Jesus gave guidelines that describe the way to live as his disciples. These are the _____.

   ○ Gospels   ○ Beatitudes   ○ Lord's Prayer

3. _____ did not believe that the other Apostles had seen Jesus.

   ○ The Apostle Thomas   ○ Mary Magdalene   ○ Joseph of Arimethea

4. On his way to _____ to persecute Christians, Saul had an experience that changed his life.

   ○ Antioch   ○ Damascus   ○ Ephesus

5. One, holy, catholic, and apostolic are the four _____.

   ○ themes of Catholic social teaching   ○ marks of the Church   ○ models of holiness

6. The Apostle _____ was chosen to take Judas's place.

   ○ Matthias   ○ Paul   ○ Jerome

7. As a Christian prophecy, the Book of Revelation deals with _____.

   ○ the ministry of the Apostles   ○ the life and work of Jesus   ○ Christ's Second Coming

8. The work to promote the unity of all Christians is called _____.

   ○ ecumenism   ○ social justice   ○ holiness

9. We call the power of God's love coming into the world and into our lives the _____.

   ○ Gospels   ○ Kingdom of God   ○ marks of the Church

10. For Christians the _____ is the new Passover of God's People.

    ○ Eucharist   ○ Gospels   ○ Beatitudes

11. Christians call the day Christ died _____.

    ○ Sabbath   ○ Good Friday   ○ Pentecost

continued on next page

Write True or False for the following sentences. Then change the false sentences to make them true.

12. _____ The Gospels are effective signs given to us by Jesus through which we share in God's life, which we call grace.

_____

13. _____ It was at Antioch, about ten years after Jesus' Death, that his followers were first called Nazarenes.

_____

14. _____ The Lord's Prayer is one of the most important prayers in the Gospels and of the Church.

_____

15. _____ Catholic social teaching calls us to work for justice and peace as Jesus did.

_____

16. _____ The Apostles are all the baptized members of the Church who share in the Church's mission to bring the Good News of Christ to the world.

_____

Write a paragraph to answer each question.

17–18. If you were an early Christian and were arrested for your faith, what would you tell the Roman authorities?

_____
_____
_____

19–20. As members of the Church, each of us is called to take part in her mission. How can you, as a sixth grader, do this?

_____
_____
_____

Explain the importance to Christians of each of these passages from Scripture. Then illustrate each passage.

1. "Now this is eternal life, that they should know you, the only true God, and the one whom you sent, Jesus Christ." (John 17:3)

2. "God created man in his image;
   in the divine image
     he created him;
   male and female
     he created them."
   (Genesis 1:27)

3. "Have dominion over the fish of the sea, the birds of the air, and all the living things that move on the earth."
   (Genesis 1:28)

4. "This is the sign of the covenant I have established between me and all mortal creatures that are on earth."
   (Genesis 9:17)

5. "Do not do the least thing to him. I know now how devoted you are to God, since you did not withhold from me your own beloved son."
   (Genesis 22:12)

Across

1. Moses' brother, who helped him explain God's message to the Israelites.

3. The sweet, bread-like food God provided to the Israelites in the wilderness.

5. Poetic prayers intended to be chanted or sung in public worship.

8. David's son, who succeeded him as king of Israel.

11. The first king of Israel, chosen by God and anointed by Samuel.

12. David's father, who summoned his son from the fields at Samuel's command.

13. The center of worship of the one true God that Solomon built in Jerusalem.

14. A Moabite woman whose story shows us that sadness can be turned into joy when we follow God's plan for us.

Down

1. The _____ of the covenant, the box in which the tablets of the Ten Commandments were kept.

2. The land God promised to the Israelites.

4. The night on which God spared the Israelites as he struck down the firstborn of the Egyptians.

5. Delilah, who betrayed Samson, was a _____ woman.

6. The man to whom God spoke from a burning bush, calling him to lead his people from slavery.

7. The son of Hannah whom God called to be a prophet.

9. Through God's actions and her firm faith in him, _____ helped free Israel from its enemies.

10. A poem or song expressing sorrow, mourning, or regret.

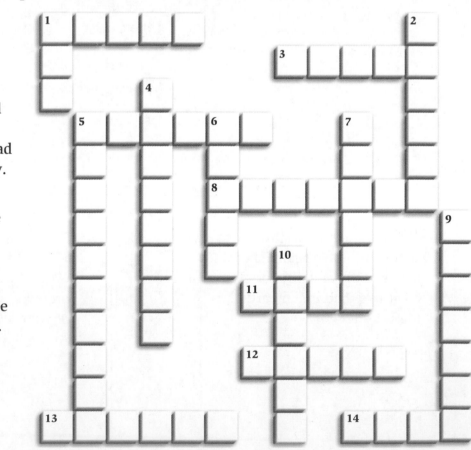

ALTERNATIVE ASSESSMENT

Amos	Elijah	Elisha	Ezekiel	John
Habakkuk	Isaiah	Jeremiah	Malachi	Micah

Write the name of the prophet that fits the description below.

1. This man was the first prophet sent by God to the northern kingdom of Israel to preach that the one true God is the only God; his name means "Yahweh is my God."

2. God summoned this shepherd from the southern kingdom of Judah to call the people of the northern kingdom back to God.

3. When God's people were in exile in Babylon, God told them that Babylon was an instrument for purifying Judea of its sins.

4. The prophet Elijah anointed this man and threw his cloak over him as a sign that he was called to the mission of a prophet.

_____ _____ _____ _____

5. This prophet was accused of blasphemy, attacked, and imprisoned by God's people, but he continued to speak out against the sins he saw around him.

6. This prophet mentioned a messenger who would prepare the way for repentance and true worship.

7. This prophet and priest warned God's people against all forms of social injustice, idolatry, and superstition.

_____ _____ _____

8. This great prophet foretold that salvation would come only through the suffering of a servant of the Lord. This servant would be without sin.

9. This prophet foretold that a new David would restore the Chosen People.

10. This son of Elizabeth and Zechariah preached and prophesied throughout Judea to prepare the way for the coming of the Messiah.

_____ _____ _____

As a member of the Church, you are called to continue Jesus' ministry. Choose four from the following and write a summary:

- the Lord's Prayer
- the Beatitudes
- Spiritual Works of Mercy
- Corporal Works of Mercy
- the Seven Sacraments
- the seven themes of Catholic social teaching
- the Bible.

_____

_____

_____

_____

_____

_____

_____

_____

_____

_____

_____

_____

_____

_____

_____

Then describe ways that each of the four you have summarized above can be used to spread the Good News of Jesus Christ. Present your ideas in the form of a demonstration, a poster, or a song.

CONGRATULATIONS ON COMPLETING YOUR YEAR AS A GRADE 6 DISCIPLE!

Fold on this line.

A RECORD OF MY JOURNEY AS A GRADE 6 DISCIPLE

_____
Name

✂ Cut on this line.

As a disciple of Jesus, I am called to make loving choices.

This year I made a loving choice in interacting

- with my family _____

_____

- with my friend(s) _____

_____

- in school _____

When I heard about the needs of others, I chose to

_____

_____

_____

As a disciple of Jesus, I pray every day.

A prayer I like to pray from the

- Old Testament is _____

_____

- New Testament is _____

_____

I like to pray

○ by myself

○ with friends and family

○ with my parish

A prayer for guidance I will pray this summer

is _____

_____

This year I learned about God's actions in the lives of his people throughout history.

I learned about

- the patriarchs _____

_____

- Moses and the Exodus _____

_____

- the prophets _____

_____

- Jesus _____

_____

2

Cut on this line.

As a disciple of Jesus, I share my faith with others.

I can share stories from the Bible with

○ a younger child or children

○ a close friend

○ my family

○ _____

Three of my favorite stories I would like to

share are _____

_____

_____

6

As a disciple of Jesus, I live out my faith by following ancestors of faith.

An ancestor of faith who is an example

- of asking God for forgiveness _____

_____

- of being just and fair _____

_____

- of caring for the needs of others _____

_____

- of being Jesus' disciple _____

_____

I will continue to live out my faith by

_____

_____

7

As Jesus' disciple I celebrate the sacraments with the Church.

I have received the Sacraments of

_____

_____

I celebrated these sacraments with

_____

_____

I am preparing to receive the Sacrament of

_____

_____

I am preparing by _____

_____

_____

3

PROJECT DISCIPLE

Pray
Learn
Celebrate
Share
Choose
Live

End-of-Year Prayer Service

✝ We Gather in Prayer

🎵 **Though the Mountains May Fall**

Though the mountains may fall
and the hills turn to dust,
yet the love of the Lord will stand
as a shelter for all who will call on his name.
Sing the praise and the glory of God.

Leader: Let us gather together to give thanks to our God.

All: God, we thank you for faithfulness and love. We thank you for our ancestors in faith, who have shown us your ways of love.

Leader: God, we thank you for revealing yourself to us through the words and actions of your Son, Jesus Christ.

All: God, help us continue Jesus' mission and share the Good News of your love with everyone we meet.

Leader: God, we ask for the Holy Spirit's guidance in being loving and faithful disciples.

As we look forward to a safe and happy summer, help us to remember that Jesus is with us.

All: Amen!

The Lives of the Saints

Saint Joan of Arc

⇒ **Born:** January 6, 1412 ⇒ **Died:** May 30, 1431 ⇒ **Feast Day:** May 30

What she said

"About Jesus Christ and the Church, I simply know they're just one thing, and we shouldn't complicate the matter."

What the world was like

Joan of Arc lived at the time of the beginning of the Renaissance, which was a revival of classical art, architecture, literature, and learning. This was a time of transition from medieval times to modern times.

When Joan of Arc was born, France was involved in the Hundred Years War with England. Because of this war, much of the farmland in France was ruined and people were starving because of lack of food. During Joan's life, many people in France died from the Black Death, a deadly plague that was spreading throughout Europe. People lived in fear of not only the English and the plague, but also of local French people who raided towns and villages.

Who she was

Joan of Arc grew up in France. Her father was a farmer. Although she did not have much formal education, her mother taught her prayers. Joan always listened to her parents and tried to do what they asked of her. She attended Mass every day and she tried to help the poor. She was quiet and preferred to play alone rather than with others. She enjoyed playing in the woods and she was good at spinning and weaving cloth.

While Joan was growing up, there was a war going on between France and England. This war had lasted almost one hundred years. France was divided and had no king. Joan began hearing the voices of Saint Michael, Saint Catherine, and Saint Margaret. They told Joan that she was chosen by God to unite France and to help Charles be crowned king. Joan was very surprised because she knew nothing about politics or about the military. She wanted to serve God, but she did not know how to help her country. Finally, she realized that this was God's will and he would lead her.

At first she was laughed at, but soon Joan was leading the French army with a banner that said "Jesus and Mary." She began winning battles. Soon the English were gone from many towns in France. The French soldiers loved Joan. Eventually, she saw Charles crowned the king of France.

Later Joan was captured and became a prisoner of the English. She was sentenced to death. Although she was afraid, Joan remained faithful to God and calmly went to her death holding a crucifix.

What this saint means to us today

Joan of Arc was faithful to God's will in her life. Even when she was laughed at, she kept her focus on God and what he asked her to do. It seemed to be impossible for a teenage girl to become a soldier, lead an army, and unite the country of France, but Joan did just that because of her faith.

When things seem to be impossible in our lives, we can be like Joan and let our faith guide us.

The Lives of the Saints

Name _____

Saint Joan of Arc

Joan of Arc grew up in France when her country was at war with England. She was the daughter of a farmer and lived a very simple and quiet life. She attended Mass every day and loved God very much. As a teenager, she heard the voices of Saint Michael, Saint Catherine, and Saint Margaret telling her that God had a special mission for her. God wanted Joan to unite France and to help Charles be crowned the king. Though this seemed impossible, Joan became the leader of the French army and won many battles. She was brave and helped to defend and unite her country. Because of her victories, Charles was crowned king of France with Joan by his side.

In the space below, write about a time that you found the courage to do something that you thought was right.

_____

_____

_____

_____

_____

_____

_____

_____

_____

_____

For saints, games, study guides and more,
visit www.webelieveweb.com.

PROJECT DISCIPLE

Congratulations! Throughout your **We Believe** program you have learned, celebrated, prayed, chosen, shared, and served as a disciple of Jesus Christ.

Now, you are moving toward a more mature faith and a deeper relationship with Jesus Christ and the Catholic Church. As a junior high student, you will be experiencing a continuation of the **We Believe** program that is especially designed for you: **We Live Our Faith**.

There are two texts, one for each junior high year: **We Live Our Faith** as *Disciples of Jesus* and **We Live Our Faith** as *Members of the Church*.

Both texts are based on questions that real junior high students—like you—asked. You will have the opportunity to learn about what your faith can mean to your life as an older student.

The most important things I have learned about my faith this year are:

_____

_____

As a junior high student, I want to learn more about Jesus and the Church. Here is a question I hope to get answered.

_____

_____

_____

We are blessed to be disciples of Jesus Christ and members of the Church!

Prayers and Practices

Glory Be to the Father

Glory be to the Father
and to the Son
and the Holy Spirit,
as it was in the beginning
is now, and ever shall be
world without end. Amen.

Our Father

Our Father, who art in heaven,
hallowed be thy name;
thy kingdom come;
thy will be done on earth
    as it is in heaven.
Give us this day our daily bread;
and forgive us our trespasses
as we forgive those
    who trespass against us;
and lead us not into temptation,
but deliver us from evil. Amen.

Hail Mary

Hail Mary, full of grace,
the Lord is with you!
Blessed are you among women,
and blessed is the fruit
    of your womb, Jesus.
Holy Mary, Mother of God,
pray for us sinners,
now and at the hour of our death.
Amen.

Morning Offering

O Jesus, I offer you all my prayers,
works, and sufferings of this day
for all the intentions of your most
Sacred Heart. Amen.

Evening Prayer

Dear God, before I sleep
I want to thank you for this day,
so full of your kindness and your joy.
I close my eyes to rest
safe in your loving care.

Apostles' Creed

I believe in God, the Father Almighty,
Creator of heaven and earth,
and in Jesus Christ, his only Son, our Lord,
who was conceived by the Holy Spirit,
born of the Virgin Mary,
suffered under Pontius Pilate,
    was crucified, died and was buried;
he descended into hell;
on the third day he rose again from the dead;
he ascended into heaven,
and is seated at the right hand
    of God the father almighty;
from there he will come to judge
    the living and the dead.

I believe in the Holy Spirit,
    the holy catholic Church,
    the communion of saints,
    the forgiveness of sins,
    the resurrection of the body,
    and life everlasting. Amen.

Find other versions of some of these
prayers at **www.webelieveweb.com**

The Angelus

The angel spoke God's message to Mary,
and she conceived of the Holy Spirit.
Hail Mary. . . .

"I am the lowly servant of the Lord:
let it be done to me according to your word."
Hail Mary. . . .

And the Word became flesh
and lived among us.
Hail Mary. . . .

Pray for us, holy Mother of God,
that we may become worthy of the promises
of Christ.

Let us pray.
Lord,
fill our hearts with your grace:
once, through the message of an angel
you revealed to us the Incarnation of your Son;
now, through his suffering and death
lead us to the glory of his resurrection.
We ask this through Christ our Lord.
Amen.

Hail, Holy Queen

Hail, holy Queen, mother of mercy,
hail, our life, our sweetness, and our hope.
To you we cry, the children of Eve;
to you we send up our sighs,
mourning and weeping in this land of exile.
Turn, then, most gracious advocate,
your eyes of mercy toward us;
lead us home at last
and show us the blessed fruit of your womb, Jesus:
O clement, O loving, O sweet Virgin Mary.

The Canticle of Mary, The Magnificat

"My soul proclaims the greatness of the Lord;
   my spirit rejoices in God my savior.
For he has looked upon his handmaid's lowliness;
   behold, from now on will all ages call me
      blessed.
The Mighty One has done great things for me,
   and holy is his name.
His mercy is from age to age
   to those who fear him.
He has shown might with his arm,
   dispersed the arrogant of mind and heart.
He has thrown down the rulers from their thrones
   but lifted up the lowly.
The hungry he has filled with good things;
   the rich he has sent away empty.
He has helped Israel his servant,
   remembering his mercy,
according to his promise to our fathers,
   to Abraham and to his descendants forever."

(Luke 1:46–55)

Memorare

Remember, most loving Virgin Mary,
never was it heard
that anyone who turned to you for help
was left unaided.

Inspired by this confidence,
though burdened by my sins,
I run to your protection
for you are my mother.
Mother of the Word of God,
do not despise my words of pleading
but be merciful and hear my prayer.
Amen.

Note:
The Ten Commandments are found on page 110.
The gifts of the Holy Spirit are found on page 147.
The Beatitudes are found on page 251.
The Seven Sacraments are found on pages 288–289.
The seven themes of Catholic social teaching are found on pages 290–291.
The Prayer to the Holy Spirit is found on page 281.

Nicene Creed

I believe in one God,
    the Father almighty,
    maker of heaven and earth,
    of all things visible and invisible.

I believe in one Lord Jesus Christ,
    the Only Begotten Son of God,
    born of the Father before all ages.
    God from God, Light from Light,
    true God from true God,
    begotten, not made, consubstantial
        with the Father;
    through him all things were made.
    For us men and for our salvation
        he came down from heaven,
    and by the Holy Spirit
        was incarnate of the Virgin Mary,
           and became man.

For our sake he was crucified
        under Pontius Pilate,
    he suffered death and was buried,
    and rose again on the third day
        in accordance with the Scriptures.
    He ascended into heaven
        and is seated at the right hand
           of the Father.
    He will come again in glory to judge
        the living and the dead
        and his kingdom will have no end.

I believe in the Holy Spirit, the Lord,
    the giver of life,
    who proceeds from the Father and the Son,
    who with the Father and the Son is
        adored and glorified,
    who has spoken through the prophets.
    I believe in one, holy, catholic
        and apostolic Church.
    I confess one Baptism for the
        forgiveness of sins
    and I look forward to the resurrection of the
        dead and the life of the world to come.
    Amen.

The Rosary

A rosary is made up of groups of beads arranged in a circle. It begins with a cross followed by one large bead and three small ones. The next large bead (just before the medal) begins the first "decade." Each decade consists of one large bead followed by ten smaller beads.

Begin the Rosary with the Sign of the Cross. Recite the Apostles' Creed. Then pray one Our Father, three Hail Marys, and one Glory Be to the Father.

To pray each decade, say an Our Father on the large bead and a Hail Mary on each of the ten smaller beads. Close each decade by praying the Glory Be to the Father. Pray the Hail, Holy Queen as the last prayer of the Rosary.

The mysteries of the Rosary are special events in the lives of Jesus and Mary. As you pray each decade, think of the appropriate Joyful Mystery, Sorrowful Mystery, Glorious Mystery, or Mystery of Light.

The Five Joyful Mysteries
1. The Annunciation
2. The Visitation
3. The Birth of Jesus
4. The Presentation of Jesus in the Temple
5. The Finding of the Child Jesus in the Temple

The Five Sorrowful Mysteries
1. The Agony in the Garden
2. The Scourging at the Pillar
3. The Crowning with Thorns
4. The Carrying of the Cross
5. The Crucifixion and Death of Jesus

The Five Glorious Mysteries
1. The Resurrection
2. The Ascension
3. The Descent of the Holy Spirit upon the Apostles
4. The Assumption of Mary into Heaven
5. The Coronation of Mary as Queen of Heaven

The Five Mysteries of Light
1. Jesus' Baptism in the Jordan
2. The Miracle at the Wedding at Cana
3. Jesus Announces the Kingdom of God
4. The Transfiguration
5. The Institution of the Eucharist

Stations of the Cross

From the earliest days of the Church, Christians remembered Jesus' life and Death by visiting and praying at the places where Jesus lived, suffered, died, and rose from the dead.

As the Church spread to other countries, not everyone could travel to the Holy Land. So local churches began inviting people to "follow in the footsteps of Jesus" without leaving home. "Stations," or places to stop and pray, were made so that stay-at-home pilgrims could "walk the way of the cross" in their own parish churches. We do the same today, especially during Lent.

There are fourteen "stations," or stops. At each one, we pause and think about what is happening at the station.

1. Jesus is condemned to die.
2. Jesus takes up his cross.
3. Jesus falls the first time.
4. Jesus meets his mother.
5. Simon helps Jesus carry his cross.
6. Veronica wipes the face of Jesus.
7. Jesus falls the second time.
8. Jesus meets the women of Jerusalem.
9. Jesus falls the third time.
10. Jesus is stripped of his garments.
11. Jesus is nailed to the cross.
12. Jesus dies on the cross.
13. Jesus is taken down from the cross.
14. Jesus is laid in the tomb.

The Canticle of Zechariah

"Blessed be the Lord, the God of Israel,
for he has visited and brought redemption
    to his people.
He has raised up a horn for our salvation
within the house of David his servant,
even as he promised through the mouth of his
    holy prophets from of old:
    salvation from our enemies and from the
    hand of all who hate us,
        to show mercy to our fathers
    and to be mindful of his holy covenant
and of the oath he swore to Abraham our father,
and to grant us that, rescued from the hand
    of enemies,
without fear we might worship him in holiness
    and righteousness
    before him all our days.
And you, child, will be called prophet of the Most High,
for you will go before the Lord to prepare his ways,
to give his people knowledge of salvation
    through the forgiveness of their sins,
because of the tender mercy of our God
    by which the daybreak from on high will visit us
to shine on those who sit in darkness and
    death's shadow,
    to guide our feet into the path of peace."

(Luke 1:68–79)

Act of Contrition

My God,
I am sorry for my sins with all my heart.
In choosing to do wrong
and failing to do good,
I have sinned against you
whom I should love above all things.
I firmly intend, with your help,
to do penance,
to sin no more,
and to avoid whatever leads me to sin.
Our Savior Jesus Christ
suffered and died for us.
In his name, my God, have mercy.

Prayer for Vocation

Dear God,
You have a great and loving plan
for our world and for me.
I wish to share in that plan fully,
faithfully, and joyfully.

Help me to understand what it is
you wish me to do with my life.
Help me to be attentive to the signs
that you give me about preparing for the future.

Help me to learn to be a sign
of the kingdom, or reign, of
God whether I'm called to the
priesthood or religious life,
the single or married life.

And once I have heard and understood
your call, give me the strength
and the grace to follow it
with generosity and love. Amen

The Precepts of the Church

1. You shall attend Mass on Sundays and holy days of obligation and rest from servile labor.

2. You shall confess your sins at least once a year.

3. You shall receive the Sacrament of the Eucharist at least during the Easter season.

4. You shall observe the days of fasting and abstinence by the Church.

5. You shall help to provide for the needs of the Church.

Corporal Works of Mercy

Feed the hungry.
Give drink to the thirsty.
Clothe the naked.
Visit the imprisoned.
Shelter the homeless.
Visit the sick.
Bury the dead.

Spiritual Works of Mercy

Admonish the sinner.
   (Give correction to those who need it.)

Instruct the ignorant.
   (Share our knowledge with others.)

Counsel the doubtful.
   (Give advice to those who need it.)

Comfort the sorrowful.
   (Comfort those who suffer.)

Bear wrongs patiently.
   (Be patient with others.)

Forgive all injuries.
   (Forgive those who hurt us.)

Pray for the living and the dead.

The Holy Days of Obligation

(as celebrated by the Church in the United States.)

Solemnity of Mary, Mother of God (January 1)

Ascension (when celebrated on Thursday during the Easter Season)*

Assumption of Mary (August 15)

All Saints Day (November 1)

Immaculate Conception (December 8)

Christmas (December 25)

*(Some dioceses celebrate the Ascension on the following Sunday.)

Glossary

ark of the covenant (p. 113)
a wooden box in which the tablets of the Ten Commandments were kept

Beatitudes (p. 250)
teachings of Jesus that describe the way to live as his disciples

Bible (p. 24)
the written record of God's Revelation and his relationship with his people

blasphemy (p. 190)
a thought, word, or act that refers to God without respect or reverence

Blessed Trinity (p. 22)
the Three Persons in one God: God the Father, God the Son, and God the Holy Spirit

Book of Genesis (p. 33)
the first book in the Bible

Canaan (p. 68)
an area in western Palestine that included most of present-day Israel

Catholic social teaching (p. 290)
the teaching of the Church that calls all members to work for justice and peace as Jesus did

conscience (p. 38)
the ability to know the difference between good and evil, right and wrong

covenant (p. 32)
an agreement between God and his people

Divine Inspiration (p. 24)
the special guidance that the Holy Spirit gave to the human writers of the Bible

Divine Revelation (p. 22)
God's making himself known to us

ecumenism (p. 297)
the work to promote unity among all Christians

exodus (p. 97)
the biblical word describing the Israelites' departure from slavery to freedom

faith (p. 68)
a gift from God that enables us to believe in him and accept all that he has revealed

free will (p. 38)
the freedom and ability to choose

Gospel (p. 56)
the Good News about God at work in Jesus Christ

holiness (p. 298)
sharing in God's goodness and responding to his love by the way we live; our holiness comes through grace

hope (p. 198)
a gift from God that enables us to trust in God's promise to be with us always; it enables us to be confident in God's love and care for us

human dignity (p. 38)
the value and worth that comes from being made in God's image and likeness

idolatry (p. 173)
giving worship to a creature or thing instead of to God

Incarnation (p. 224)
the truth that the Son of God, the Second Person of the Blessed Trinity, became man

Kingdom of God (p. 248)
the power of God's love coming into the world and into our lives

lamentation (p. 196)
a sorrow that is expressed in the form of a poem

Last Supper (p. 260)
the Passover meal that Jesus shared with his disciples on the night before he died

manna (p. 109)
a sweet bread-like food that God provided for the Israelites in the desert

marks of the Church (p. 296)
the four essential features of the Church: one, holy, catholic, and apostolic

martyr (p. 276)
person who dies rather than give up his or her belief in Jesus Christ

miracle (p. 109)
an extraordinary event that is beyond human power and brought about by God

monarchy (p. 134)
kingdom or empire ruled by one person, either a king or a queen

Mount Sinai (p. 108)
a mountain peak in the rocky southern part of the Sinai peninsula

Nazirite (p. 124)
a person consecrated to God who promised not to drink wine or strong drink, touch anyone or anything that had died, or cut or shave his or her hair

Original Sin (p. 50)
the first sin that weakened human nature and brought ignorance, suffering, and death into the world; we all suffer from its effects

parable (p. 210)
short story that has a message

Passover (p. 102)
the event in which God passed over the whole of Egypt, taking the lives of every firstborn Egyptian and sparing the Israelites

patriarch (p. 68)
a father, or founder, of a clan, a group of related families

Pentecost (p. 272)
the day on which the Holy Spirit came upon the first disciples

pharaoh (p. 74)
the king of Egypt

prophet (p. 132)
someone who speaks on behalf of God, defends the truth, and works for justice

proverb (p. 200)
a brief saying that gives wise advice

providence (p. 74)
God's plan for and protection of all creation

psalm (p. 150)
a poetic prayer designed to be sung or chanted to some kind of musical accompaniment

Resurrection (p. 264)
the mystery of Jesus' being raised from the dead

sin (p. 50)
a thought, word, deed, or omission against God's law

soul (p. 44)
the invisible spiritual reality that makes each of us human and that will never die

steward (p. 47)
a person who is given both the authority over what he or she cares for and the responsibility for seeing that it lives and grows

superstition (p. 196)
the false belief that living creatures or things possess powers that in fact they do not have

Ten Commandments (p. 110)
the laws of God's covenant given to Moses on Mount Sinai

Torah (p. 203)
the Hebrew name for the first five books of the Old Testament

Tradition (p. 25)
the Revelation of the Good News of Jesus Christ as lived out in the Church, past and present

vocation (p. 190)
God's call to serve him in a special way

wisdom (p. 147)
the knowledge and ability to recognize and follow God's will in our lives

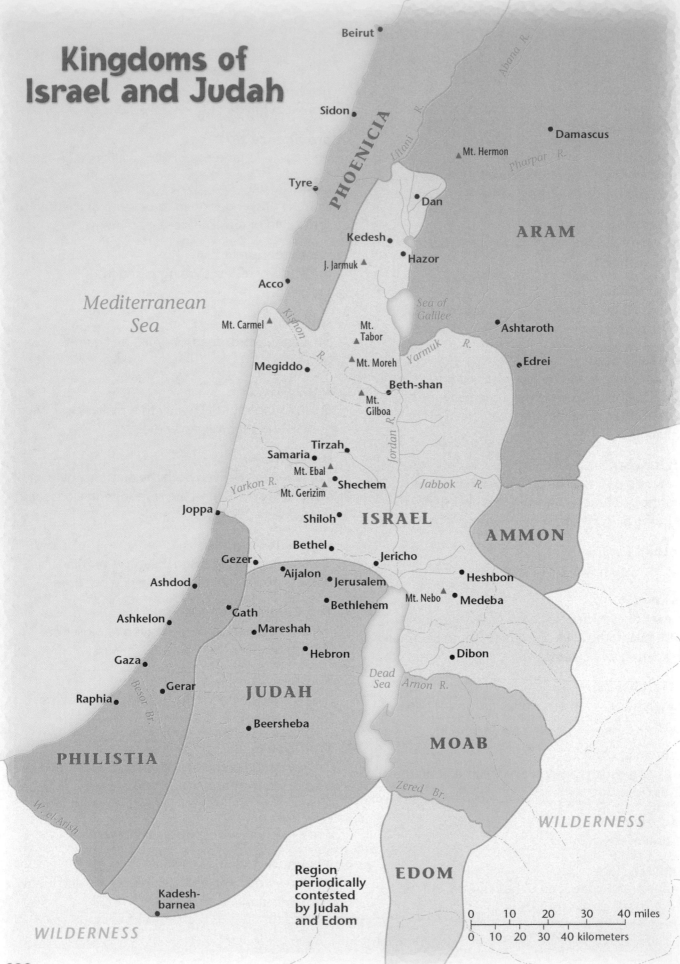

Kingdoms of Israel and Judah

Beirut

Sidon

PHOENICIA

Damascus

Mt. Hermon

Tyre

Dan

ARAM

Kedesh

Hazor

J. Jarmuk

Acco

Sea of Galilee

Ashtaroth

Mediterranean Sea

Mt. Carmel

Mt. Tabor

Edrei

Mt. Moreh

Megiddo

Beth-shan

Mt. Gilboa

Tirzah

Samaria

Mt. Ebal

Shechem

Jabbok R.

Mt. Gerizim

Shiloh

ISRAEL

AMMON

Bethel

Jericho

Joppa

Gezer

Heshbon

Aijalon

Jerusalem

Mt. Nebo

Medeba

Ashdod

Bethlehem

Gath

Ashkelon

Mareshah

Gaza

Hebron

Dibon

Gerar

JUDAH

Dead Sea

Arnon R.

Raphia

Beersheba

MOAB

PHILISTIA

Zered Br.

W. el-Arish

WILDERNESS

Kadesh-barnea

Region periodically contested by Judah and Edom

EDOM

WILDERNESS

0   10   20   30   40 miles
0 10 20 30 40 kilometers

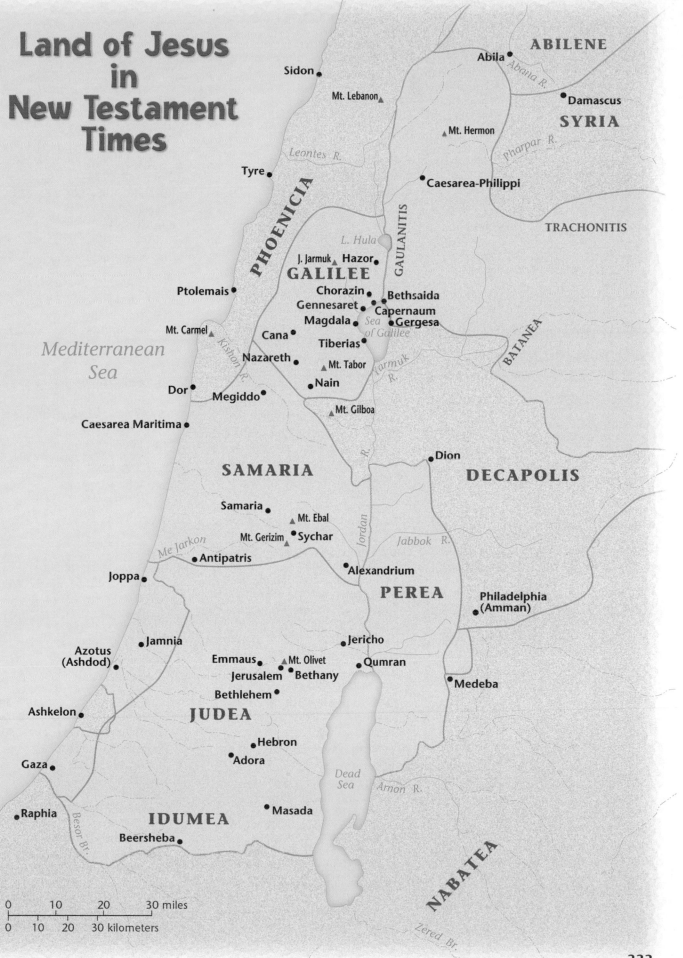

Land of Jesus in New Testament Times

ABILENE

Abila

Abana R.

Damascus

SYRIA

Sidon

Mt. Lebanon

Mt. Hermon

Leontes R.

Pharpar R.

Tyre

PHOENICIA

Caesarea-Philippi

GAULANITIS

TRACHONITIS

L. Hula

J. Jarmuk   Hazor

GALILEE

Chorazin   Bethsaida

Ptolemais

Gennesaret   Capernaum

Magdala   Gergesa

Sea of Galilee

BATANEA

Mt. Carmel

Cana

Tiberias

Mediterranean Sea

Kishon R.

Nazareth

Mt. Tabor

Jarmuk R.

Dor

Nain

Megiddo

Mt. Gilboa

Caesarea Maritima

Dion

DECAPOLIS

SAMARIA

Samaria

Mt. Ebal

Jordan

Mt. Gerizim   Sychar

Jabbok R.

Me Jarkon

Antipatris

Joppa

Alexandrium

PEREA

Philadelphia (Amman)

Jamnia

Jericho

Azotus (Ashdod)

Emmaus   Mt. Olivet

Qumran

Jerusalem   Bethany

Ashkelon

Bethlehem

Medeba

JUDEA

Hebron

Gaza

Adora

Dead Sea

Arnon R.

Raphia

IDUMEA

Masada

Besor Br.

Beersheba

NABATEA

Zered Br.

| 0 | 10 | 20 | 30 miles |
| 0 | 10 | 20 | 30 kilometers |

Index

The following is a list of topics that appear in the pupil's text.
Boldface indicates an entire chapter or section.